THE RAGAS OF NORTH INDIA

ASIAN STUDIES RESEARCH INSTITUTE
DENIS SINOR, DIRECTOR

ORIENTAL SERIES, No. 1

THE RAGAS OF NORTH INDIA ❧

By WALTER KAUFMANN

Published for the
INTERNATIONAL AFFAIRS CENTER BY
INDIANA UNIVERSITY PRESS · BLOOMINGTON · LONDON

PREFACE

The aim of this book is to offer a detailed survey of the rāgas of
North India. A definition of rāga, the remarkable and prominent
feature of Indian music, cannot be offered in one or two sentences.
A detailed description will be given on pages 1-25. Here in the pre-
face it must suffice to state that the rāga is the dominant feature in
Indian art music and that the usual description, "melody pattern," is
not fully adequate. From a musical point of view: (1) A rāga may be
represented by a scale which may or may not possess the same notes
in ascent and descent; most rāgas differ from each other in their specific tone material. (2) There are some rāgas which cannot be represented by simple scale forms because their scales ascend and/or
descend in a more or less irregular manner, e. g., in a zigzag.
(3) Certain notes within the tone material of a rāga have greater,
others lesser, importance; in some instances several rāgas with
identical tone material are distinguished from each other only by the
different emphasis given to specific notes. (4) Numerous rāgas are
characterized by certain typical phrases, other rāgas by certain
typical intonations of some of their notes. (5) All rāgas are performed
to the sound of characteristic drones.

In addition to these musical characteristics, there are a number
of extra-musical considerations, some of which have lost their importance: (1) Many rāgas, if performed correctly, are believed to
possess magic powers. (2) Numerous rāgas have to be performed at
specific times of the day or night, and some rāgas have to be sung or
played at particular seasons of the year—one speaks of morning- or
evening-rāgas, of spring-, autumn-, rainy season-, winter-rāgas,
and so forth. (3) A considerable number of rāgas are believed to
represent persons, usually various deities of the Hindu pantheon, and

are shown in the form of pictorial representations. (4) Each of a
large number of rāgas has its own characteristic mood (rasa).

Part I of this volume is an introductory section. Part II presents
a comparatively brief review of some important Sanskrit and Hindi
theoretical works of North Indian music. I have kept it brief because
a large number of the works mentioned have been described in books
that are easily accessible; a detailed discussion would for the most
part only repeat statements already made by other authors. Part III
contains a careful, detailed discussion of the North Indian rāgas as
they are performed at the present time. Analyses of tone materials,
song examples, and diverse matters of Auffuehrungspraxis are presented here. A second volume, to be offered at a later date, will
deal in a similar manner with the sources and rāgas of South Indian
music.

Some readers may object to the detailed discussions of the
hundreds of rāgas and argue that it would be better to include fewer
details and more generalizations. This objection must be answered
at once. It is exactly this great multitude of details which requires
our special attention. In comparing a violet and a rose, we might
generalize that both are flowers and both have a sweet fragrance. In
addition, however, each has many interesting and distinguishing details of its own. Similarly, each rāga has its own characteristic
features, often a surprising wealth of small details which are of tre-
mendous importance to Indian musicians and audiences. Vague generalizations will not serve our purpose and, in any case, can already
be found in numerous books of past and contemporary vintage.

Some Sanskrit sources indistinctly refer to both northern and
southern systems, and a strict division of the sources dealing with
the music of the two areas is difficult. This first volume, which
deals with northern rāgas, will now and then refer to a theoretical
work listed in the second volume, and vice versa.

In colloquial language and in numerous books the Hindi term
rag is used. I prefer, however, to use the Sanskrit form, rāga.
Rāga represents in this text not only old but also modern forms,
and is also used, whenever indicated, for rāginī, putra, etc.

The note rsabha (rishabha) can be notated in various ways,
either as RI or, in the contemporary manner, as RE. In dealing with

Sanskrit sources I shall employ the old form, RI; in the discussion
of modern rāgas I shall employ the commonly used RE.

Whether the lowest note of a melodic curve belongs to the
descent or to the subsequent ascent, and whether the highest note
of a curve is part of the descent or still belongs to the ascent, are
questions answered by Indian music theorists in the following manner:
the lowest note of a melodic curve belongs to the subsequent ascent,
and the highest note of a melodic curve belongs to the descent immediately following.

The indicated notes E, C, and D belong to the ascending line, G and F
to the descending.   This method will be used in the discussions below.

The ālāp examples which precede the song specimens contain
whole-, half-, quarter-, eighth-, etc., notes not in order to indicate
durational values but only to distinguish between more and less important notes.   Long durational values represent "strong" notes;
short ones represent "weak" notes.

Certain ornaments are notated simply as appogiaturas.   It
must be added, however, that many of these "appogiaturas" may
have a different meaning from that of related ornaments in the music
of the West.   They may, for instance, indicate starting points of
gliding steps which lead to the main notes which follow; they may
indicate microtonal alterations of the following notes, or various
forms of vibrato.   In my discussions of the rāgas, directives are
given for the interpretation of the diverse ornaments.

The composers of most song examples, particularly in the
North, are unknown, and one cannot speak of authorship in the
Western sense of the word.   A song melody, usually of traditional
origin, is common property and may move from one musician to
another and undergo manifold modifications.   The song specimens
generally represent only "skeletons" which serve the performing
artists as bases for further elaboration.   Many of the North Indian

song specimens, which I have transcribed into western notation, can
be found in North Indian notation in the Hindusthani Sangit Paddhati,
compiled by the eminent Pandit Vishnu Narayana Bhatkhande. I
have identified these song specimens with the letters BH. The
Roman numeral following BH indicates the volume, and the Arabic
number refers to the page in Bhatkhande's work. Specimens from
other sources are so marked.

    The manner of writing of the Sanskrit authors, copyists, and
later interpreters is not uniform. Variants such as Malaśrī,
Malavaśrī; Todī, Tudī; Gaudī, Gouda; Velāvalī, Velāulī, Bilaval;
Saverī, Savarī; Vangāla, Bangala; also amśa or aṁśa, and many
more, have to be kept in mind. In dealing with the rāgas of the
present time (Part III), an anglicized form has been adopted (e. g.,
Malaśrī will be written Malashri, Pañcama will become Panchama,
rāga will be written raga, etc.), because the majority of contemporary works employ this style. When in doubt, the reader may
find help by consulting the Sanskrit-English Dictionary by Sir
Monier Monier-Williams (Oxford, 1899, 1956, 1960).

    As the title of my book indicates, this text focuses on the rāgas.
Discussions of Indian notations and drummings have been omitted.
They may be found in my Musical Notations of the Orient (Indiana
University Press, 1967).

    It is my pleasant duty to acknowledge the encouragement I have
received from Professor Denis Sinor and the assistance give to me
by the Indiana University Graduate School and the Ford International
Program (Indiana University). I further wish to express my deep
gratitude to India's great musician and scholar, the late Pandit V.
N. Bhatkhande, who more than thirty years ago helped me with his
excellent advice and generously allowed me to quote from his works.
I am equally indebted to my friend Professor B. R. Deodhar (Bombay),
one of the great scholar-musicians of Northern India, as well as to
numerous Indian musicians of All India Radio (Bombay, Delhi, etc.).
I wish to thank Dr. Jack Sewell, Director of the Oriental Division of
the Art Institute of Chicago; he kindly gave me permission to photo-
graph and later reproduce in Plates I-XX and XXII-XXVIII a number
of his beautiful rāga-mālās. I am indebted to Mr. Terence Bech, a
former student at Indiana University, who made for me a number of

photographs of another group of rāga-mālās, preserved in the Bir
Library, Khatmandu, Nepal, and obtained for me permission to present a few of them in Plates XXIX-XXXV. I wish to acknowledge my
indebtedness to Dr. David Sheldon for reading through my manuscript
with a critical eye.

Last but not least I wish to extend my deep gratitude to Mrs.
Edith G. Albee, Editor of the International Affairs Center Publica-
tions, Indiana University Press, and to her untiring assistant Miss
Anita Johnson.

Walter Kaufmann

Indiana University
Bloomington, Indiana

To
WILFRED C. BAIN

CONTENTS

ILLUSTRATIONS

NOTE ON THE PLATES: Under each plate is a rough translation of the Sanskrit inscription that appears above the picture.   In several instances (Plates II, IX, XXII) the main figures shown in the pictures are male even though the inscriptions refer to them as female.

Chaupayi indicates a Sanskrit stanza consisting of four lines.   The endings of the second and fourth lines form a rhyme.

Doha is a rhyming couplet giving the essence of the chaupayi.

INTRODUCTION

SOURCES AND HISTORY

I

INTRODUCTION

The art music of India has evolved entirely within the realm of mono-
phonic modality and, with the exception of some instances of contemporary popular and film music, has not been noticeably influenced by
the polyphonic and harmonic tendencies of Western music. The vertical
element in Indian music is represented only by a rigid, unchangeable
drone bass, which has no direct influence upon the flow of the melodic
line. This Oriental emphasis upon the horizontal extension of music
has created an art exceedingly rich in scales, motives, melody formulas,
and subtle refinements which, up to recent times, has found comparatively little appreciation in the West.

This remarkable art can best be observed in the enormous
wealth of rāgas, in the multitude of scales, formulas, and ornaments,
in the microtonal alterations of certain tones and intervals, and in
the manifold rhythmic modes.

The concept rāga, which appeared for the first time in its musical
connotation in the Br̥haddeśi,[1] a work by the Sanskrit author Mataṅga
(who lived sometime between the fifth and seventh centuries), has
dominated the entire art music of the Indian peninsula up to the present
day. The word rāga,[2] or its colloquial and Hindi form rāg, originally
denoted "color" or "atmosphere." It is derived from the Sanskrit
word raṅga, "color." Theoretically, Indian music possesses thousands
of rāgas. Practically, however, only a few hundred are known. The
average Indian musician may probably know most of them, but experience has shown that some of the very famous North Indian artists
usually do not perform more than about a dozen rāgas each. This
rather limited use of rāgas is not surprising if we keep in mind the
long and tedious manner of Indian musical instruction. The master
sings a certain phrase and the pupil tries to repeat it. Only when this
phrase is performed to the teacher's complete satisfaction will another

1

phrase be proffered. Generally the student is not told any characteristic details of the rāga he is studying; his task is rather to learn,
phrase by phrase, one or more melodies. A great deal of time may
be taken before another rāga can be presented in the same manner.
It is remarkable that many of the great artists I met would hesitate
to describe the essential features of a rāga. When consulted, they
would avoid verbal explanations and present instead the entire melody
or a set of phrases.

Most definitions of "rāga" will first state that a rāga consists
of a fixed, unchangeable number of notes which frequently are presented in the form of an ascending and descending scale. The number
and pitches of scale degrees may change from one rāga to another,
although there exist several rāgas which possess identical tone material.
Generally there should be a minimum of five or a maximum of seven
degrees in the ascending (ārohana or āroha) and descending (āvaro-
hana or āvaroha) forms of the scale. We find indeed, all nine possibilities utilized:

Ascending scale	Descending scale
5 degrees	5 degrees
5 degrees	6 degrees
5 degrees	7 degrees
6 degrees	5 degrees
6 degrees	6 degrees
6 degrees	7 degrees
7 degrees	5 degrees
7 degrees	6 degrees
7 degrees	7 degrees

Some exceptional rāgas may employ four or eight degrees in one
or the other form of the scale. Pentatonic scales are called odava;
hexatonic, shādava; and heptatonic, sampūrna. A rāga which, for
instance, possesses five tones in the ascending, and seven in the descendi
cending, scale is called odav-sampūrna. Words such as sampūrna,
which indicates the completeness of the scale (seven degrees in ascent
and descent), and shadāva (or shāshtaka), which indicates six degrees,
raise no doubt about the number of degrees. The word odava (or audava),

however, does not appear in any Indian language, and is believed to
be of foreign origin.[3]

In several rāgas it is impossible to demonstrate the tone material in the form of a scale because some steps have to be performed
vakra (zigzag). For instance, in rāga Mīyān-ki-Mallār the basic
material is represented by:

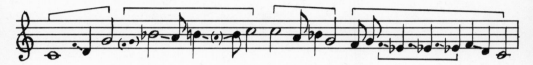

If we wish to ascend in rāga Mīyān-ki-Mallār from C to G, we have
to interpolate the notes F and D. The note E is avoided. A direct
ascent (C D F G) is not permissible and would destroy the character
of this particular rāga. In order to ascend from G to the upper c, we
have to avoid, first of all, the note A, use in its place the note B♭,
and follow this B♭ by the notes A and B. From B we can reach the
upper c with a brief detour to A. Similar vakra steps can be observed
in the descent of this rāga: the progression from the upper c to C
aims first at A, then at B♭ and G; the descent from G to C calls first
for a brief touch of F, whereupon the line returns to G. Then follows
the note E♭, usually repeated three times and beginning each time
with a tiny gliding step from F, after which the final gliding step F-
D leads to the lower C. Deviations from this pattern are not allowed
and are considered to be harmful to the character of this rāga. The
performer is thus bound by the aforementioned rules and can move
his improvised melody only within a strictly delineated framework.

The musical rendition of each rāga has to be accompanied by
an invariable bourdon bass, which consists of three notes. If the
scale of the rāga contains a pure fifth, the bass consists of the fifth,
the tonic, and the upper octave of the tonic:

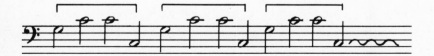

If the scale possesses no fifth but has a pure fourth, the bass will be:

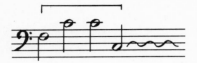

If the scale possesses neither a fifth nor a pure fourth, the major
seventh is substituted in the following manner:

These bourdon basses are played mostly without interruption, irrespective of the rhythm and tempo of the melody, on a tanbura, a
fretless lute with a long neck and four thin metal strings. The long
strings of the instrument are touched gently in succession in such a
manner as to produce a whirring, metallic, slightly nasal pedal effect. Above this "plain" of the bourdon bass rises and falls the melody
of the soloist. A performance of a rāga without this bourdon accompaniment is unthinkable. Only some popular and folk melodies may
be sung or played without it.

      Absolute pitches are not in use in Indian music. The ancient
Sanskrit theorists, for instance Sārṇgadeva in his famous work
Saṅgīta-Ratnākara,[4] did try to establish a system whereby the notes
of the scale were compared to the cries of certain animals. This
unreliable system was as follows: the first note of the scale, Sadja
(Shadja), abbreviated SA, corresponds to the call of the peacock;
Rsabha (Rishabha, RI or RE), the second degree of the scale, corresponds to the sound of the chataka, the fever bird, which can be
heard during the rainy season; Gāndhāra (GA), the third scale degree,
to the call of the goat; Madhyama (MA), the fourth note of the scale,
to the call of the crane; Pañcama (PA), the fifth note to the sound of
the koil, the Indian woodpecker; Dhaivata (DHA), the sixth degree,
to the call of the frog in love; and Nisāda (Nishada, NI), the seventh
note of the scale, to the call of the elephant when he is beaten on the
head by his rider.[5] Even the duration of the matra (metrical unit)
was compared to the duration of an animal call.

During the nineteenth century Western missionaries imported
into India a small, portable harmonium which became exceedingly
popular. Up to the middle of the twentieth century this instrument
was used by almost every music-loving family in India. One must
acknowledge the efforts of All India Radio in discouraging the use
of this practical but, for the fine intonations of Indian music, thorough-
ly unsuitable instrument. The only useful function of this harmonium
was (and still is) that its white and black keys served musicians as
a basis for the definitions of absolute pitches. At the beginning of
a concert, musicians discussed which SA (tonic) would be convenient
for singer and accompanists. "White One," for instance, referred
to the first white key on the harmonium, C. "White Two," represented
D, "Black One" stood for C# (D♭), "Black Two" for D# (E♭), and
so forth.

The tone material of a rāga remains unchanged, as we have
seen, and "modulations" from one scale to another within one rāga
are strictly forbidden. Each scale possesses notes of greater and
lesser significance, which Indian musicians call "strong" and "weak,"
respectively. This does not imply that "strong" notes are performed
louder than "weak" ones. This terminology indicates that strong notes
appear frequently, that they can become "recitation notes" or may
have "finalis" functions, while weak notes are of little importance,
are treated lightly, and appear less frequently. The strong notes'
are the SA, the first note of the scale, and the predominant vādī
("speaker") or amsa. Usually at an interval of a fifth or fourth from
the vādī appears the samvādī ("consonance"), a slightly less important note. All other notes of the scale are called anuvādī ("incomplete consonance") and are of lesser importance. The term vivādī
denotes a "dissonant" note, one which usually does not appear in the
scale of a particular rāga. When it does, however, it gives the rāga
its characteristic "flavor." For instance, the tone B♭ in rāga Deshkar[6]
does not belong in its scale but appears as a slight ornament, which
if omitted would deprive Deshkar of its peculiar feature. The following Sanskrit verse describes the strong and weak notes:

Vadi raja svarastaya samvādī syad amatyat

Satrur vivādī tasy syad anuvādī ca bhrtyavat.[7]

Freely translated, this verse states: The vādī is the king of the notes;
the samvādī is the minister; the vivādī is the enemy; and the anuvādī
is the vassal.

 The old Sanskrit terms graha ("initial note") and nyāsa ("final
note") have no significance at the present time. Today, the central
note of the melody (aṃśa) is called vādī.

 In order to illustrate some of the finer differences between
rāgas, the formulas of four rāgas which all have the same scale,
C D E G A, are shown below. The differences between the four
rāgas can be observed in the various positions of the strong and weak
notes, in the vakra steps, in fine ornamentations, glides, and other
features:

The strong note, the vādī, in rāga Bhupali, is GA (E). Most
Bhupali melodies end either on E or on the tonic of the scale (C).
The importance of the vādī is indicated by its "strength" and can be
intensified on certain occasions by a special complex beat on the

drums. Similar to the vādī and the SA, this beat is not performed
louder than the other drum beats, but is treated in a particular manner whereby both drums of the tabla pair or both drumheads of the
mridanga are beaten in a manner which differs noticeably from the
other beats. This beat, which is performed in different ways in
the various rhythmic modi, is called sam.[8]

   Further characteristics of rāga Bhupali are the gliding step[9]
in the descent from D to C and the weak notes D and G. Neither D
nor G can be employed as sustained notes and must not be performed
with the sam.

   Rāga Deshkar uses the same tone material as rāga Bhupali.
In Deshkar appear two strong notes. The first is the vādī, the note
A, which has to be approached from above (roughly from B♭—a vivādī)
by means of a short gliding movement. Although B♭ does not appear
as a scale degree in Deshkar (as a matter of fact it is a "wrong" note
in the rāga), it nevertheless has considerable importance as a grace
note which precedes the vādī. The second strong note is G, an exception called a vishrantisthan. It has the same functions as the vādī.
In contrast to Bhupali the note E in Deshkar is of little importance and
receives a "weak"treatment.

   Rāga Shuddh-kalyan, with the same tone material as Bhupali
and Deshkar, has E as vādī. This rāga differs from the two previously discussed by the vakra steps in its ascent and by the use of a faint
trace of F#, which appears in a characteristic gliding movement
between G and E. Although B♭ in Deshkar and F# in Shuddh-kalyan
are vivādīs, they are of considerable importance in the correct interpretation of the two rāgas. If these two very weak grace notes
were omitted, the representation of Deshkar and Shuddh-kalyan would
be imperfect.

   The following example may serve to show some further characteristic features of rāgas. Rāga Vasant has as vādī the high c. Vasant
melodies almost always begin with this high note in a descending movement. The Vasant formula is:

Rāga Vasant

Another example is the formula of rāga (formerly rāginī)[10] Todī. The vādī is A♭. Of interest are the "slightly low" intonations of the notes D♭, E♭, and A♭, and the "slightly high" treatment of F# and B:

Rāga Todī

I purposely use the vague terms "little low" and "little sharp." Although the theoretical works of the Indian past do contain various termini technici which could be utilized in creating a modern terminology, I abstain from using them because the musicians of the present time have little or no awareness of these ancient words and no acquaintance with music theories of the Sanskrit authors of the past. The musicians do not describe the notes they play in terms denoting exact mathematical standards. During my long stay in India, I frequently had the opportunity to observe famous and highly revered Indian singers and instrumentalists. After completing their recitals, these performers insisted on receiving their remuneration in bare coin, never in the form of checks. Most of these great artists came to the broadcasting studio in the company of young persons who were able to count the coins, because, as the older artists sometimes confessed, they were unable to perform this task themselves. It would, therefore, be quite erroneous to assume that these artists determine any microtonal alterations by mathematical calculations. It is important to note that in the whole music literature of classical India there exists not one single mathematical calculation which describes

exact intervallic distances.[11] Furthermore, none of the Indian notational systems possess symbols which denote microtonal alterations.
In spite of these vague standards, however, experienced musicians
executed the microtonal alterations in a manner that will create distinctly the prescribed mood of a raga. While it is possible that one
singer may intone a certain note a "little higher" than another singer,
who treats the same note only a "very little higher," it is nevertheless
possible to feel in both renditions the characteristic mood of the raga.
Even if the microtonal alterations vary from one performer to another.
no violation of the traditional mood of the raga can be noticed.

Similar microtonal alterations can be observed in the vocal
and string music of Western civilization. Let us assume, for example, that the interval of a major third, C-E, is to be performed.
If the note C is fixed, the E may become subject to fine alterations
if certain moods are involved. Assuming that the note E is performed
in a tender, gentle, loving sentiment, we find that it will have, for
instance, n vibrations. If we change the mood to a virile, strong,
driving sentiment, the vibration number of E will be slightly higher,
for instance, n + m, producing a "slightly higher" tone. In the West
these two manners of intonation could be described as "soft" or
"hard," "singing" or "metallic," but we find no specific, exact terms
or mathematical definitions for the descriptions of these microtonal
differences.

For many centuries Indian theorists have written and argued
a great deal, trying to reach a clear definition of the śrutis, micro-
tones, or microtonal intervals, to describe the "slightly high" and
"slightly low" intonations of certain notes. Despite the numerous
arguments and calculations brought forth by Indian and Western
authors, Indian performing musicians pay no attention to these matters
and are guided solely by the rasa, the sentiment and mood of a rāga,
in order to achieve the required intonations. They refuse to define
microtonal alterations by means of mathematical speculations.

During my fourteen year stay in India as Director of Music
at All India Radio, Bombay, I had ample opportunity to investigate
the microtonal alterations in certain rāgas. Measurements showed
that various singers, when performing the same rāga, differed considerably in their microtonal alterations of certain intervals. There

were even noticeable differences in intonation when the same artist
performed the same rāga on different occasions. Careful measurements of these alterations were made by N. A. Jairazbhoy who, together with A. W. Stone, published the results of his investigations
in an article, "Intonation in Present-day North Indian Classical Music"[12]
Jairazbhoy shows, that the interval SA GA, for example, a major
third, in rāga Yaman,[13] had 439 cents in the performance by Pannalal
Ghosh and 375 cents in the performance by Ustad Umrao Khan. Both
artists were fully acknowledged and highly respected, and in both
performances not only was the rāga clear, but even its rasa raised
no doubt in the minds of the listeners.

Besides the musical characteristics of rāgas there are several
extra-musical features such as rasa, personification, often deifica-
tion, pictorial representation, magic properties, and fixed performance times. Rasa (Sanskrit: "taste," "prevailing sentiment") was
an important feature in ancient Hindu drama and poetry and eventually
also in music. It represents the psychological reaction, the "rever-
beration," in the spectator or listener when confronted with a drama,
poem, or piece of music. The primary emotion inherent in the drama
was called bhava ("state of mind," "way of feeling"). Bhava and its
response in the spectator, rasa, are two different phenomena in
drama and poetry, while in music rasa is assumed to represent both
primary and responding emotions.[14] It is hardly necessary to point
out the resemblance of rasa to the ethos of ancient Greece, or to similar phenomena in the music of the Renaissance and Baroque periods
of the West, particularly to the Affektenlehre of the late eighteenth
century. In order to prove that the use of a fixed scale does indeed
create a certain rasa, an experiment is suggested: we select a scale
which may consist of any number of degrees. Let us assume that it
has five notes, C E F# A B (c). We can even complicate the matter
by introducing into the scale some vakra steps, for instance C F# E
A B A c. If we improvise with these five tones for a while, we can
observe that a certain mood is created which, although quite distinct, can hardly be described in words. If, after the rasa has been
established, we suddenly use a foreign note, for instance E♭ or F,
we notice how painfully wrong this "vivādī" is and how severely it de-
stroys the previously established sentiment.

If we consider that the performance of an Indian art song may
last at least half an hour, or if we think of the ancient dhrupad[15] which
may have lasted several hours, it becomes plausible that as one particular rasa is uninterruptedly projected upon the listener, he may
believe a rāga to be a representation of a person, particularly a
divine being. There are many rāgas which have become "personified"
and, as certain divine beings are revered at certain seasons or days,
have also become associated with certain seasons and even with certain periods of the day and night. Furthermore, rāgas were believed
to possess magic properties.

Many centuries before the Islamic invasions in India, perhaps
as early as the second century, there existed short poetical descriptions of rāgas, usually in the form of brief prayer verses. Although
these verses do not yet indicate pictorial representations of the rāgas,
they show the trend toward musical-poetical-pictorial associations.
The earliest known source which contains such verses and shows
personifications of certain rāgas is the Rāga-Sāgara,[16] a work of the
second (?) century ascribed to the Sanskrit authors Dattila and Nārada.
The following example is a free translation of the verses from the
Rāga-Sāgara (3,1)[17] describing rāga Bhairava:

> The ocean of notes and śrutis [filled] with the delight of
> the varieties of all rhythmical features [expressing] the
> consummation of the adoration of Shiva. His body, eter-
> nally covered with ashes, with matted locks, the brilliancy
> of the young moon about his head, adorned with a string of
> skulls; I venerate Bhairava, the accomplished divine dancer.[18]

Rāga Bhairava (or Bhairav) represents the giant Bhairava,
an incarnation of the god Shiva, who is one of the three awe-inspiring
guardians of the mythical "City of Kailasa" where Shiva and his wife,
Parvati, reside. The rasa of this rāga is terror, grandeur, and
seriousness, which in the course of the subsequent centuries gradually changed to quiet, yet awe-inspiring adoration.

Since about the thirteenth century, Sanskrit writers have evolved
a remarkable iconography of important rāgas. From this time on,
nearly one and a half milleniums after the Rāga-Sāgara was written,
we find numerous Sanskrit pictorial descriptions of rāgas, or rāga-
mālās, for instance, the Pañcama-Sāra-Samhitā by Nārada, written

about 1440;[19] the Rāga-Mālā by Puṇḍarika Viṭṭhala, written in 1576
during the reign of Akbar the Great;[20] the Saṅgīta-Darpaṇa by Dāmodara
Miśra;[21] the Anūpa-Saṅgīta-Vilāsa and the Anūpa-Saṅgīta-Ratnākara,
both by Bhāva-Bhaṭṭa (1674-1701);[22] and the Saṅgīta-Mālā by an
anonymous author, written about 1750.[23]   In addition to these and
numerous other Sanskrit texts, we find an impressive number of
rāga-mālā texts in Hindi and in other Indian languages.

     Not far removed from the personifications and deifications and
the resulting poetical descriptions and pictorial representations of
the rāga-malas is the belief that certain rāgas possess magical properties. The concept of magic is strong not only in the world of
primitive man but in civilizations of higher levels. Ways of dealing
with sickness, death, natural disasters, and other events are often
irrational, and are believed to be controlled by magic formulas, rites,
charms, spells, dances, processions, certain songs, and so on.

> On the island of Gaua in the New Hebrides it is said that
> formerly old men used to stand by with bows and arrows
> and shoot at every dancer who made a mistake.[24]

Accuracy in the practice of magic has to be strictly observed and
finds its reflection in the strictly prescribed performance practice
of certain rāgas. We cannot dismiss the belief in the magical attri-
butes of rāgas as utter nonsense if we consider the healing powers
that music was supposed to have had in ancient Greece. We have
only to recall the dance music that aimed at purification and then
turn to the twentieth century and the function music has in modern
psychotherapy. The personifications and particularly the deifications
of certain rāgas led, as can be expected in a deeply devout India, to
the belief that certain rāgas, if correctly performed at the prescribed
times of day or night, work miracles and bring divine beings down
into the melody and so into performers and listeners. The rāgas
therefore become powerful tools of magic.

     India has a great wealth of stories and legends which describe
the magical features of the rāgas. We are told, for instance, that
the famous singer Naik Gopal, who lived during the sixteenth century
at the court of Akbar the Great, was ordered by his monarch to sing
rāga Dipak. There are still some Indian musicians who insist that
Dipak creates fire if correctly performed. Naik Gopal begged his

emperor to release him from this dangerous task, but Akbar remained
adamant. The despairing singer, so the story goes, placed himself
in the river Jumna in such a manner that the water reached up to his
chin; then he began to sing. We are told that the water became increasingly hot and that suddenly flames burst from the artist's head
and he perished. The Mallār rāgas, if correctly sung, were believed
to create rain. These rāgas had to be performed during the rainy
season, probably for the simple reason that at such a time the chance
of sudden rain was infinitely greater than during the dry season. If
a Mallār rāga was sung during the rainy season and no rain occurred
after the performance, the orthodox musician could have offered two
excuses: he could have stated that his performance of the rāga at the
wrong time made its powers ineffective or that the rendering of the
rāga was faulty. Another rāga with magic powers was Kedar, which
was supposed to cure diseases and to melt stones. Some musicians
relate smilingly that Kedar melodies were taught by prison wardens
and their assistants to those prisoners who were able to pay an adequate remuneration to the music teacher. If, by chance, the singing
of Kedar did not melt the stones of the prison walls, the teacher
would say that the rendition of the rāga was not absolutely correct.

Much less mysterious and abstruse are the performance times
of the rāgas. It is well known that most of the important rāgas can
be performed only at certain fixed times during the day or night. The
older generation of Indian musicians in particular still believes that
disaster will be invoked if, for instance, an evening-rāga is performed in the morning, or vice versa. The belief that there exists a re-
ciprocal effect between the rāga and the forces of the universe is
widely accepted and has prevailed throughout the centuries.

There is little doubt that the source of the concept of proper
performance times reaches back to the ritual chant of the Vedas.
Irrespective of the Vedas, however, performance times of certain
rāga melodies were linked with seasonal festivities and ceremonials
of spring, summer, harvesting, the solstices, and so forth, each of
which had its own fixed prayers, songs, and dances. It is remarkable
that the first Sanskrit author who dealt seriously with a time relationship of rāgas, the royal Someśvara of the twelfth century,[25] established six seasonal rāgas. At the end of his list he informs his

readers that these "melodies" may also be sung in other seasons for the sake of pure enjoyment.

Performance times usually were ascribed to certain periods of the day and night. As early as in the Saṅgīta-Makaranda, a work written by Nārada, who lived sometime between the seventh and eleventh centuries,[26] the reader is threatened that if the rāgas are not performed at their correct times of the day and night, disastrous consequences are to be expected. After Nārada, this theory of performance times flourished and expanded, and it is only at the present time that we observe a certain neglect of these ancient rules.

The musical aspect of this theory is of interest and deserves some attention. Theorists divided the twenty-four hours of the day and night into eight three-hour watches (praharas). There are some musicians and authors who begin the cycle of these watches at 6 a.m., the time of sunrise in India; others begin it an hour later. The division into these eight watches is not too rigorously observed, but the times of sunrise, sunset, noon, and midnight are distinctly maintained. In order to explain this matter we shall use the comparatively simple seven-tone scales of ten particular rāgas which Pandit Bhatkhande, in his work Hindusthani Sangit Paddhati postulates as thāta-rāgas,[27] parent rāgas:

1.	Kalyan	C D E F# G A B c
2.	Bilaval	C D E F G A B c
3.	Khamaj	C D E F G A B♭ c
4.	Bhairav	C D♭ E F G A♭ B c
5.	Purvi	C D♭ E F# G A♭ B c
6.	Marva	C D♭ E F# G A B c
7.	Kafi	C D E♭ F G A B♭ c
8.	Asavari	C D E♭ F G A♭ B♭ c
9.	Bhairavi	C D♭ E♭ F G A♭ B♭ c
10.	Todi	C D♭ E♭ F# G A♭ B c

The difference between thāta and rāga is that in the rāga the scale is "alive": it may stress or neglect and omit or add certain

notes; it may use certain vakra (zigzag) steps, ornaments, characteristic phrases, and special intonations.   The thāta is an "impersonal"
scale which always has seven notes and is used as a "headline," a basic
scale which serves mainly for classification purposes.   For instance,
while the thāta scale of Khamaj is C D E F G A B♭ c, the scale of
Khamaj omits the note D in ascent, stresses the notes E and B♭, and
also occasionally employs the note B.   The following table shows the
relationship between the ten thāta-rāgas and the eight praharas.   The
second column shows their appropriate performance times.

Prahara	Time	Thāta	C	D♭	D	E♭	E	F	F#	G	A♭	A	B♭	B	c
I	7-10 (a. m.)	Kalyan	x		x		x		x	x		x		x	x
		Bilaval	x		x		x	x		x		x		x	x
II	10-1	Bhairavi	x	x		x		x		x	x		x		x
		Todi	x	x		x			x	x	x			x	x
		Asavari	x		x	x		x		x	x		x		x
		Kafi	x		x	x		x		x		x	x		x
III	1-4 (p. m.)	Kafi	x		x	x		x		x		x	x		x
		Todi	x	x		x			x	x	x			x	x
IV	4-7	Purvi	x	x			x		x	x	x			x	x
		Marva	x	x			x		x	x		x		x	x
		Bhairav	x	x			x	x		x	x			x	x
V	7-10	Kalyan	x		x		x		x	x		x		x	x
		Bilaval	x		x		x	x		x		x		x	x
VI	10-1	Khamaj	x		x		x	x		x		x	x		x
		Kafi	x		x	x		x		x		x	x		x
VII	1-4 (a. m.)	Asavari	x		x	x		x		x	x		x		x
		Bhairavi	x	x		x		x		x	x		x		x
VIII	4-7	Purvi	x	x			x		x	x	x			x	x
		Marva	x	x			x		x	x		x		x	x
		Bhairav	x	x			x	x		x	x			x	x

The notes C and G remain unchanged in all rāgas. Our brief investigation can thus be confined to the notes D E F A and B and their chromatic alternatives. The most characteristic periods of the twenty-
four hours of day and night are sunrise and sunset. Other characteristic periods are noon, midnight, morning, and evening. Although
there are hundreds of rāgas in the North, we shall limit ourselves to
the scales of the ten thāta-rāgas and indicate the chromatic changes
that occur at the above-mentioned periods. The chromatic changes
of the notes D E F A and B are graphically shown below in relation
to the various periods of day and night:

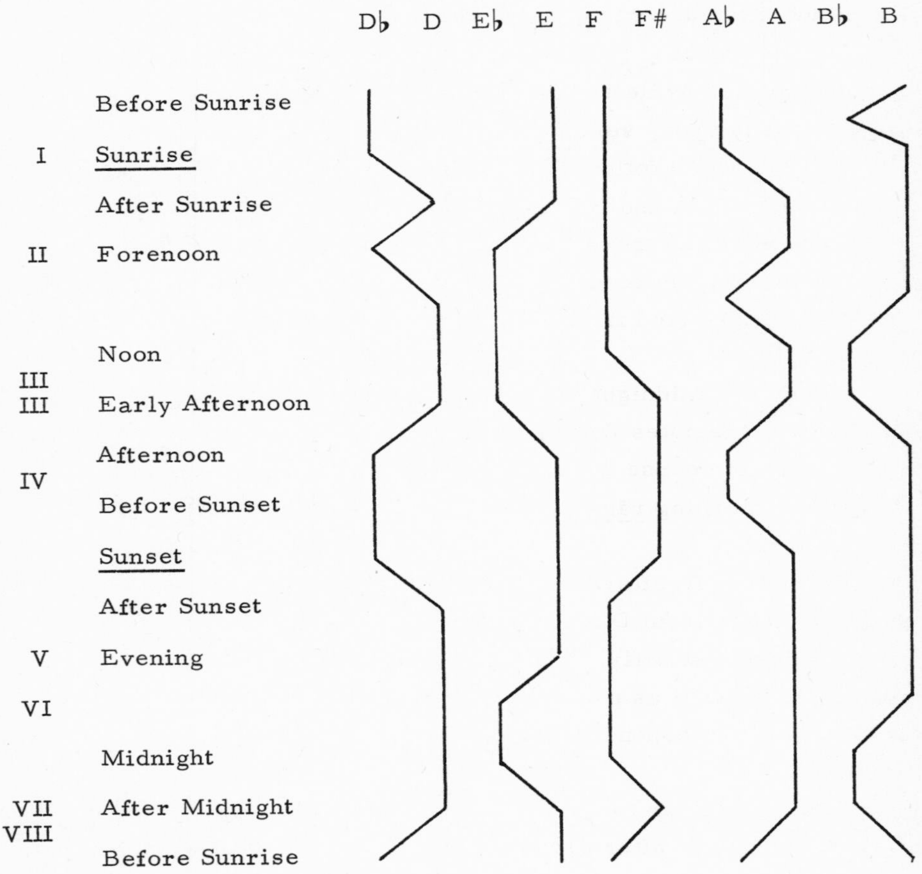

The Sandhiprakash[28] rāgas, rāgas to be performed at sunrise
and sunset, employ, as a rule, Db, occasionally also Ab. A further

characteristic is the fluctuation from F to F# (or F# to F); the sunrise rāgas usually employ F, those of the sunset period tend toward
F# and, after sunset, gradually return to F. The number of sunrise
rāgas with F# is very limited in contrast to the sunset rāgas, where
this note assumes an almost predominant position. The sunrise rāgas
do not omit the notes D and A at the same time (a feature which cannot be observed in our table but which will become evident in our
later presentation of rāgas). Similarly, the sunset rāgas do not omit
E and B at the same time. One or the other of each pair of notes
must be used.

   The pre-sunrise and pre-sunset rāgas stress the notes C, F
and G and often use one of these three notes as their vādī. As has
already been stated, the notes Db and Ab are important and stressed
to some extent, while E, and still more, B, are "weak," that is,
they are little used, serving mainly as "passing notes."

   Rāgas which follow the sunrise and sunset groups often employ
the notes D, E, A and B. If we consider the changes which occur
from sunrise to later morning and from sunset to evening, we observe
clearly the swaying from Db to D and from Ab to A in both sunrise
and sunset rāgas and from F# to F in the sunset and early evening
rāgas.

   Noon and midnight rāgas employ either Eb or Bb. In addition,
we find that the notes D, F and A are used. D becomes very strong,
while A and of course E become very weak or are omitted.

   Late morning rāgas tend to avoid Eb in ascent, but use it strongly in descent.

   In the early-afternoon and in the after-midnight rāgas we observe a change from D to Db, from Eb to E, from F to F#, and,
although less distinctly, from A to Ab and from Bb to B. Early-
afternoon, as well as pre-sunset, rāgas stress the notes C, F and/
or G, while corresponding rāgas of the past-midnight period stress
the note E.

   Our list is far too limited to substantiate our findings here, but
it can be enlarged after the hundreds of rāgas presented below have
been considered. It is obvious that there are deviations from the
rules stated above, but the great majority of rāgas obey them. One
of the serious disadvantages of our limited list is the fact that it

does not indicate stressed and weak notes; neither can we observe
the vakra (zigzag) steps, the various ornamentations, characteristic
"wrong" notes which enhance the "flavor" of certain rāgas, and so
forth.

South Indian rāgas, too, are ascribed certain performance times,
but their indistinct time system is based entirely upon tradition, not
upon characteristic musical features. However, a rāga-rasa relationship does exist in the South and was originally based upon the
same principles as in the North.

The concept of performance time is deeply ingrained in the
minds of the older generation of Indian musicians, and the belief that
a rāga performed at the wrong time will bring poverty and disaster
to all listeners and shorten their lives, cannot be better illustrated
than by a conversation I had in 1934 with a very famous old musician
in Bombay. The old man said, "Do you know that you people in the
West will soon experience a most terrible disaster? And do you know
why?" When I shrugged my shoulders, the old man thundered, "Because you people in the West abuse music and perform it at wrong
times and occasions! You play funeral marches and sing dirges when
there is no funeral and no cause for sadness, you sing love songs
and spring songs when there is neither love nor spring, you play
nocturnes during the day, wedding music when there is no wedding!
How long," he roared, "will the universe tolerate this abuse of music,
music, mind you, a most sacred thing?" This, probably the most
unusual reason ever offered for the outbreak of the Second World War,
illustrates better than anything else the unshakeable belief old Indian
musicians have in "that sacred thing," their music.

The names of rāgas are derived from various sources.[29] For
instance, the earliest forerunners of the rāgas, the jātis of Bharata,
as he mentions them in his Nātyasāstra, derive their names from the
Sanskrit tone names Sadja, Rsabha, Gāndhāra, Madhyama, etc., and
thus become Sadjī, Ārsabhī, Gāndhārī, Madhyamadī, etc. Other
rāga names are derived from the names of Indian tribes, for instance,
Ābhīrī, Āndhrī, Gūrjarī, Sāverī, etc. A remarkable name is Vela-
ullī, which appears for the first time in the Mānosollāsa[30] of the
twelfth century. Vela-ullī is derived from the tribe of the Velāva,
who wandered to the South, into the realm of Tamil speaking people.

Velāval eventually became the well-known rāga name Bilaval. The
rāga name Takka comes from the tribe of the Takkas or Tauk, who
dwelled in the Punjab. It is a name that may possibly be related to
the very ancient city name Taxila. Numerous rāga names are derived from the names of provinces, counties, cities, and villages. Desh,
Deshī, Deshkar refer to the Sanskrit Desa ("Country"); Votta comes
from Bhotta (Tibet); Karnāta from the South of India; Khambāvati from
the old city name Cambay; Kukubh from an ancient village (in the district of Gorakhpur) which became famous during the Gupta period;
Todī comes from Tuddi; Pūrvī refers to the East; Gauda indicates
East Bengal; Bangal comes from Bengal; Saindhvi from the Sindh
province; Sorath from Saurashtra; Tilang has its origin in the name
Trilinga, the land of the three lingams, also called Telang, with
its predominantly Telugu speaking inhabitants. Mallār refers to
Mallahara or Mallari, the Shiva lingams on the hills of the South;
the God Shiva was occasionally called Mallahari, the conqueror of
the demon Malla, and so forth.

Other rāga names are derived from the seasons and periods
of the day: Megh indicates the rainy season; Vasant (in Bengal:
Basant) means spring; Shrī refers to the autumnal harvest festival
which has a pronounced religious character; Panchamā implies spring,
when the Indian cuckoo produces his single note, panchama; and
Shyām-kalyān may imply evening-Kalyan. We observe numerous other
words which found their way into rāga names, such as Hindol, which
means "swing" and refers to the swing of God Krishna; Sarparda,
derived from svarparda, "tones which come from a foreigner," a
rāga supposedly created by Amīr Khosru[31] in the early fourteenth
century. Sohini is derived from Soni ("Beautiful"), a word which may
show a relationship to the mythical lover Soni Mahiwal of the Punjab;
Jogiya refers to Yogi; Lachhasakh may be related to sakha ("friend");
Jayjayvanti refers to jay ("victory"); and Kamod ("that which is desirable") may have various origins.

Some rāga names are or include mutilated words, probably as
a result of faulty copying. Sankīrna rāgas are "mixed" rāgas which
were in fashion several centuries after Bharata's time. Sankīrna
eventually became Sankara (Shankara), thus assuming an entirely
different meaning. Similarly, Desakhya became the Hindi rāga

name Devsakh (or Deosakh); Hamvir was turned into Hamir; Addānā
became Ādāna; and the ancient Prathama-mañjarī ("the first buds
in spring") became Pata-mañjarī or Patmañjarī. In the Rāga-Sāgara[32]
we find the name Madhuma-vati which through faulty copying became
Madhu-madhavi, whereby its meaning was completely altered, because Madhava refers to the God Krishna.

Other rāga names utilize the names of animals, trees, and
flowers: Bihāgdā is derived from the bird Vihaṅgadā; Kokila from
the Indian cuckoo; Hansadhvani comes from hamsa-dhvani, the
"voice of the swan"; Pilu may be derived from the tree salvadora
indica. A number of rāgas are named after famous musicians and
kings. For example, Miyān-ki-Mallār is named after Miyān Tānsen,
the celebrated court musician of Akbar the Great; Mirabai-ki-Mallār
is named after the famous Mirabai; Bahaduri-Todī after Sultan Baz
Bahadur of Malwa (sixteenth century); Jaunpuri-Todī (or Jivanpuri-
Todī) after the kings of Jaunpur (Jivanpur) who reigned between
1394 and 1479; Sarang after Sārṅgadeva,[33] etc.

Rhythm and Form in North Indian Music

Before we turn to the sources and, later, to the descriptions
of present-day rāgas, it is of importance to survey briefly the rhythmical and structural features of North Indian music.

The Sanskrit word tāla, which represents "rhythm," literally
means the palm of the hand or the clapping of hands. In Vedic times
two types of tāla were distinguished: mārga (lit. "to seek," "to arrive
at"), which refers to the free recitation of liturgical texts; and desī,
which refers to "country music," dance music, and other secular
types performed to the accompaniment of drums. The mārga tālas
have arisen from the Sanskrit prose and are not relevant to the clapping of hands or to regular beats.[34] The desī tālas, which became recognized during or soon after the time of Bharata, led gradually toward the fascinating system of tālas known today. Dāmodara,[35] of the
early seventeenth century, writes about tāla-jātis which may possibly
reach back to the time of Bharata, or immediately thereafter.

Indian art music, with a few insignificant exceptions, does not
employ what Curt Sachs calls "divisive" rhythms. A "divisive"

rhythm is a simple metrical organization in which the successive
bars are linked to each other like beads on a string; it is the type of
rhythm common to marches, valses, and most Western compositions
up to the twentieth century.

The Indian musician tends strongly toward the "additive" principle in rhythm, in which groups of bars (āvarta, "enclosure") recur
over and over again until the song or instrumental piece comes to an
end. While in the "divisive" form each bar (vibhāga, "division") has
the same number of metrical units as the next one, in the "additive"
form the number of metrical units may not only differ from one vibhāga
to the next but may assume different musical significance, such as
the bar containing the sam and the one containing the khāli beat.[36] The
following example, Dhamar-tāl, is an ancient rhythmic modus which
is often employed in dhrūpad[37] songs. Every āvarta in Dhamar-tāl
consists of four vibhāgas which differ from each other in the following
manner:

The above āvarta, which contains five, two, three, and four metrical
units in succession, is repeated over and over again until the song
comes to an end. Each of these four vibhāgas within each āvarta has
its own meaning. The first vibhāga is characterized by its first beat,
the sam (lit. "with," "together"), which in notation is usually indicated
by an X. The sam is a musically emphasized beat. Its significance
lies in the fact that the soloist has to perform on it either the vādī,
occasionally the samvādī, or the SA, the basic note, or, in some instances, the vishrantisthan; in short, an important note of the rāga
is used. In a performance great care has to be taken that drummer
and soloist coincide on the sam, the soloist with his important note
and the drummer with his special beat which indicate the sam. The
first beat of the second vibhāga is of lesser importance, although the
character of its first drum beat is clearly prescribed; it is notated
with the number 2. The first beat of the third vibhāga is called the
khāli, the "open beat," and is notated with the symbol 0. It is, more

or less, a warning signal for the soloist that after a certain fixed
number of metrical units the <u>sam</u> will return. The <u>khāli</u> has its own
drum sound, usually a dull, somewhat deadened effect which is distinctly recognizable.

A second example of <u>tāla</u> is <u>Tintāl</u> or <u>Tritāl</u> (<u>tin</u>, <u>tri</u>: "three,"
a "three-rhythm"). Its <u>āvarta</u> contains sixteen metrical units grouped
into four <u>vibhāgas</u>, each containing four beats.

Superficially there appears to be a similarity between <u>Tintāl</u> and the
common meter (4/4) of the West, but the different values of the four
<u>vibhāgas</u> of <u>Tintāl</u> show the attentive listener that he is dealing with
a <u>tāla</u> and not with a "divisive" Western feature. This modus is called
a "three-rhythm" because theoretically the <u>khāli</u> beat (and <u>khāli</u> vibhāga) is not counted. In practice there are, of course, four <u>vibhāgas</u>
and a total of sixteen metrical units in the <u>āvarta</u>. The sequence of
the four <u>vibhāgas</u>, notated as X 2 0 3, has to be kept intact. If the
song begins with an "upbar," for instance with 0, the sequence has
to maintain the same order as before, that is, 0 3 X 2.

There are some <u>tālas</u> which contain two or more <u>khāli</u> bars.
The following list shows the <u>āvartas</u> of some frequently used <u>tālas</u> of
North India:

<u>Ādachautāl</u>
| 1 2 | 3 4 | 5 6 | 7 8 | 9 10 | 11 12 | 13 14 |
| X | 2 | 0 | 3 | 0 | 4 | 0 |

<u>Brahmtāl</u>
1 2	3 4	5 6	7 8	9 10	11 12	13 14	15 16
X	0	2	3	0	4	5	6
17 18	19 20	21 22	23 24	25 26 27 28
0	7	8	9	10　　 0

<u>Chautāl</u>
| 1 2 | 3 4 | 5 6 | 7 8 | 9 10 | 11 12 |
| X | 0 | 2 | 0 | 3 | 4 |

<u>Dādra</u>
| 1 2 3 | 4 5 6 |
| X | 0 |

<u>Dhamar-tāl</u>
| 1 2 3 4 5 | 6 7 | 8 9 10 | 11 12 13 14 |
| X | 2 | 0 | 3 |

Dipchandi | 1   2   3 | 4   5   6   7 | 8   9   10 | 11 12 13 14 |
           | X | 2 | 0 | 3 |

Ektāl | 1   2 | 3   4 | 5   6 | 7   8 | 9   10 | 11 12 |
           | X | 0 | 2 | 0 | 3 | 4 |

Jhampa | 1   2 | 3   4   5 | 6   7 | 8   9   10 |
           | X | 2 | 0 | 3 |

Jhaptāl | 1   2 | 3   4   5 | 6   7 | 8   9   10 |
           | X | 2 | 0 | 3 |

The difference between Jhampa and Jhaptāl lies in the drum beats, which are executed differently in each tāla. Panjabi has the same structure as Tintāl, but employs differently performed drum beats.

Rūpak | 1   2   3 | 4   5 | 6   7 |
           | X | 2 | 3 |

Rūpak, Dādra, and Tivra are popular tālas. The brevity of their āvartas does not require a khāli feature. In Rūpak this is clearly noticeable, but Dādra, too, can be notated with X 2 instead of X 0.

Shikar | 1   2   3   4   5   6 | 7   8   9   10 11 12 | 13 14 15 16 17 |
       | X | 0 | 3   4 |

The second vibhāga (2) in Shikar-tāl is often not notated. One usually finds instead the sequence X 0 3 4, in which 2 is omitted.

Sultāl | 1   2 | 3   4 | 5   6 | 7   8 | 9   10 |
           | X | 0 | 2 | 3 | 0 |

Tilvada | 1   2   3   4 | 5   6   7   8 | 9   10 11 12 | 13 14 15 16 |
           | X | 2 | 0 | 3 |

Tivra | 1   2   3 | 4   5 | 6   7 |
           | X | 2 | 3 |

As we know, in Tivra there is no indication of a khali feature.

Tintāl or | 1   2   3   4 | 5   6   7   8 | 9   10 11 12 | 13 14 15 16 |
Tritāl | X | 2 | 0 | 3 |

A comparison between Tilvada and Tintāl shows that although both tālas contain sixteen metrical units that are grouped into four vibhāgas each, the basic drum beats in each tāla are different.[38] The tabla bols

("drum words") which indicate the <u>Auffuehrungspraxis</u> of the drummer
are as follows:

	1 X	2	3	4	5 2	6	7	8
<u>Tilvada</u>	DHA	TUKA	DHAN	DHAN	DHA	DHA	TI	TI
<u>Trital</u>	TA	DHAN	DHAN	DHA	TA	DHAN	DHAN	DHAN

	9 0	10	11	12	13 3	14	15	16
	TA	TUKA	DHAN	DHAN	DHA	DHA	DHAN	DHAN
	DHA	TIN	TIN	TA	TA	DHAN	DHAN	DHA

The drumming of the <u>sam</u> in the two <u>talas</u> shows that it is <u>DHA</u> in
<u>Tilvada</u> and <u>TA</u> in <u>Tintal</u>. The drum word <u>DHA</u>, in no way related
to the tone name <u>DHA</u> (<u>Dhaivata</u>), represents two beats performed
simultaneously on both drums of the <u>tabla</u> pair. They are <u>TA</u>,
performed on the right-hand drum, and <u>GHE</u>, on the left-hand drum,
the <u>Bayan</u> (<u>Banya</u>). In <u>Tintal</u>, however, the <u>sam</u> is performed only
by <u>TA</u> on the right-hand <u>tabla</u>.[39]
     North Indian <u>talas</u>, in contrast to those of South Indian music,
are not organized into groups of related types. One can assume that
this freedom was caused by the various foreign, particularly Islamic,
influences on northern music.
     The two important forms of North Indian music are the older
<u>dhrupad</u> and the more recent <u>khyal</u>. The word <u>dhrupad</u> is derived
from the Sanskrit <u>dhruva</u> ("firm," "enduring") and <u>pada</u> ("quarter-
verse"). The <u>dhrupad</u> represents a verse which is often repeated,
a characteristic which however, can also be observed in the <u>khyal</u>.
Indian musicians used to say that only a man who has the strength of
five buffaloes can sing <u>dhrupad</u>. Today <u>dhrupad</u> singing is very rare;
it requires unusual perseverance of the singer because a <u>dhrupad</u>
performance may last many hours. It avoids all ornamentations and
virtuoso elements and asks for a particularly clear and firm intonation. If there are doubts concerning the correct performance of a
certain <u>raga</u>, Indian musicians will never consult the works of the
Sanskrit theorists but refer instead to the classical <u>dhrupad</u>.
     It is uncertain when the <u>dhrupad</u> came into existence. We know
that it represents the ancient, classical song form and that in it the

rāga is shown in its clearest and purest form. Its formal structure
resembles the Western rondo form and, in spite of many variants,
is also the basis of the modern North Indian khyāl and of the South
Indian kīrtana.[40] The dhrūpad is only sung in one of the following four
talās: Chautāl, Dhamar-tāl, Surphakta (Sulphakta),[41] and Tevra.[42]

    The texts of dhrūpads are frequently of a religious nature.
Occasionally singers may employ the meaningless syllables "nom"
and "tom." The dhrūpad, always rendered in a slow and dignified
manner, is invariably accompanied by a mridanga (or by a pakhawaj),
the ancient barrel drum of India, never by a tabla pair.

    The form of the dhrūpad consists of an ālāp, a prelude, followed
by four sections: the asthāyī (or sthāyī), the antara, the sanchārī,
and the ābhog. In the ālāp the drum is silent; only the bourdon bass
of the tanbura is used as accompaniment. This rhythmically free
prelude is a representation of the essential features of the rāga. Step
by step, the singer shows the ascent and descent of the scale, the
strong and weak notes, and characteristic phrases and typical ornaments. It is usually performed in two sections: the first one presents the material of the lower tetrachord of the scale and the second
one emphasizes the notes of the upper tetrachord. The only exception
can be observed in rāgas where the melodies have to begin with the
upper SA (c), as, for example, in rāga Vasant. In such instances
the singer begins with the upper and continues with the lower tetrachord. The ālāp has no text; usually the syllables "ah" or "nah" are
employed. In the subsequent song one can now and then observe some
minor deviations from the rules of the rāga. These irregularities,
often caused by the textual syllables which may compel the musician
to prolong a basically short note or shorten a stressed note, never
occur in the wordless ālāp. The ālāp has for the Indian musician a
greater significance than that of a mere prelude, because in it the
rāga is manifested in its most distinct and faultless manner. It is
the ālāp that prepares the foundation of the prevailing rasa. The
duration of the ālāp is left to the discretion of the soloist. When the
soloist feels that he has presented all the essential features of the
rāga and has thus firmly established the required mood, he will,
without interrupting his singing, begin the first part of the song, the
asthāyī ("at home"). With the beginning of the asthāyī, the drummer

starts his beats. Even an inexperienced listener will recognize this
point because after the rhythmically free ālāp the sudden appearance
of rhythm and distinct drum beats can have a surprising and electri-
fying effect. From now on soloist (with tanbura) and drummer perform together. Both are intent that the sam and vādī (or samvādī,
SA or vishrantisthan) coincide. In the asthāyī the soloist deals
mainly with the notes of the lower tetrachord, except in those rāgas
which have to begin with the upper SA (c). The asthāyī can begin
with any beat of the āvarta but has to end on the sam.

The second part of the song, the antara ("interval," referring
to the notes of the upper tetrachord), follows the asthāyī usually
without any interruption. If the melody of the asthāyī has come to
an end before the āvarta is completed, the soloist has to wait until
the drummer has concluded his drum phrase (theka). In the antara
the notes of the upper tetrachord of the scale prevail, except in
those rāgas which begin with the high SA (c), where the notes of the
upper tetrachord are used in the asthāyī.

A link similar to that between asthāyī and antara can be observed between the antara and the third part of the song, the sanchārī
("alternation"). The name sanchārī refers to the use of the notes of
both tetrachords, which may (or may not) appear in some alternating
fashion. This part resembles to some degree a development of
the previously stated material.

The concluding part of the song is the ābhog ("coda") in which
a return of the melody to the asthāyī can be noticed. The song ends
either on the vādī or SA, with the sam of the drummer.

The dhrūpad does not employ any variations or ornaments, nor
do we find any virtuoso features. Tempo and meter may change
toward the end of the song, showing a speeding up. In the "coda"
the singer may first perform the dugan, in which all note values are
shortened to one-half of their original duration. After the dugan may
follow the ād in which the original note values are shortened to a
third, and in the following chaugan to a quarter. In some rare cases
one may still hear the kuar in which all original note values are
shortened to a sixteenth.

The second, less ancient form of the North Indian art song is
the khyāl. The words khayāl karo could be translated as "imagine,"

"take heed," or "pay attention." Indian musician used to say "khyāl karo" to each other when they sang or played a new piece. This exclamation is supposed to have been the origin of the word khyāl. Arnold Bake, in his article on Indian Music,[43] believes that the name khyāl may be of Arabic-Persian origin (Arab., Kayal, "fantasy").

While the heavy dhrūpad remained free of Mohammedan influences, the lighter khyāl is said to have had its origin with Mahmud Sharqi of Jaunpur (1401-1440). Mahmud Sarqi created this form in free imitation of the dhrūpad. The khyāl experienced its golden age during the Mohammedan period of North India, but even today it is still the most important form of North Indian art songs and instrumental pieces. The khyāl resembles the Western rondo form more than does the dhrūpad. Its texts deal with love and admiration of, or grief about the absence of, the beloved and can now and then contain religious sentiments also. In the text of the antara pseudonyms of Indian musicians may occasionally appear. For instance, "Sadarangile," which stands for Niamat Khan; "Sarasranga" for the great Tansen: "Ram Priya" for the famous Fayyaz Khan; "Kisan Priya" for the excellent Professor Deodhar of Bombay; and so forth.

The drums used in the khyāl performance are invariably the tabla pair. In addition to the solo (vocal or instrumental) part, tanbura bass and drums, we often find one or more accompanying melody instruments, mostly string instruments, such as the sarangi. The accompaniment is executed in the following manner. As has already been mentioned, the tanbura performs the bourdon bass and the tablas provide the rhythmical foundation. The third player, however—let us assume it is a sarangi player—imitates the melody of the soloist. It is understandable that his accompaniment limps a little in time after the notes of the solo part. This manner of accompaniment, although at first hearing surprising, is not at all disturbing, because the sarangi player is fully aware of all the rules and regulations of the rāga and can frequently anticipate the notes which the soloist is going to perform. Particularly at the sam, the sarangi player will anticipate the vādī and perform this note synchronously with the soloist. When the sam has been passed, the accompanying string player will again be slightly behind the vocal part in time. This somewhat heterophonic method of accompaniment represents

a more or less vague delineation of the melody. As the accompanist
does not perform any notes which are foreign to the rāga, the end
effect is neither unpleasant nor confusing. At times when the singer
is stopped, the string player will perform his part in strict rhythm
with the drum part until the singer starts again. Then the sarangi
will continue to follow the vocal line like a musical shadow.

The form of the khyāl is, of course, related to the dhrūpad.
In the khyāl, however, numerous melismas, variations, ornaments,
and other musical "fireworks" which are strictly forbidden in the
severe dhrūpad.

The form of the khyāl is as follows:

1. The ālāp of the khyāl is shorter than that of the dhrūpad.
Its performance is the same as that of the dhrūpad; only soloist and
tanbura perform, while the tablas remain silent. The soloist first
deals with the notes of the lower tetrachord, then with those of the
upper, thereby presenting to his listeners the strong and weak notes,
characteristic phrases, etc., of the rāga.

2. At the beginning of the asthāyī the drummer usually starts
with a prescribed sequence of beats. This opening drum phrase,
called peshkar, is a brief, ornamented feature which leads into the
proper sequence of beats (theka). In contrast to the dhrūpad, where
only a few rhythmic modi are permissible, khyāls can be in a large
number of tālas.

3. As in the dhrūpad, the asthāyī of the khyāl is followed by
the antara. Both of these sections have approximately the same
duration. In the antara the melody of the soloist moves up to the
notes of the upper tetrachord. When the antara is completed, the
soloist returns to:

4. A brief repetition of the asthāyī. Usually the soloist will
perform here only one āvarta of the asthāyī, which extends from one
sam to the next.

5. After this interpolation of an asthāyī segment, the so-called
proper or big ālāp follows. This ālāp differs from the first one by
the addition of a drum accompaniment. Although the vocal line is
rhythmically free, the drummer performs his thekas, and when the
sam occurs, the "floating" melody of the soloist touches either the
vādī or the SA. This ālāp consists of two sections. The first is the

rāga ālāp, in which, similar to the first ālāp, is shown the tone
material of the rāga, the strong and weak notes, characteristic
phrases, etc.; the second is the rūpaka ālāp, in which the formal
structure of the whole song is shown in miniature. It shows in
diminutive form the sequence of asthāyī, antara, sanchārī, and ābhog.
All these are presented by the soloist in a rhythmically free manner
(to the accompaniment of the tablas). The syllables "ah" or "nah"
and occasionally also the names of the notes (SA, RE, GA, MA, PA,
etc.) appear here as text. This is the part of the song that often
leads to angry arguments between soloist and drummer, because
while the singer has to move freely, the drummer, not to be outdone,
indulges in complex variations which eventually can mislead the singer
and cause him to miss a sam and perform a wrong note on this important beat. This proper ālāp, which may last longer than all the
other parts of the song, ends with:

6. A repetition of both asthāyī and antara. This interpolation
is often avoided in contemporary performances.

7. The next part of the khyāl is the bol-tans. Tan, or tana
("uninterrupted succession," "melodic figuration"), is a sequence of
notes performed at a fast speed; it may be a variation or any form of
"fioritura." In this part of the song the singer utilizes the text words
(bolna, "to speak") in a manner similar to the Italian opera of the late
seventeenth or eighteenth centuries. Words are repeated and move
about in order to provide a convenient textual setting of the increasingly complex tans. The bol-tans are presented in two groups, the
small bol-tans and the big bol-tans. In the small bol-tans the figurations are comparatively brief, while in the big bol-tans more extensive and bolder forms appear. The bol-tans are followed by:

8. A repetition of the asthāyī and antara which, at the present
time, is frequently omitted.

9. The following part of the khyāl is the real or proper tans.
In this part we observe complex figurations and variations which are
all performed in strict rhythm but without text, only to the syllables
"ah" or "na." This part offers the soloist an opportunity to show his
artistry. His improvisation within the strictly delineated confines
of the rāga leads here to fast colorature passages which, according
to their shape, the Indian musician describes as zigzags, elephant-calls,

garlands, waterfalls, fountains, rainbows, etc. This part signifies
for performer and audience the climax of the performance. These
real tans are grouped again into small and big ones which correspond
in character to the small and big bol-tans.

After this part the performer has two possibilities of continuing the khyāl.

10. Either he will introduce a new melody with its own asthāyī
and antara, or the khyāl will conclude here with the first phrase of
the old asthāyī on the sam. In the first instance, when a new theme
is introduced, we find that it is performed in a faster tempo than that
of the preceding song. It may even contain a few brilliant tans which
roughly correspond to the stretta of an Italian operatic aria. In the
other instance, when the first āvarta of the old asthāyī is repeated,
the khyāl often comes to an unexpected, occasionally rather abrupt
conclusion.

We observe that in the khyāl the dhrūpad parts sanchārī and
ābhog are generally avoided. Their appearance in the rūpaka ālāp
is so fleeting and so brief that they are hardly noticed by an unin-
formed listener.

As a conclusion to this brief description of the important
North Indian song forms, a considerably shortened form of a khyāl
in rāga Durga[44] is shown below. This type of rāga Durga belongs to
the Bilaval thāta (another type of rāga Durga is ascribed to the
Khamaj thāta[45]) and has, as an exception, the note PA (G) as vādī,
although usually MA (F) assumes this function. The scale of this
rāga is C D F G A c. In the descending scale two characteristic
gliding steps, c-A and F-D, appear. The tāla is Jhaptāl.

KHYĀL IN DURGA (Bilaval Thāta; Jhaptāl)

Ālāp

Asthāyī

Antara

Asthāyī repeated

1. Proper ālāp

Beginning of the asthāyī

2. Ālāp

Beginning of the asthāyī

3. Ālāp

Beginning of the asthāyī

4. Ālāp

Beginning of the asthāyī

5. Ālāp

End of the ālāp and opening phrase of the asthāyī

1. Small bol-tan

2. Small bol-tan

3. Small bol-tan

Beginning of the asthāyī

4. Big bol-tan

Beginning of the asthāyī

5. <u>Big bol-tan</u>

The complete <u>asthāyī</u>

1. <u>Small proper tan</u>

2. <u>Small proper tan</u>

3. <u>Small proper tan</u>

4. <u>Small proper tan</u>

Beginning of the <u>asthāyī</u>

5. Big tan

Beginning of the asthāyī

6. Big tan

Beginning of the asthāyī

7. Big tan

Beginning of the asthāyī

8. Big tan

Beginning of the asthāyī

Conclusion on the vādī

x

II

SOURCES AND HISTORY

Up to the end of the twelfth or the beginning of the thirteenth century the whole of India had more or less one system of art music. With the Islamic conquest of the northern parts of the peninsula, however, Arabic-Persian musical elements were imported which, although stimulating, caused considerable confusion. Some Mohammedan rulers employed their own as well as Hindu musicians and encouraged a fusion of the two musical styles. This led to competition between Islamic and Hindu artists who were striving to gain the favor of the sovereigns at all costs, and resulted in the distortion of old, and the creation of new, rāgas and forms. This new musical trend showed sparks of genuine inspiration, but nevertheless impeded a uniform development of North Indian music. No orderly system evolved from these endeavors to amalgamate the two styles. As a matter of fact, a variegated disorder ensued, particularly in the classification of rāgas. Only after more than half a millennium of manifold efforts toward achieving some order was a comparatively stable system of North Indian rāgas established.

The ancient music of the Hindus, as it existed before the Mohammedan invasions, found refuge in the South where, although subject to some local influences, it was little disturbed and could evolve into a remarkably orderly system which was more or less finalized in the seventeenth and eighteenth centuries and is still in use at the present time.

Attempts to write a comprehensive history of Indian music will continue to meet with severe difficulties until a great number of historical and theoretical works are freed from the dust of libraries and made available to scholars. The libraries of the former Maharajahs of Bikaner and Kashi, the libraries of Trivandrum and Tanjore, the Government Oriental Library of Mysore, numerous libraries in

Calcutta, Madras, Khatmandu, and many private collections contain
valuable documents which probably could fill the embarrassingly
large gaps in our present knowledge of the musical past of India.[1]

Another difficulty, not as easily solved as the rescue of works
from libraries, is created by the fact that the great majority of
Sanskrit authors left us only lists with rāga names along with some
vague descriptions which permit only indefinite and ambiguous interpretations. Thus, surveying these works would confine us to a
mere enumeration of rāga names, with very little chance of being
able to describe their scales. The destroying and building forces
that became manifest during the Islamic invasion of India are reflected, for instance, in the postulation of varying basic scales.
The choice of the fundamental scales that serve as starting points
for the descriptions of derivative scales still requires much investigation. We know that these basic scales occasionally changed not
only from one region to another but even from one author to another.
We face instances where the fundamental scale an author uses is so
poorly defined that all other scales derived from it become far too
vague to be of any value. Authors from the South, attracted by the
splendor of the courts of the Mogul emperors, came to the North
and wrote their learned books there; yet they used as fundamental
scales their southern scales—without mentioning this fact. Even at
the present time scholars are still uncertain whether the works of
certain authors should be described as southern or northern.

Before turning to a description of the rāgas, it would be desirable to make a survey of some of the important northern Sanskrit
and Hindi sources and trace the history of the rāgas, their evolution,
classifications, and other features throughout the centuries up to
the present time. Such an endeavor would require an extensive separate volume far beyond the scope of this study. Much of the survey,
however, has already been made by several scholars, particularly
by O. C. Gangoly in his book Rāgas and Rāginīs (Bombay, 1935), and
by Pandit V. N. Bhatkhande in his "A Comparative Study of Some
Leading Music Systems of the 15th, 16th, 17th and 18th Centuries,"
and in his A Short Historical Survey of the Music of Upper India
(Bombay, 1934). It would be of little value to repeat their information. Instead, a list of a few important Sanskrit and Hindi sources,

in an approximately chronological order, is shown below, with some
comments which may be helpful, particularly if used in conjunction
with the above-named works.

———

Bharata, Nātyasāstra; Kāvya Māla Series, No. 42 (Bombay, n.d.);
Kashi Sanskrit Series, No. 60 (Benares, 1926); English translation
by Manmohar Ghose (Calcutta: The Royal Asiatic Society of Bengal,
1950). This is the earliest known work on theater, dance, and music,
and was written either in the second century B.C., or in the second,
third, or even fifth century A.D. The work is probably a collection
of treatises by several Bharatas, "dancer-actors," such as Bharata
Nandikesvara and Bharata Kohala. The work offers information
about scale degrees (XXVIII, 23), "consonances" and "dissonances"
(XXVIII, 24), and basic grāmas defined by means of srutis (XXVIII,
25-28). In XXVIII, 31-33 the mūrchhanās (from the Sanskrit murch,
"increase," "enlarge," referring to the regulated up and down of a scale;
in works written several centuries later, mūrchhanā is also used to
indicate the ornamentation of a note; see Fox-Strangways, p. 106),
seven-degree scales, are derived from the grāmas. Later, seven
jātis were employed (Sanskrit: "kind," "sort," "manner," "mode";
the term jāti is used for two concepts—scales, and certain groups
of srutis with the same or similar rasas). Bharata's jātis are
scales which differ from the mūrchhanās by having several characteristic features such as initial notes (graha), final notes (nyāsa),
central notes (amsa), secondary final notes (apanyāsa), etc., and
thus become indeed the forerunners of the rāgas. (See Gangoly, pp.
10 ff., and pp. 175 f. for a list of jātis; see also E. Clements, Introduction to the Study of Indian Music [London, 1913], which contains an
English translation of XXVIII, 22-35.)

Dattila, Untitled Sanskrit Text; Trivandrum Edition, CII (1930), 5,
49-54. Dattila's work, written in the second (?) century, mentions
eighteen jātis. Dattila's name appears several times in the
Bharatanātyasāstra, and Gangoly (p. 11) writes about an ancient
tradition according to which Dattila is considered to be one of the
"Five Bharatas" (the others are Nandi, Kohala, Bharata, and Matanga).
(See Gangoly, pp. 11 ff.; list of jātis, p. 175.)

The Kuḍumiyamālai Inscription; described by P. R. Bhandarkar in
"The Kuḍimiyamālai Inscription of Music," Epigraphia Indica, XII
(Calcutta, 1914), 226-37. This famous sixth- or seventh-century
South Indian rock inscription, discovered in 1904 in the province
of Pudukōṭṭai, contains seven rāgas (or jātis) notated with the tone
syllables SA, RA, GA, A (for antara GA), MA, PA, DHA, NA, and
KA (for kākali NI). Many centuries later some South Indian theorists
again employed similar vowel changes in their tone syllables in
order to denote alterations of pitches, but it is most unlikely that
this method was derived from the tone syllables of the Kuḍumiyamālai
Inscription. Bhandarkar describes the notes of the inscription as
C, D, E♭, E, F, G, A, B♭, and B. None of the seven rāgas of the
inscription (their names are mentioned in Gangoly, p. 15) are mentioned by Bharata. They appear, however, in the Nāradīyā-Śikṣā
(Calcutta, 1890; Benares Sanskrit Series, 1893; Mysore, 1946).
This latter work, written perhaps as early as the Bharatanātyaśāstra
and with little justification ascribed to Nārada, is one of the first
mentioning microtonal intervals (śrutis) and creates a bridge between
the sāmavedic chant (including ritual and mudrās) and early art
music. (See Swami Prajnanananda, A History of Indian Music
[Calcutta, 1963], pp. 16, 36, 38, 45, 68.)

Mataṅga, Bṛhaddeśi; Trivandrum Sanskrit Series, XCIV (1928),
82-133. A work on secular music written sometime between the fifth
and seventh centuries. Mataṅga is the first Sanskrit author to employ the word rāga as a musical term. He groups his gītis ("melodies");
among them are rāga-gītis) into main and subordinate forms. He
also provides information about the rasas of his rāgas. (See Gangoly,
pp. 16 ff.; lists of gītis, etc., pp. 177 f.)

Nārada, Saṅgīta-Makaranda; Gaekwad's Oriental Series, XVI, M. R.
Telang, ed. (Baroda, 1920). This work, written some time between
the seventh and eleventh centuries, presents two groupings of rāgas,
one stating eight main rāgas, subordinating to each rāga three "female"
ones; the second postulates six main rāgas and subordinates to each
rāga six "female." Nārada uses the terms rāga or pumliṅga for his
main rāgas, strī or yosit for the "females," and napumsaka for a
few "neutral" ones. Nārada writes about performance times and

divides his rāgas into morning-, noon-, afternoon-, and night-rāgas (III, 10-23). (See Gangoly, pp. 21 ff.; lists of rāgas, pp. 179 ff.)

Someśvara, Abhilāsārtha-Cintamaṇī or Mānasollāsa. Sections of this work (omitting the two chapters on music) were reprinted in the Mysore Oriental Publication Series, 69 (1926), and in Gaekwad's Oriental Series, 28, I (Baroda, 1925). A complete manuscript is preserved in the Bhandarkar Research Institute, Poona. The work was written in 1131; the author writes about śuddha-rāgas, bhinna-rāgas, gauda-rāgas, etc., without offering any distinct classification. Someśvara also deals with the rasas and refers the performance times of his rāgas to the six seasons of India. (See Gangoly, pp. 19 ff.; list of rāgas, pp. 184 f.)

Pañcama-Sāra-Samhitā. Several handwritten copies of this work are extant. One, in Bengali, is in the collection of the Bangīya Sahitya Parisad, Calcutta (No. 716); another, older copy, made in 1440, is preserved in the Library of the Asiatic Society of Bengal (Calcutta), No. 5040. The time of origin (perhaps sometime between the seventh and eleventh centuries) and the authorship (Nārada?) are uncertain. The author implies that some of his rāga names refer to melodies prevalent in his time in Rajputana, Gujarat, Cutch, and Meerut. The Pañcama-Sāra-Samhitā is most probably the first Sanskrit work in which the subordinate forms, the "wives" of the rāgas, are called rāginīs. The work mentions six rāgas, each having six rāginīs. (See Gangoly, pp. 24 f.; list of rāgas, pp. 191 f.)

Nātya-Locana. One unclearly written manuscript is preserved in the Library of the Asiatic Society of Bengal (Calcutta), No. III, E. 158. The unknown author of this work deals with theater, drama, and music. It was written some time between the ninth and eleventh centuries. The 44 (?) rāgas mentioned are not yet subject to the rāga-rāginī organization. They are grouped into six śuddha, sixteen śālamka, and twenty-two (?) sandhi rāgas. Śuddha, as we know, means "pure" and refers to the main rāgas; śālamka points to altered forms; and sandhi (transitional) may either mean mixed rāgas (miśra or saṅkīrna) or refer to performance times at sunrise and sunset. The term sandhi appears also in the work of Bharata, where

it is applied to the jāti-sādhārana forms and where no attention is
paid to performance times. One should assume that the sandhi types
of the Nātya-Locana are musically transitional types standing between main rāgas and derivative forms. A similar feature can be
noted in the bhāsā-gītis of Mataṅga (see above and Gangoly, p. 177).
(See Gangoly, pp. 25 f.; list of rāgas, pp. 182 f.)

Nānyadeva, Sarasvatī-Hrdāyālamkāra. The only manuscript extant
is preserved in the Bhandarkar Oriental Institute, Poona, in 221
folios as No. 111, 1869-70, and is catalogued under the title Bharata-
bhāsya (Commentary to the Bharatanātyaśāstra). The treatise, written
between 1097 and 1133, is based upon the works of Nārada, Mataṅga,
and others. It describes the structure of the rāgas, their Auffuehrungspraxis, and classification (Chapters VI and VII). The royal
author employs the terms mūla-rāga ("root-rāga"), svarākhya-rāga
(in which the name of the rāga is derived from the name of a svara,
a note; e. g., rāga Dhaivatī, derived from the note Dhaivata, abbreviated
DHA, etc.), and desākhya-rāga (from desa, "country," referring to
folk and other melodies of certain regions and provinces). (See
Gangoly, pp. 29 f.; list of rāgas, pp. 183 f.)

Locanakavi, Rāga-Tarangini; E. D. Joshi, ed. (Poona, 1918). This
work was written in 1162 (or 1375) in Maithili, a Hindi dialect. Of
the one hundred pages of the book, sixty-two are devoted to verses
of Vidyapati, a celebrated poet. Locanakavi introduces each poem
with a short sloka ("verse") which prescribes the required rāga
and tāla. The terminology of Locanakavi is southern, but the names
of the rāgas are generally northern. The author speaks of twelve
melas (main rāgas) and seventy-seven janya rāgas (subordinate
forms). Bhatkhande believes that the basic scale of Locanakavi is
C D E♭ F G A B♭ c, which corresponds to the North Indian rāga
Kafi. (See Bhatkhande, "A Comparative Study. . . ," pp. 13 ff.;
and Gangoly; list of rāgas, pp. 196 f.)

Śārṅgadeva, Saṅgīta-Ratnākara; Anandasrama Sanskrit Series (Poona,
1896); Adyar Library (Madras, 1943). This work, often considered
to be the "Liber Magnus" of medieval North Indian music, was
written in the first half of the thirteenth century. Śārṅgadeva's

grandfather, a learned man, is said to have come from Kashmir
and settled in Devagiri (the present Daulatabad) in the Deccan.
Sārṅgadeva's father was in the services of the Yādava kings Bhillama
and Sinhaladeva, and Sārṅgadeva himself lived at the court of
Sinhaladeva in Devagiri.   The Saṅgīta-Ratnākara, the "Ocean of
Music," was and is subject to severe controversy, the main dispute
being whether the work represents northern or southern music.
It deals mainly with the art of singing and dancing, and a few statements are made about drama and music.   Among these statements
appear some strange remarks concerning dramatic gestures.   Eval-
uations of the work are so diverse that at least one opinion, that of
Pandit Bhatkhande, may be mentioned here:

> Even at this day. . . the Southerners always talk about
> Sharangadeva as one of their own writers.   But what is
> it that we observe in the northern part of the country?
> The name and fame of the Ratnākara are of course known
> there, but no sensible attempts seem to have been made
> anywhere to penetrate the mysteries of the book.   None
> of our northern professionals seem to know what the
> book contains.   It is only in the last century that we find
> one or two attempts at translating the work into the
> Hindi language, but the translators never seem to have
> understood even the shuddha scale of Sharangadeva and
> have, therefore, absolutely failed to follow his music.
> It would certainly be interesting to know why such a
> great work like the Ratnākara should have become ab-
> solutely unintelligible everywhere within about a hun-
> dred and fifty years of its completion.   Our wonder is
> only increased when we see that Kallinatha, Sharanga-
> deva's great commentator, and the other subsequent
> southern writers who freely quote from his work, the
> Ratnākara, should not be in a position to explain any
> of the rāgas described in it, notwithstanding the fact
> that many of the latter were such as they themselves
> perhaps constantly sang and played.   (A Short Historical
> Survey. . . , pp. 16 f.)

Sārṅgadeva describes the degrees of his scales by śruti numbers
and string divisions (III, 13-16).   In III, 48 the author endeavors
to describe the pitches by comparing them to the cries of animals.
Sārṅgadeva states that each of his jātis is distinguished by twelve
characteristics (graha, nyāsa, etc.), instead of the ten postulated
by Bharata.   His theoretical considerations are followed by four
lists of rāgas.   Although Nānyadeva in his Sarasvati-Hrdāyālamkāra

mentions relationships between some of his rāgas and deities, the
Saṅgīta-Ratnākara is usually considered to be the first Sanskrit work
which distinctly associates rāgas with deities and patron saints and,
as many authors have done before, relates rāgas to specific performance times. (See Gangoly, pp. 31 ff.; list of rāgas, pp. 185 ff.)

Pārśvadeva, Saṅgīta-Samayasāra; T. G. Śastri, ed., Trivandrum
Sanskrit Series, LXXXVII (1925). This work was written some time
between 1165 and 1330. The author speaks of 101 rāgas which are
presented as āṅga ("similarity," "likeness") types: rāgāṅgas,
bhāsāṅgas, upāṅgas, and kriyāṅgas. Originally bhāsāṅga connotated
a rāga from a certain district which showed characteristics of simple
folk music. Hence bhāsāṅga was also referred to as deśāṅga rāga,
a "country-type rāga." During the last three centuries, the term
bhāsāṅga has changed its meaning and signifies an upāṅga type which
has one or more foreign notes in its primary scale. Kriyāṅga is a
term which at the present time has lost its significance. Dāmodara
in his Saṅgīta-Darpana (seventeenth century) states that kriyāṅgas
are rāgas which invoke exaltation in performers and listeners.
Other authors, however, apply this term to rāgas with vakra features,
and another group of writers uses kriyāṅga only when referring to
rāgas whose names end with the syllables -kriya, such as Devakriya,
Ramakriya, etc. The term kriyāṅga has been erroneously used to
refer to janya rāgas which employed foreign notes. Pārśvadeva
divides all his rāgāṅgas, bhāsāṅgas, upāṅgas, and kriyāṅgas into
sampūrna (heptatonic), sādava (hexatonic), and odava (pentatonic)
forms. (See Gangoly, pp. 34 f.; list of rāgas, pp. 187 f.)

Rāgārnava. The original text of this work is lost. Its material has
been quoted in a Sanskrit encyclopedia, the Śārṅgadhara-Paddhati,
compiled in 1363 (Gangoly, p. 190). The anonymous author lists six
main rāgas, each having five subordinate types. It is remarkable
that in this work subordinate forms are not called rāginīs or uparāgas,
but are simply designated as rāgas. (See Gangoly, pp. 35; list of
rāgas, pp. 190 f.)

Subhamkara, Samgāna-Sāgara. According to Gangoly (p. 36) the
manuscript is preserved in the Library of the Asiatic Society of

Bengal (Calcutta).   The fragmentary work was written in Newari
script on palm leaves in 1308.   The author was in the service of
Maharajah Bhumalla Deva in Nepal.   Subhamkara speaks of thirty-
four rāgas and eighteen jātis and derives his information mainly from
the work of Someṡvara.

Joytirīṡvara, Varna-Ratnākara.   The work is discussed by S. K.
Chatterjee in "The Varṇa-Ratnākara of Joytirīṡvara Kaviṡekharācārya,"
Proceedings of the Fourth Oriental Conference, II (Allahabad, 1928),
553-621.   This unique palm-leaf manuscript, written in the old
Maithili language, is preserved in the Government Collection of
the Asiatic Society of Bengal (Calcutta), as No. 48134.   Its colophon
indicates 1507 as the year of its origin.   The seventh part of this
encyclopedic work deals with poetry, music, and dance.   The author
presents the popular rāgas of the early sixteenth century without
grouping or classifying them.   (See Gangoly, pp. 36 f.)

   Occasionally Persian maqamat and North Indian rāgas were
combined into new forms even before the Mohammedan invasions.
The impact of Islamic music upon the music of northern India became distinctly noticeable during the period of the early Sultans of
Delhi, and still more in the fifteenth century, the period of the later
Sultanates of Delhi, Kashmir, Jaunpur, Bengal, Malwa, Gujarat,
Deccan, etc.   This trend continued in splendor at the courts of the
Mogul Emperors of the sixteenth and seventeenth centuries.   The
music of South India remained comparatively free of foreign influences and provides even today some semblance of Indian music as
it may have been before the fateful invasions.   There are many
Indian musicians who decry the mixture of Indian and Mohammedan
styles, and South Indian musicians who insist that their disciples be
kept away from the "corrupted and disfigured" music of the North.
An impartial observer, however, will notice that the fusion of the
two styles has been the cause of numerous fascinating new forms
which an undisturbed evolution of purely Indian music would probably
not have created.
      The Mohammedan invaders had little intention of studying
Indian music, and Indian musicians serving under the great sultans

and emperors were not interested in presenting to their new patrons
the ancient jātis and rāgas. The Indian artists were more or less
compelled to make manifold modifications of their own scales, melodies, rhythms, and forms, only to be able to compete with the imported music of the Mohammedan court musicians. Out of these
endeavors there arose a "modern" music of the Indian North that
eventually found favor with the Mohammedan rulers. Among the
rulers who fostered this new music were particularly Sultan Alā'-
ud-dīn (1295-1316) and his contemporary, the famous poet Amir
Khosru of Delhi (1254-1325), Sultan Husain Shurquee of Jaunpur; and,
later, Sultan Bahadur of Gujarat (1526-36) and, finally, Akbar the
Great (1556-1605). The poet Amir Khosru, who was strongly influenced by Muslim mysticism (Sufism), was an experienced and ingenious musician. He probably had little interest in preserving the
revered ancient Indian jātis and rāgas but attempted the creation of
new rāgas by fusing Indian and Persian musical elements (the singing
of these mixed rāgas was called qavali). The names of some of
these newly created rāgas are listed in Gangoly, p. 40. In addition
to the invention of new rāgas, Amir Khosru and his Sultan Alā'-ud-
dīn are believed to have been the creators of the Khyāl, the "modern"
form in Indian art music.

Kallinātha, Saṅgīta-Ratnākaratikā; Adyar Library (Madras, 1945).
This work, written in 1460, is a partly obscure commentary on
Sārṅgadeva's Saṅgīta-Ratnākara, which has equally obscure sections.
Pandit Kallinātha lists six head rāgas, each having six subordinate
rāginīs. The complete list of these rāgas can be found in Gangoly,
pp. 192 f.

Kṛṣṇa Kīrtana ("Songs of Krishna"). Manindra Mohan Basu discusses
these manuscripts in "Srī Kṛṣṇa Kīrtaner Navāviskṛta Puthi" (in
Bengali), Sāhitya Parisad Patrikā XXXIX, 3 (Calcutta, 1939), 176-
194. Toward the end of the fourteenth century there began in Bengal
a strong religious movement which caused the creation of numerous
Vaishnavitic songs. The movement culminated in the famous
Vaishnavitic preacher Chaitanya (1485-1533), who condemned many
Hindu rituals and the caste system and appeared to reach out toward
the ideals of Islam. The most interesting and dramatic person of

this movement, whose fame was still undiminished a few years ago
when he was made the hero of a motion picture, was the poor priest
Candidas (Chandi Das). He lived about 1400 and became famous
through his Kr̥sna Kīrtana. These songs, which for the first time
raised Bengali to the level of a literary language (other vernacular
languages, particularly Hindi, had been in literary use since the
eleventh century), possess an unusually religious-passionate-romantic
character. Candidas' attitude, and the fiery, revolutionary character of his love songs were the cause of his excommunication by the
Brahmins. A repentent Candidas eventually agreed to renounce at
a public ceremony his songs and his love for his adored Rami.
During the ceremony, however, Candidas saw Rami standing among
the people in front of him. Instead of renouncing his love, he sank
upon his knees before her with folded hands and compared her
beauty and charm to the ideals of Brahmanism. A list of the rāgas
in which the Kr̥sna Kīrtana were to be sung may be found in Gangoly,
p. 45. (See Gangoly, pp. 44 f.)

Kumbhakarṇa, Saṅgīta-Rāga. The manuscript is preserved in the
collection of the Bhandarkar Oriental Research Institute, Poona,
as No. 365 (1879-80). Rāṇā Kumbhakarṇa of Mewar (ca. 1419-60)
writes about thirty bhāṣā-gītis and makes a clear distinction between
gīta ("song") and rāga. He states that only those gītis may be called
rāgas which possess the ten characteristics of Bharata's jātis. The
royal author ascribes to each of his rāgas a characteristic tāla
which, in his opinion, brings out the true and "happiest" nature of
the rāga. (See Gangoly, pp. 46 ff.)

Kṣema Karṇa (or Meṣa Karṇa), Rāga-Mālā. The manuscript is
preserved in the Government Collection of the Asiatic Society of
Bengal (Calcutta), as No. 1195 (211). Another copy of the manuscript
is to be found in the India Office (No. 1125-15165), ascribed to an
author named Kṣemakarṇa Pāṭhaka. After the beginning of the sixteenth century there appears to have been a notable increase in the
number of works dealing with the pictorial representations of rāgas.
The Rāga-Mālā, a frequently used title, was written in 1509 (or,
according to Fox-Strangways, p. 105, in 1507). The author, who
lived in Rewa State, groups his material into six head rāgas, each

having five rāginīs and eight "sons." (See Gangoly, pp. 49 f.; list
of rāgas, pp. 194 f.)

Mān Singh, Mān-Kutūhala ("Rarities of Man"). A manuscript of
this work (in Hindi) is in the possession of H. H. the Nawab Saheb
of Rampur (Gangoly, p. 50). Raja Mān Siṃha Tomar (Raja Mān
Singh) of Gwalior (1486-1517), the author, was particularly concerned with "mixed" (sankirna) rāgas. Four of his rāgas have the
name Gujari. Gujari points to Gujarat, the home of Raja Mān's
queen Mṛga-Nenā ("the one with the eyes of a deer"). The musical
life of this period, particularly of Gwalior, was highly praised and
famous. The fame of Gwalior prevailed up to the middle of the
present century. Many musical achievements (true or invented)
were ascribed to the celebrated court musicians of Gwalior, such as
the invention of new rāgas, the creation of a particular style of
singing (to be discussed at the end of this work, on p.   ), and
the dhrūpad. (See Gangoly, pp. 50 f.)

———

The music of the North reached a peak during the reign of
Akbar the Great (1556-1605). This famous sovereign assembled at
his court numerous important artists, among whom were 31 (or 32)
Mohammedan and four (or five) Hindu musicians.. Perhaps the
greatest of all these musicians was Tannamiśra or, as he was called
after his conversion to Islam, Mīyān Tānsen. Tānsen was a pupil
of the poet-musician Haridās Swāmī, a pious figure about whom
many legends have circulated. Tānsen was the first musician who
openly dared to alter the ancient revered jātis and rāgas and to use
foreign notes in old established scales. For instance, Tānsen performed rāga Mallār with the notes GA komal (E♭), NI komal (B♭),
and NI śuddha (B). This form of Mallār is known today as Mīyān-
ki-Mallār ("Mallār of Mīyān Tānsen"). The creation of rāga Mīyān-
ki-Todī and raga Darbārī-kānadā, an altered form of rāga Kānadā
(Kānnarā), and of the rāgas Shuddh-kalyan, Shuddh-sarang, Shuddh-
nat, Shuddh-mallār, Shuddh-bilaval, and others has also been ascribed to Tānsen. From his school (Tānseni mat) came a Hindi work
with the familiar title Rāg-Mālā (Rāg-Mālā prasiddha Mīyān Tān Sen
racita, Lahiri Press [Benares, 1907]). Some scholars believe that

Tānsen himself was its author.

> Pandit Bhatkhande believes that this is a spurious work
> compiled by some later authors and fathered on Tān Sen
> to lend a halo of authority to the work. The fact that the
> name of Tān Sen is introduced somewhat aggressively in
> almost every alternate line throws ample doubts on the
> authenticity of the attribution. (Gangoly, p. 53 n.)

If the work were really written by Tānsen, we should have to call
it a disappointment: in contrast to Tānsen's bold and always inspired attitude, this work contains no new thoughts. It is based
mainly upon the principles and teachings of Bharata and Mataṅga.
(See Gangoly, pp. 52 ff.)

Puṇḍarika Viṭṭhala, a) Sadrāga-Candrodaya

b) Rāga-Mālā

c) Rāga-Mañjari

d) Nartana-Nirnāya

These four treatises were written at the end of the sixteenth and at
the beginning of the seventeenth centuries. The first three works
were published by Pandit Bhatkhande in Bombay. The manuscript
of the Rāga-Mālā is preserved in the Collection of the Bhandarkar
Oriental Research Institute, Poona, as No. 1026 (1884-87).

a) The Sadrāga-Candrodaya deals with southern and northern
music. In order to facilitate the reading of Bhatkhande's list ("A
Comparative Study. . . ," p. 46), where the terms are written in
Nagari script, the following table cites the śuddha (basic) and
vikrta (altered) notes of Puṇḍarika (who employs southern terms)
and compares them with the corresponding (northern) terms of
Locanakavi and their Western equivalents (SA is considered to be C):

Śuddha Notes

Pundarika	Locanakavi	Northern tone syllables	Western notes
Śuddha SA	Śuddha SA	SA	C
Śuddha RI	Komal RI	RI (RE) komal	Db
Śuddha GA	Śuddha RI	RI (RE)	D (Ebb)
Śuddha MA	Śuddha MA	MA	F

Śuddha PA	Śuddha PA	PA	G
Śuddha DHA	Komal DHA	DHA komal	A♭
Śuddha NI	Tivra DHA	DHA	A (B♭♭)

Vikṛta Notes

Laghu SA	Tivratama NI		C less 1 śruti
Laghu MA	Tivratama GA		F less 1 śruti
Laghu PA	Tivratama MA		F#
Sādhārana GA	Śuddha GA	GA komal	E♭
Antara GA	Tivratar GA	GA	E
Kaiśika NI	Śuddha NI	NI komal	B♭
Kākali NI	Tivratar NI	NI	B

Puṇḍarika's śuddha scale is that of the old southern rāga
Mukhari (or the modern southern rāga Kanakangi: C D♭ E♭♭ F G
A♭ B♭♭ c).   He establishes nineteen thātas; a list of their names
and notes can be found in Bhatkhande ("A Comparative Study. . . ,"
pp. 49-50).   The scale degrees are described by the terms shown
in the table above, and a few vikṛta notes are described as trisruti
and catuśruti notes (three and four śruti intervals distant from the
lower degrees).   The thatas possess subordinate janya rāgas.

b)   The Rāga-Mālā is discussed in the Annals of the Bhandarkar
Research Institute, XIII (1931-32), 337-46.   The Rāga-Mālā deals
only with rāgas of the North; it uses, however, the same (southern)
śuddha scale as the Sadrāga-Candrodaya does.   Puṇḍarika groups
his rāgas into six male (puruṣa) rāgas, each of which possesses
five female (bhāryā or strī) rāgas and five sons (putras).   According to Puṇḍarika this classification of rāgas is the only correct one
in the North.   The list of these rāgas can be found in Gangoly, pp.
199-200.   In this work Puṇḍarika's terminology for śuddha notes is
sthiti and for vikṛti notes, gati.

c)   The Rāga-Mañjari; Puṇḍarika lists twenty thātas with their
subordinate janya rāgas.   The names mentioned in the list and the
use of the terms mela and janya point to the music of the South.
However, at the end of the work the author mentions some Persian
(parada, "foreign") rāgas which, of course, are northern.   Among
them are Huseni, Yaman, and Sarparda.   Although the creation

of rāga Sarparda is generally ascribed to Amir Khosru, Puṇḍarika
lists it here as a new form.   The list of the thāta-melas can be
found in Bhatkhande ("A Comparative Study. . . ," pp. 58 ff.).

       d) The Nartana-Nirnāya is of lesser interest to the musicol-
ogist because it contains the same musical information as the Rāga-
Mālā; the rest of the work deals with the art of dancing. (See Gangoly,
pp. 54 ff., 86-87 [performance times]; p. 111 f. [pictorial represen-
tation]; pp. 199-200. Bhatkhande, "A Comparative Study. . . ," pp. 51 ff.)

Cattvārimsacchata-Rāga-Nirūpanam; M. S. Sukthankar, ed., Arya
Bhusan Press (Bombay, 1914); a sixteenth century work by an author
who adopted the name Nārada.   The author is in no way related to
the authors of the Saṅgīta-Makaranda and the Pañcama-Sārasamhita.
One manuscript is preserved in the Tanjore Palace Library (no. 6651).
The author builds his system upon ten janaka rāgas ("father rāgas,"
a southern term).   Each janaka has five wives and four sons, and
each son has one wife. It may be of interest that Sārṅgadeva has
already dealt with janakas (and bhāsās) in his fourth list of rāgas.
Rāgas which cannot be listed among the janakas or among the bhāsās
pose a problem which Sārṅgadeva solves by creating a separate cate-
gory which he names anukta-janaka ("of unknown parentage").   The
present Nārada does not need to create an anukta-janaka group because he can place his "superfluous" rāgas into the categories of
sons or wives of sons. The complete list of rāgas, wives, sons, and
wives of sons can be found in Gangoly, pp. 201 ff. (See Gangoly,
pp. 57 f., 112 ff. [dhyānas, poetic-pictorial descriptions], pp. 201 ff.)

Dāmodara Miśra, Saṅgīta-Darpana; S. M. Tagore, ed., Stanhope
Press (Calcutta, 1881). The Saṅgīta-Darpana ("Mirror of Music"),
a short and popular work, was written about 1625.   Parts of this
work were translated into Persian (under the title Toft-ul-Hind,
"A Present from India") by Mirza Khan under the auspices of Aazem
Shah.   Pandit Bhatkhande states (A Short Historical Survey. . . ,
p. 26) that the work does not stand in high esteem in western India.
There are some musicians who have learned Dāmodara's text by
heart, but despite their diligence they are unable to comprehend
fully the rāgas described in the book.   The confusion is caused by

extended quotations, particularly from Śārṅgadeva's famous work;
and Dāmodara's text is as unclear as that of the Saṅgīta-Ratnākara.
Sir William Jones in his "On the Musical Modes of the Hindus" (in
Hindu Music from Various Authors, S. M. Tagore, ed. [Calcutta,
1882], 123 ff.) bases much of his information on the Saṅgīta-Darpana.
Dāmodara presents three lists of rāgas, one with twenty head-rāgas
and the two others with six head-rāgas each. Each of the six head-
rāgas of Dāmodara's second and third lists have five or six rāginīs.
(See Gangoly, pp. 59 f. ; list of rāgas, p. 206)

Somanātha, Rāga-Vibodha; Purusottama Gharpure (Poona, 1885).
A revised edition (M. S. Aiyar, ed.) appeared in Madras (Triplicane)
in 1933. The work is discussed by K. B. Deval in his Theory of
Indian Music as Expounded by Somanātha, Arya Bhusan Press (Poona,
1916). Palkuriki Somanātha was a Telugu author who lived sometime
between the twelfth and fourteenth centuries; he wrote two works
(Basavapurāna and Panditaradhyacarita) which were published by
the Andhra Patrika Office in 1926 and 1929. The Rāga-Vibodha is
an important Sanskrit work and was written during the reign of
Jehangir (1605-27), probably in 1609. Somanātha's terminology is
entirely South Indian and many Indian musicians and writers consider him as a representative of southern music. Bhatkhande assumes
that despite the southern terminology Somanātha referred in his
scale and rāga descriptions to the music of the North. Somanātha
does indeed mention some of the "Persian" rāgas (Husseini, Navroj,
Zeeluf [Zhilaf], Erakh, and others), which, of course, are northern.
He describes his śrutis (and scale degrees) by means of the string
divisions of his vina. He then presents twenty-three melas and
seventy-six subordinate janya rāgas. Although Somanātha's terminology deviates from that of his predecessors (e. g., mrdu instead of
Pundarika's laghu), there are no difficulties in identifying the scale
degrees. His first mela is again the old Mukhari (C Db Ebb F G Ab
Bbb c). A table showing the śuddha and vikrta notes compared with
North Indian tone syllables, and a list of the twenty-three melas
and their notes, both in Nagari script, can be found in Bhatkhande
("A Comparative Study. . . ," pp. 93, 94). A few verses of the Rāga-
Vibodha (V, 7-10) deal cursorily with performance times. (See
Gangoly, pp. 58 f., 88 ff.; list of rāgas, pp. 204 f.)

Hṛdaya Nārāyaṇa Deva,   a) Hṛdayakautaka

                         b) Hṛdayaprakāśa

Both texts are edited by D. K. Joshi and published by the Arya Bhusan
Press (Poona, 1918). Bhatkhande states that the two manuscripts
are preserved in the Palace Library of Bikaner (A Short Historical
Survey. . . , p. 33). Both treatises were written in the second half
of the seventeenth century. In his first work Hṛdaya bases his rāga
descriptions on Locanakavi's Rāga-Tarangini. He postulates twelve
thātas and adds the scale of a rāga of his own invention, which he
calls Hṛdaya-rāma. In the Hṛdayaprakāśa the author rearranges
the order of the twelve thātas and uses his new rāga Hṛdaya-rāma
instead of rāga Dipak. The omission of Dipak in a seventeenth
century work shows the continued belief that this rāga is considered
to be dangerous. Hṛdaya's description of notes contains little new
information. He states that vikrta notes are made by raising the
suddha notes by one, two, or three śrutis. A high alteration by one
śruti is called tivra; by two śrutis, tivratara; and by three śrutis,
tivratama. If low alterations are intended, the one-śruti lowering
of a suddha note is called komal, and the lowering of a suddha note
by more than one śruti is called atikomal. In the terminology of
modern North Indian music, tivra denotes a high alteration by a
semitone, and komal a low alteration by a semitone. In the early
system of southern music, the suddha notes always indicate the
lowest sounds (e. g., c, D♭, E♭♭), and the vikrta notes invariably
represent high alterations of the suddha notes; while in the northern
system, the suddha notes assume more or less central positions, and
vikrta notes may appear above and below the suddha notes.

          After descriptions of the terms vādī, samvādī, sampūrna,
sadava, and odava (frequently stated information), the author discusses the length of the strings of his vina, which he uses to determine
pitches. He reports that the notes SA-PA, RI-DHA, GA-NI, and
MA-SA constitute pure fifths and thus stand in the samvādī ("consonance") relationship. If SA is described with the string length of 36
units, RI has 32, GA has 30, MA 27, PA 24, DHA 21 1/2, NI 20, and
the upper SA 18—which shows that Hṛdaya's suddha scale is not that
of the old Mukhari but that of the northern rāga Kafi (C D E♭ F G A
B♭ c). If we check the samvādī relationships, we find indeed that

PA (24) is 2/3 of SA (36), DHA (21 1/2) is about 2/3 of RI (32), and
so forth. (See Gangoly, p. 61; list of rāgas, pp. 207 f; and Bhatkhande,
"A Comparative Study. . . ," pp. 22 ff.)

Ahobala, Saṅgīta-Pārijāta; Jīvānanda Vidyāsāgara, ed. (Calcutta:
Sarasvati Press, 1884). The work was written in 1665, and although
it contains several rāga names which belong in the system of southern
music, there is little doubt that the Saṅgīta-Pārijāta deals mainly
with the music of the North. Pandit Ahobala, like so many other
writers, came from the South and settled in the North. His work
was translated by one Pandit Dinanath into Persian in 1724. This
translation is preserved in the State Library of Rampur; it shows
the seal of Mohammed Shah, who reigned in Delhi between 1719 and
1724.

Ahobala's śuddha scale is identical with that of Hṛdaya. His
list contains 122 rāgas, but the author does not point out which ones
are thātas or melas and which ones are subordinate forms. He occasionally uses the term thāta, which proves that he is acquainted
with the method his predecessors used to group rāgas.

In his list of scales Ahobala uses different terms for high and
low vikrta notes: if a śuddha note is high altered by one śruti, it
is called tivra; if raised by two śrutis, it becomes tivratara; if raised by three śrutis, it is tivratama; and if raised by four śrutis, it
becomes atitivratama. In low alterations Ahobala uses komal if the
note is lowered by one śruti and purva if the note is lowered by two
śrutis. The terminology is similar to that of Hṛdaya; the term
atitivratama, although new, is easily comprehensible. The term
purva, however, does not appear either in the work of Locanakavi or
in the works of Hṛdaya.

Ahobala assembles his rāgas into three groups, according to
their performance times. In addition he lists nineteen rāgas which
can be performed at any time. (See Gangoly, p. 63.; Bhatkhande,
"A Comparative Study. . . ," pp. 30 ff.)

Sri Nivasa, Rāga-Tatva-Vibodha. According to Bhatkhande ("A
Comparative Study. . . ," p. 36), who describes the work without
stating where it is preserved, it was written soon after the Saṅgīta-
Pārijāta. Pandit Śri Nivasa quotes Ahobala's work extensively.

Of some interest is Śri Nivasa's use of the old term mūrchhanā.
Because Bhatkhande explains it (ibid., pp. 36 ff.), the information
will not be repeated here.

Bhavabhatta,   a) Anūpa-Saṅgīta-Vilāsa

               b) Anūpa-Saṅgīta-Ratnākara

               c) Anūpa-Saṅgītaṅkuśa

Anūpa-Saṅgīta-Vilāsa was reprinted in Bombay in 1921; the other two
were reprinted in Bombay in 1916.   All three works were edited by
Joshi and Sukthankar.   These three somewhat unclear treatises were
written in the late seventeenth century.   Bhavabhatta, who served
at the court of Raja Anup Singh (1674-1701) at Bikaner, relies in his
long-winded descriptions of śrutis, grāmas, mūrchhanās, jātis, etc.,
too much upon the indistinct verses of Sārṅgadeva's work (Bhatkhande,
A Short Historical. . . , p. 31) and on the texts of Locanakavi, Hṛdaya,
Somanātha, etc., and offers no new information.   The only exception
are a few of Bhavabhatta's pictorial descriptions of rāgas in the first
two treatises.   Although some of them are quoted from earlier texts,
there are several which appear for the first time in the works of
Bhavabhatta (Gangoly, p. 114).   (See Gangoly, p. 114; list of rāgas,
pp. 210 f; Bhatkhande, "A Comparative Study. . . ," pp. 69 ff.)

———

Works dealing with eighteenth century music as a rule offer
little or no new information.   Most authors confine themselves to
referring to or quoting from earlier works, and the confusion caused
by the indiscriminate use of southern and northern terms and by the
unclear descriptions does not help the study of the music of this
period.   In the nineteenth century, at the time of the British East
India Company when many of the white foreigners rejected Indian
music, there began something like a renaissance among Indian
musicians.   The trend was to clear away the innumerable ambiguities
and the confusion in music and to create a solid and satisfactory
system.   The first sign of this sober effort toward clarity can be
observed in:

Muhammed Rezza Khan, Naqmat-e-Asaphi.   This work was written
in 1813 in Persian.   Muhammed Rezza was a nobleman (Gangoly calls

him a prince) of Patna.   The work exists only in copies; both Gangoly
and Bhatkhande mention it but do not state where it can be examined.
One clue may be a speech of Bhatkhande, given in 1916 at the All
India Music Conference in Baroda; he stated: ". . . our worthy presi-
dent has fortunately procured a copy of this work. . . ." Rezza de-
clares the rāga-rāginī (husband-wife) system absurd and attacks
numerous ancient Sanskrit works because of their confused texts,
and he makes the (at his time) "sacrilegious" statement that information given by Bharata, Sārṅgadeva, Kallinātha, and Someśvara
is useless.   He groups the rāgas according to the tonal relationships
shown in their scales.   Each group has its head-scale (and rāga) which
indicates the common or related tone material of all its subordinate
rāgas.   Although Rezza rejects the rāga-rāginī system, he uses
the terms by employing rāga for head-rāga and rāginī for subordinate
rāga.   Rezza's śuddha scale, representing a most important and
far-reaching innovation, is the scale of rāga Bilaval.   This, as we
know, is a scale which comes very close to the Western major scale
if we ignore subtle deviations which occur in the actual performance
of rāga Bilaval.   This Bilaval scale (C D E F G A B c) is even today
the basic scale of North Indian music.   (See Gangoly, p. 67)

Sawai Pratapa Singha Deva, Saṅgīta-Sāra; (Poona: Arya Bhusan Press,
1910-12).   The court musicians of Maharajah Pratap Singh of Jaipur
(1779-1804), who wrote the book in Hindi for their sovereign in the
late eighteenth century, aimed at a grouping of rāgas similar to that
established by Rezza.   They too employ the Bilaval scale as basic material.   Although their work does not offer any historical data and provides little opportunity to study the immediate past and development of
rāgas of the eighteenth century, its brief descriptions of rāgas are
of value.   The Saṅgīta-Sāra shows that Pratap Singh and his musicians
were interested in creating a reliable work which, at least in pictorial representations of rāgas, tries to establish some order.   (See
Gangoly, pp. 66 f.; list of rāgas, pp. 215 f.)

Krishnānanda Vyās, Saṅgīta-Rāga-Kalpadruma; new edition in two
volumes by the Baṅgīya Sāhitya Parisad (Calcutta, 1916).   This work
is discussed by Gangoly in "Date of the Saṃgīta-Rāga-Kalpa-Drumh,"
Annals of the Bhandarkar Oriental Research Institute, XV, 1-11 (Poona,

1934), 117. The Saṅgīta-Rāga-Kalpadruma was first published in
1842 in Hindi and Bengali by Krishnānanda Vyās of Udaipur. It represents an encyclopedia originally written in Sanskrit, which contains songs from various parts of India. Of interest are the numerous
Hindi and Persian "songs" which are added to the chapter of rāgas.
Unfortunately, only the texts on these songs are given. The śuddha
scale of this work is the same as that of Rezza and Pratap Singh:
the Bilaval scale. Vyās discusses thirty-six rāgas and rounds off
each description with a brief prayer formula which denotes the rasa
and pictorial characteristics in a manner similar to that of the descriptions in the Saṅgīta-Darpana. (See Gangoly, pp. 67 f.)

Sourindro Mohun Ṭagore, Saṅgīta-Sāra-Samgraha (Calcutta, 1875).
Tagore's basis for this work is the Saṅgīta-Ratnākara, the Saṅgīta-
Darpana, and several other similar works. As is to be expected,
the text is unclear but the prayer formulas describing rasas and
pictorial features of the rāgas are of some interest. (See Gangoly,
p. 68)

———

Toward the end of the nineteenth century and in the early twentieth century several works appeared in English which are well known
and require no discussion. A survey of these works was made by
Harold S. Powers in Ethnomusicology, IX, 1965, pp. 1-12.

———

Looking back at the source material and a few specimen works
mentioned above, it can be observed that despite the confusion, a
few points gradually become clear. The principle of head-rāgas
(thātas in the North, melas in the South) becomes increasingly distinct. The scales of the great majority of rāgas consist of a maximum of seven and minimum of five notes. The rāga-rāginī-putra
system gradually disappears and parent scales with tonally subordinate forms become the basis of rāga classification. After much
experimentation, the śuddha scale of the North becomes the Bilaval
scale, while in the South the śuddha scale is that of mela Kanakangi.
With the exception of some light and popular forms, all northern
rāgas have their vādīs and samvādīs. Pictorial representation and
performance time, both of which played an important role in the

past, gradually lose their significance. At the present time, while musicians of the older generation still observe the performance times of the important rāgas, younger musicians pay little attention to these matters.

THE RAGAS
OF NORTH
INDIA ❧

III

THE RAGAS OF NORTH INDIA

And Their
Auffuehrungspraxis

A final, satisfactory classification of the North Indian ragas was achieved by Pandit V. N. Bhatkhande in his three works. Srīmal-Laksya-Saṅgītam,[1] Abhinava-Rāga-Mañjari,[2] and particularly in his Hindusthani-Sangit-Paddhati.[3] Bhatkhande, by far the most important figure in North Indian music of the early twentieth century, follows the direction set by Muhammed Rezza and bases his classification of ragas to some extent upon Veṅkaṭamakhin's Caturdandī-Prākaśikā,[4] an important work dealing with the music of the South. Bhatkhande establishes ten thatas which head all his other ragas. The thatas are:[5]

Kalyan thata	C D E F# G A B c
Bilaval thata	C D E F G A B c
Khamaj thata	C D E F G A Bb c
Bhairav thata	C Db E F G Ab B c
Purvi thata	C Db E F# G Ab B c
Marva thata	C Db E F# G A B c
Kafi thata	C D Eb F G A Bb c
Asavari thata	C D Eb F G Ab Bb c
Bhairavi thata	C Db Eb F G Ab Bb c
Todi thata	C Db Eb F# G Ab B c

THE KALYAN THATA

<u>Raga Kalyan or Yaman (Yemen, Iman[a], Yamun [a])</u>

    <u>Kalyan</u> is the Indian (Sanskrit), <u>Yaman</u> the Persian, name. This raga should be performed during the first quarter of the night. The pictorial descriptions show several variants, even contradictions. In the <u>Rāga-Sāgara</u> (3, 56)[6] the following description appears:

> Always I sincerely pray to the goddess of all adornment,
> Yamuna, who sits on the left side of Lord Vishnu, the
> victor over the demon Madhu. Lord Vishnu has won over
> Yamuna by his graces. She holds a drum in her hands
> and is beautifully attired.

In the <u>Rāga-Kalpadruma</u> (p. 32)[7] we read:

> The sages say that <u>Kalyan raga</u> is red to look at and is
> terrible in appearance. Robed in gold, his forehead
> marked with the sign of victory and holding a sword in
> his hand, he enters the battlefield.

    Today <u>Kalyan</u> is considered to be a blessing, luck-bringing, and soothing raga. For this reason it is usually performed in the evening at the beginning of a concert or theatrical performance.

    Its <u>vadi</u> is <u>GA</u> (E); the <u>samvadi,</u> a comparatively weak note, is <u>NI</u> (B). The scale of the raga is the same as that of the <u>thata</u>, C D E F# G A B c. Although <u>Kalyan</u> has no characteristic phrases or particular features, there are at the present time many musicians who avoid in the ascending scale the notes <u>SA</u> (C) and <u>PA</u> (G) or treat them very weakly. One can often hear (B) D E F# A B c, c B A G F# E D C. <u>Kalyan</u> is one of the few ragas which permits the performer comparative freedom.

      RAGA KALYAN (YAMAN)   (Trital)   BH, IV, 26

      Asthayi

Antara

Tone material

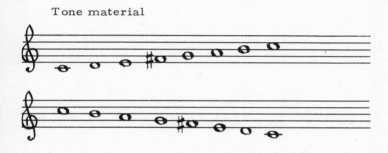

Raga Yaman-kalyan

This raga differs from raga Kalyan in its descending scale
where, occasionally, the tone MA (F) becomes interpolated between
two GA (E): GA MA GA RE SA (E F E D C). In all other instances MA tivra (F#) is used. The performance time of this raga
is not clearly established. Its strong affinity to raga Kalyan
prompts musicians to perform it during the first quarter of the night.

Although this raga has no fixed rules, there are a few features
which appear in almost all performances: the notes MA tivra and GA
(F#-E) are frequently linked in descent by a small gliding step; the
lower SA (C) is approached in ascent by the vakra turn NI RE SA
(B D C), and the upper SA (c) is often reached by the sequence PA
NI DHA SA (G B A c).

RAGA YAMAN-KALYAN   (Trital)   BH, II, 25-26

Asthayi

Antara

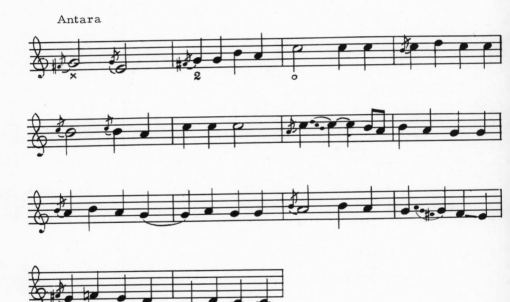

In the foregoing song example we observe the following organization
of vibhagas: 0 3 X 2 in the asthayi and X 2 0 3 in the antara.
In a performance the singer has two ways of progressing from the
end of the asthayi to the beginning of the antara. He either stops
singing when the fourth measure of the second line of the asthayi has
been completed and allows the drummer to perform alone (with the
tanbura) the khali measure 0 and measure 3 in order to join the

drummer again on the next sam (X) when the antara begins; or, after the last measure of the asthayi, the singer repeats the first two measures of the first line of the asthayi (0 and 3), which enables him to join the drummer on the sam when the antara begins. The rule is that the sequence X 2 0 3 has to remain intact, irrespective of the fact that the melody may end before the avarta is completed.

The vadi (or the samvadi, or the SA) has to coincide with the sam. In the alap proper this is always the case, because there the raga is presented in its purest form. In a song it may happen that exceptions occur where a certain amount of liberty is granted to the singer. In the asthayi of the foregoing example, we notice that the notes NI (B), the samvadi, and GA (E), the vadi, coincide, according to the rule, with the sam. But in the antara (first line, measure one) a deviation occurs: the note PA (G) with an ornamenting MA tivra (F#) is made to coincide with the sam. This is a liberty which may be taken in songs, particularly in ragas of lighter character. In the second, third, and fourth lines of the antara we observe on the sam the note NI (B) with an ornamenting SA (c), the notes permissible because NI (B) is the samvadi and SA can always be used; DHA (A) with the here important appoggiatura of NI (B); and GA (E), the vadi, with an ornamenting MA tivra (F#).

Tone material

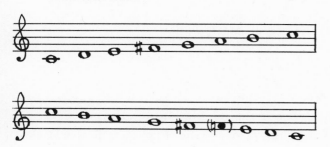

Although we have already mentioned the ragas Bhupali, Shuddh-kalyan, and Jayat-kalyan in the introduction, we shall now consider them more carefully.

Raga Bhupali

Bhupali is subordinated to the Kalyan thata. The Sanskrit syllable bhu indicates "land, " "earth, " and the syllable pa[8] refers to "protector, " "father. " The denotation protector of the land, the king,
gives this raga a royal, courtly character. Bhupali is always performed at night in a slow and dignified tempo.

Pictorial descriptions of this raga can be found in the Rāga-
Sāgara,[9] the Rāga-Kalpadruma,[10] and in the Sangīta-Darpana. [11]   In
the Rāga-Sāgara (3, 5) we read:

> I always pray to Bhupala, seated on his throne, surrounded
> by members of his big family and being fanned with fly-
> whisks by lovely women who have eyes like deer.

In Rāga-Kalpadruma (p. 32)

> With a gleaming fair body anointed with fragrances, and
> high breasted, with her face radiant like the moon,
> Bhupalika is in great grief about the absence of her
> lover, and constantly thinks of him.   Bhupalika is full
> of the shanta rasa.

Another description can be found in N. A. Willard, "Treatise on the
Music of Hindustan":[12]

> This is some happy nymph engaged in dalliance with her
> lover.   A white saree is thrown over her body, which is
> stained with the fragrant saffron.   A garland of flowers
> adorns her bosom.   The favoured youth sits by her side,
> round whose neck her arms are folded.

Theoretically and in pictorial representations there are two ragas:
Bhupali and Bhupala.   Originally Bhupali was "female" while Bhupala
was considered to be "male. " The description in the Rāga-Sāgara
refers to Bhupala, while that in the Rāga-Kalpadruma represents
Bhupali.   Bhupala (the raga is usually called Bhupal-todi now[13]) has
the pentatonic scale of C D♭ E♭ G A♭ c both in ascent and descent
and is ascribed to the Bhairavi thata.   In the music of South India we
find a raga Bhupala(m) which today is subordinated to the fifteenth
mela. [14] It has the notes C D♭ E G A♭ c.

In the North raga Bhupali has assumed the important "royal"
form.   Performing musicians consider it to be the prominent raga

which, despite its name, has now a dignified, male character. The
scale of Bhupali has anhemitonic pentatonic character and is C D E
G A c, c A G E D C. The vadi is GA (E) and the samvadi is
DHA (A). Melodies or phrases usually end on either of these two
notes and, of course, also on SA (C). One frequently observes the
following approaches to the notes:

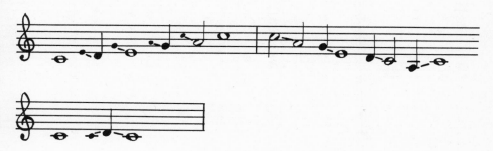

The approaches shown in the foregoing example do not constitute
fixed rules, but have become a habit. The notes of the ascending
scale are approached from above by tiny gliding steps, while the descending notes are usually performed without approaches but linked
with gliding steps (mind). In numerous performances of Bhupali there
are small ornamentations which employ minute vivadis in the following
manner:

These ornamentations use the "foreign" notes MA (F) and NI (B).
Both notes are only very lightly touched. When Indian musicians are
consulted about these vivadis, they generally deny them and insist that
both ornamentations are performed as follows:

Careful observation proves that in actual performance these foreign
notes do appear.

RAGA BHUPALI   (Trital)   BH, III, 18-19

Asthayi

Antara

Raga Shuddh-kalyan

At the court of Akbar the Great were many famous musicians.
Among them were two brothers who called themselves Suresh Khan

and Chand Khan (suraj, "sun"; chand, "moon"). These two artists
were highly respected and celebrated and often appeared in musical
contests with the famous musician Tansen, whom we have mentioned
before. Suresh Khan specialized in day-ragas, and Chand Khan was
the expert on night-ragas. Tansen, so we are told, was deeply dis-
tressed about this incessant and severe competition, and he requested
his old guru to teach him new ragas. Thus, allegedly, a number of
new ragas were created, such as Shuddh-kalyan, Shuddh-sarang,
Shuddh-nat, Shuddh-maller, Shuddh-bilaval, in addition to Miyan-ki-
mallar, Miyan-ki-todi, and others where the name Miyan clearly
refers to Tansen. The word shuddha in the raga names we have just
enumerated must be taken with caution. If one of two competing persons produces new or imported forms, the second person will probably describe his own as original, unspoilt, and pure (shuddha), which
does not mean that really pure forms have been set up. The word
shuddha in these raga names most probably implies Tansen's disap-
proval of the ragas of Suresh and Chand Khan (which may have been
criticized by Tansen as foreign mixtures) and that shuddha may have
been nothing but a label that Tansen employed in order to set his ragas
apart from those of his competitors.

Shuddh-kalyan now belongs to the Kalyan thata and has to be performed at night. Its vadi is GA (E) and the samvadi is DHA (A). The
note PA (G) is "strong." Contemporary North Indian musicians frequently distinguish two types of this raga: a) Shuddh-kalyan, Yaman-
anga, Shuddh-kalyan, resembling Yaman (or Kalyan), in which the
notes NI (B) and MA tivra (F#) are employed in descent as it is in
most Kalyan types; and b) Shuddh-kalyan, Bhup-anga, resembling raga
Bhupali, in which these two notes (B and F#) are either completely
omitted or touched very lightly. In notated melodies, even of the first
type, these two notes are not indicated. They are mostly covered by
the gliding steps SA-DHA (c-A) and PA-GA (G-E). Nevertheless,
they can be noticed if the raga is performed well.

The following steps are used frequently: SA-DHA (c-A), PA-
[MA tivra]-GA RE SA (G-[F#]-E D C), SA-(NI)-DHA PA (c-[B]-A G),
PA-GA (G-E).

RAGA SHUDDH-KALYAN   (Dhamar Tal)   BH, IV, 81
Asthayi

Antara

Tone Material

Raga Jayat-kalyan (Jait or Jet-kalyan)

Jayat-kalyan is one of the less important ragas and is performed comparatively rarely. As in raga Shuddha-kalyan, the notes MA tivra (F#) and NI (B) occur only in the form of subtle ornamentations and are practically never notated. The vadi of this raga is PA (G) and the samvadi is SA (C). The note GA (E) is very "strong" and is often treated as a vishrantisthan. The note RE (D) is so weak in ascent that it is omitted in the majority of cases. The note DHA (A) is very "weak," and in both ascent and descent is only touched. Characteristic phrases of this raga are:

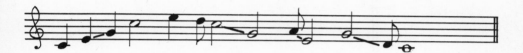

Occasionally one hears:

The weak note DHA appears repeatedly in descent in the following song specimen. This is permissible in songs but not in alaps.

RAGA JAYAT-KALYAN (Ada Chautal)   BH, V, 10-11

Asthayi

Antara

Tone material

Raga Malashri

This rare raga belongs to the Kalyan thata. In the past this raga
was considered to be a ragini of Shri-raga. N.A. Willard describes
the pictorial aspect of Malashri in the following manner:

> The fascinating creature before us . . . is clad in a
> flowing yellow robe, and sits under a mango tree, in the
> society of her female companions, enjoying the verdure
> and luxuriance of the extensive scene before her.[15]

Malashri is supposed to be performed in the afternoon. Its vadi
is PA (C), the samvadi is SA (C). The notes RE (D) and DHA (A) are
entirely omitted. The gliding steps PA-GA (G-E) and GA-SA (E-C)
are characteristic. Musicians distinguish three types of this raga:

   a) Malashri with MA tivra (F#) in descent;
   b) Malashri with MA tivra (F#) as a lightly touched ornament;
   c) Malashri with the notes SA (C), GA (E), and PA (G), whereby
      all other notes are "hidden" in descending gliding steps.

Plate I. Ragini Malashri

CHAUPAYI: Malashri is dressed in green, the color of the parrot. Her complexion is very fair, and her beautiful eyes are large. Exultant with deep love for her lord, she gracefully gathers flowers in the garden. The intricacies and elegance of her garments are beyond description; one glance at her dazzles the eyes. She has built a charming abode for herself and is surrounded by beautiful companions. She is by far the cleverest of them, and of them all is loved most by Lord Bhairava.

DOHA: Exultant with love for her lord and excited at the prospect of meeting him, she glances anxiously at the road, holding in her hands a basket of flowers with which to welcome him.

a)

b)

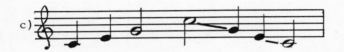

c)

The scale material of the three types is:

    a) C E G (B) c, c B G F# E C
    b) C E G (B) c, c B G (F#) E C
    c) C E G c, c G E C

The third type of this raga is remarkable because it uses less than the minimum of five notes. In this case musicians imagine the "hidden" notes in the gliding steps and thus argue that the tone material of the raga contains five notes.

    Most Malashri melodies are of the second or third types, while the first one is unusually rare. There are some musicians who insist that all three types of Malashri should be performed without the note NI (B). If, however, a raga possesses all Malashri features and uses the note NI (B) in a somewhat "stronger" manner, the raga becomes Pradipika.

    RAGA MALASHRI   First type   (Trital)   BH, V, 28

Asthayi

Antara

RAGA MALASHRI   Second type (Rupak)   BH, V, 35

Asthayi

Antara

RAGA MALASHRI   Third type (Sultal)   BH, V, 41-42

Asthayi

Antara

Raga Chandrakant

This rarely performed raga resembles <u>Shuddh-kalyan</u> and has
to be performed in the evening. Its <u>vadi</u> is <u>GA</u> (E) and the <u>samvadi</u>

is NI (B). In ascent the note MA tivra (F#) is avoided. Chandrakant
melodies generally move in the regions of the low and middle octaves.
    The following phrases are characteristic:

We observe in the first line of the foregoing example the characteristic phrase NI-DHA NI-DHA PA (B-A B-A G) and the use of MA tivra
(F#) in descent in the second line. The note MA tivra (F#) always
has to precede GA (E). Only when MA tivra (F#) is employed as a
non-notated ornament may PA (G) follow.

The note NI (B) is vakra in ascent; in order to reach the upper SA (c),
the musician has to form his melody in the following manner:

If, however, the upper SA (c) is avoided and the melody aims at a
higher note, for instance RE (d), then the direct ascent NI-RE (B-d)
is permissible:

RAGA CHANDRAKANT   (Trital)   BH, V, 2

Asthayi

Antara

The following song example utilizes the same melody as that of the previous example but shows richer ornamentation and (not shown here) a different text.

RAGA CHANDRAKANT   (Trital)   BH, V, 2-3

Asthayi

Antara

Tone material

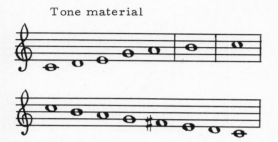

Raga Savani-kalyan

This is a comparatively recent raga. As far as we know there are only a few melodies in this raga, and the rules concerning its performance are subject to varied interpretations. The vadi of Savani-kalyan is SA (C). The samvadi is usually indicated as PA (G), but there are some musicians who insist that the samvadi is NI (B). The low DHA (A) of the mandra saptaka (lowest octave region) has the same function as a vishrantisthan, which means that melodies or phrases may end with this note. Similar to raga Chandrakant, melodies of Savani-kalyan move mainly in the regions of the mandra and madhyama saptakas.

In ascent the notes RE (D) and NI (B) are omitted and MA (F) becomes part of a vakra figure. In order to ascend from SA (C) to PA (G), the melody has to proceed in the following manner: SA MA GA PA (C F E G). Only if MA (F) is omitted can the ascent be executed in a direct line: SA GA PA (C E G). In descent RE (D) and NI (B) are employed, but MA (F) is omitted. It is possible, however, that MA (F) may appear very lightly, in the form of a tiny ornament. The same applies to the note MA tivra (F#); although this note is a characteristic feature of ragas belonging to the Kalyan thata, it does not appear in Savani-kalyan as a scale degree, but may occur in vocal music as a lightly touched ornamenting note before PA (G).

RAGA SAVANI-KALYAN   (Tilvada)   BH, V, 5

Asthayi

Antara

Tone material

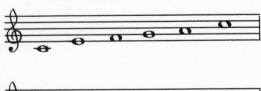

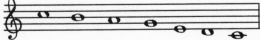

Raga Savani-bihag

This raga, ascribed to the Kalyan thata, is a derivative form of Savani-kalyan. It is very rare and its performance rules are unclear. The difference between Savani-kalyan and Savani-bihag is the fact that the latter avoids the note DHA (A) in ascent and descent and the note NI (B) in descent only.

No adequate song specimen of this raga is available.

Raga Panchkalyan

The only source which offers some information about this obscure raga is the Sangit-Kala-Prakash by R. N. Vaze.[16] Vaze states that Panchkalyan, ascribed to the Kalyan thata, has to be performed in the evening and that its vadi is SA (C) and the samvadi, PA (G). The name Panchkalyan indicates a mixture of five Kalyan types, namely Yaman-kalyan, Shyam-kalyan, Shuddh-kalyan, Hemkalyan, and Hamir-kalyan.[17] The few melodies of this raga move mainly in the mandra and madhyama saptakas.

The following song specimen shows that the note NI (B) is avoided and that MA tivra (F#), the sign of the Kalyan family, appears only once (fourth line, first measure) in the asthayi. In the antara, however, only MA (F) is used.

RAGA PANCHKALYAN   (Ektal)   Vaze, 22

Asthayi

Antara

It would be meaningless to postulate the tone material of this raga, because the mixture of five <u>Kalyan</u> types can be made in manifold ways, influencing the formation of the scale with every performance.

Raga Samantkalyan

Samantkalyan is another of the rare and little-known ragas.
Vaze[18] states that this raga belongs to the Kalyan thata, that it represents a combination of the ragas Shuddh-kalyan and Hamir,[19] and that
its vadi is GA (E) and its samvadi DHA (A). The combination of
Shuddh-kalyan and Hamir is done in such a manner that the notes of the
former raga are used in the lower tetrachord, those of the latter in the
upper tetrachord of the Samantkalyan scale.

Some musicians argue that the very few songs in Samantkalyan
end with the phrase PA MA tivra DHA (G F# A). This writer had
only one opportunity to hear this raga. On this occasion the singer
used MA tivra (F#) throughout his song with the exception of the final
note, which was MA (F). When asked, the singer stated that the final
note constitutes the characteristic element of this raga.

The following song specimen ends neither with DHA (A) nor with
MA (F).

RAGA SAMANTKALYAN   (Jhaptal)   Vaze, 24

Asthayi

Antara

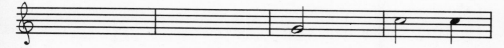

The song specimen shows that the vakra phrase NI DHA SA (B A c)
has some importance (third line, measures three and four; sixth line,
measures one and two). It further shows that RE (D) and NI (B) are
omitted in ascent and MA tivra (F#) is omitted in descent. None of
the performance rules can be stated with any certainty; hence it is of
little use to postulate a material scale.

Raga Gaurkalyan (Gorkikalyan)

This raga is another of the obscure Kalyan types which must not
be confused with raga Gorakh-kalyan.[20] Its vadi is GA (E), the samvadi is NI (B). The similarity between Gaurkalyan and Savani-Kalyan
is so strong that one is often mistaken for the other. The difference
between the two ragas lies in the fact that Gaurkalyan employs the note
MA tivra (F#) in a special, characteristic phrase and treats the note
GA (E) vakra in descent (GA MA RE SA, E F D C). The characteristic phrase using MA tivra (F#) is:

Although this phrase is essential, it must not be employed too frequently. The following example shows its use and the vakra treatment
of GA (E) in descent:

In descent the sequence PA GA RE SA (G E D C), that is, GA (E) without the vakra feature, appears only when MA (F) is omitted:

If both vadis (vadi and samvadi, E and B) are used in the descending
line, GA (E) resumes its vakra feature:

RAGA GAURKALYAN   (Jhumra)   Vaze, 26

Asthayi

Antara

Tone material

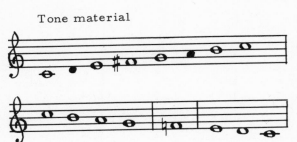

Raga Kedar (Kidara, Kedari, Kedara, Kedarika)

Kedar is one of the important ragas of the Kalyan thata and has to be performed during the first quarter of the night. The raga-mala descriptions of this raga differ considerably from each other. In the Saṅgīta-Darpana (2, 65) we find:

> Kedarika, the consort of raga Dipak, is in deep contemplation of Lord Shiva, who holds the bright crescent moon on his forehead, and has long matted hair out of which flows the river Ganga. She has the "Yogapatta" [a cloth thrown over the back and knees of an ascetic during deep meditation] on her shoulder, and snakes encircle her body.

In the Rāga-Sāgara (3, 41) the following can be read:

> We should always respectfully think of Kedarika, who is tastefully attired and sits in front of the temple of Lord Shiva, holding a book.

Plate II. Ragini Kedara

CHAUPAYI: The lovers having been parted, Kedara is in anguish. Wrapped in the dress of a hermit and smeared with holy ash, Kedara speaks of the unreal life and of living in solitude. Knowing this person to be a yogi, people gather near as Kedara teaches them the art of yoga. There is a companion there who is a yogini, and they converse about the mysteries of life. There is sorrow and sadness about Kedara, and thus, as they converse, the whole night passes.

DOHA: Listening to the music of love and knowing that the moon is now fatigued after his nocturnal round, Kedara feels no less anguish while waiting for the dawn of the day. [See "Note on Plates," p. xii.]

H. A. Popley, in his The Music of India, [21] describes Kedar in the following manner:

> . . . a group of musicians playing and singing in the moonlight. The lotus buds are all closed. There is gaiety and sadness combined. . . . It is the dewy season and it is believed that while the raga means gaiety to-day, it means also sadness in the future. The ascetic in the group [of the picture] typifies the illusoriness of the present.

N. A. Willard in his "Treatise on the Music of Hindustan" [22] offers the following description:

> The subject of the Raginee is a masculine character. The young man in white garments wields a sword in his right hand, and in his left grasps the tusk of an elephant which he has rooted out. A bard standing beside him recites the praises of his valour.

Kedar is believed to possess magic properties. It can heal diseases and melt stones.

The vadi of this raga is MA (F); the samvadi is the upper SA (c). In ascent the notes RE (D) and GA (E) are omitted. The ascending step SA MA (C F) is executed without gliding and ornamentation. The note GA (E), although forbidden in the ascending line, can appear as a small, very lightly touched ornament between the notes MA (F) and PA (G) in the following manner:

The rendition of the step PA DHA (G A), where´a lightly touched MA tivra (F#) is interpolated, is:

or

The note DHA (A) is occasionally treated in the same manner as it is in raga Deshkar: [23]

also   is possible

In order to reach the upper SA (c), the performer has to employ
the vakra phrase PA NI DHA SA (G B A c). If the melody contains a
NI komal (B♭) and if after NI komal the high SA (c) is aimed at, the
singer has first to descend via DHA (A) to PA (G), from where the
vakra ascent (G B A c) is permissible.

There are some musicians who insist that the note NI (B) is
wholly avoided in this raga. These performers direct their ascending
line directly from PA (G) to SA (c): PA DHA PA SA (G A G c).
But even these musicians usually interpolate NI in descent between SA
(c) and DHA, either by hiding it in a gliding step or by subtly touching
it:

or

The note MA tivra (F#) should appear as a short note in descent, always succeeding PA (G):

This rule is not strictly observed, as will be shown in the song example below.

The note GA (E) is omitted in descent. The gliding step MA-
RE (F-D) has to be very smooth and must not show the "hidden" GA
(E). The note RE (D) is to be used very lightly and briefly in descent,
a rule which is observed in alaps and tanas, but may be relaxed in
songs.

RAGA KEDAR   (Jhaptal)   BH, III, 113

Asthayi

Antara

In the second bars of the fourth lines of the asthayi and antara, the
note MA tivra (F#) can be observed without a preceding PA (G). Although the PA (G) is not notated, in practice we notice the following
performance:

The ascending <u>Kedar</u> scale is C F G A B A c, and the descent can be either c-A G, or c B A G followed by G F# G A G F D C. The note <u>NI</u> <u>komal</u> (B♭) may appear as a light ornament between two <u>DHA</u> (A): c-A G A B♭ A G, etc.

Tone material

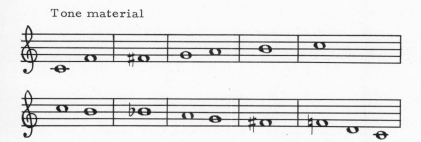

Some musicians speak about four types of <u>Kedar</u>:

a) <u>Chandani-kedar</u> is the type which has already been discussed.

b) <u>Shuddha-kedar</u> avoids the weak <u>NI</u> <u>komal</u> (B♭) entirely and uses only <u>NI</u> (B) in both ascent and descent. The <u>Deshkar</u> treatment of <u>DHA</u> (A) is avoided, and <u>MA</u> <u>tivra</u> (F#) has to be rendered in a still lighter manner than it is in <u>Chandani-kedar</u>. As far as I know, there exists not a single song of this type.

c) <u>Sangam-kedar</u> is very rare and hardly known. It is probably a recent creation. This type employs elements of the ragas <u>Nat</u>[24] and <u>Bilaval</u>,[25] which are mixed with the <u>Kedar</u> material. This type employs the notes <u>MA</u> (F) and <u>MA</u> <u>tivra</u> (F#) in immediate succession, which is a rarity in North Indian music.

RAGA SANGAM-KEDAR   (Jhaptal)   Vaze, 42 f.

Asthayi

Antara

d) Raga <u>Gaudi</u> occasionally is considered to be the fourth, another rather obscure type of <u>Kedar</u>. The following example shows that <u>Gaudi</u> consists of a mixture of elements taken from the ragas <u>Kedar</u>, <u>Bilaval</u>, <u>Sorat</u>,[26] and <u>Mallar</u>.[27]

राग नगो डी : चाचोप ध पिस रख सम गन बिरा ज त गैर : बाग स त ऋगका म
छ व सौंरी पाय की सी त ह में बो ही बा ढी : ऋानं द सहत बाग मे गा ढी : ऋ ल ख म ब र ल
फु लि जी हि बा री : म नु उ चिब ह ै द ष्टि ऋ न सार : हि म प र ह थ हु थन व ला सी पो
निप सु गं ध पौछो पस्या बा खी : द षि बि च त्र चि त्र हो डी जा ख : चि त्र बि चि त्र न ले त ढ
ला ख : चच हो ख्य र चि ब र चि चि त्र बि च त्र ग ती : सो त्ता नि ख्नि सु ख्न रा स : द खो गो ड की
हर स : ऋ प्नि न हो त प्रका स : ॥ ८ ॥

Plate III. Ragini Gaudi

CHAUPAYI: Gaudi [Gauri] is seated gloriously in full possession of the love of her lord and master. Her body glows with the warmth of love. As she proceeds to the garden, her love for him increases. In the garden countless flowers of varied colors and fragrances are arranged tastefully and fascinatingly. She places one hand on her bosom as she beholds the garden in all its glory.

DOHA: The Lord has created this woman with such care and design that she is indeed the personification of all beauty, grace, and charm. It is dazzling to behold this lovely woman.

1. shows the characteristic <u>Kedar</u> step <u>SA</u> <u>MA</u> (C F).

2. is a <u>Sorat</u> formula.

3. is a <u>Mallar</u> formula.

4. is <u>Bilaval</u> material.

The following song specimen (raga <u>Gaudi</u>) shows <u>Bilaval</u> elements up to the end of the third bar of the third line. The step F D in the fourth measure of the third line can be derived from <u>Sorat</u>, while F D G in the first and second bars of the fourth line are typical <u>Mallar</u> phrases. With the triplet A B c in the third bar of the fourth line begins another <u>Bilaval</u> sequence, etc.

RAGA GAUDI   (Jhaptal)   Vaze, 44

Asthayi

Antara

Raga Kamod (Kamoda, Kamodi, Kamodika)

This important raga has to be performed during the first quarter of the night. The Saṅgīta-Darpana (2, 68) gives this raga-mala des-scription of Kamod:

> Dressed in yellow and with long tresses of beautiful
> hair, Kamodika is in the forest and in grief cries for
> her lover. She looks around in fear and her despair
> increases when she hears the plaintive notes of a
> cuckoo.

N. A. Willard[28] offers the following description:

> Here we see a nymph . . . venture alone in the desert
> in the hideousness of night. She quits her soft bed
> and friendly neighbourhood, and traverses unaccom-
> panied the wilderness infested with ravenous beasts.
> The chance of an interview with the object of her
> love she considers well worth the risking of life and
> character. A thousand fears now mock her fortitude

Plate IV. Ragini Kamod

CHAUPAYI: Ragini Kamod is severely tortured with grief because of her separation from her beloved. She has resigned all comforts and luxuries and has found an abode on the bank of a river. It is here in this desolate place that she comprehends Govinda God Krishna, the eternal lover (who is always in her heart). There is no remedy for her other than to meet with her beloved. She desires with all her heart to become united with Shri-raga. Whenever her passions are excited and she thinks of her amorous sport with her lover, her temples become hot and burning.

DOHA: The lady has forsaken all her jewelry, ornaments, and other forms of adornment, as she has parted from her lover. She is restless, her mind is disturbed, and her body aches. All this has been caused by Kamdeva.

> when she finds herself at the place of assignation
> alone, for he on whose account she has staked all
> this is not yet there! . . . She starts at the fall of
> a leaf, and melts into tears. She has on a short
> white bodice, and passes unnoticed under cover of
> a red saree.

The vadi of this raga is PA (G), the samvadi, RE (D). Although the
vadi appears in the upper tetrachord of the scale, Kamod is considered
to be an evening raga. In contrast to Kedar, the note MA (F) is here
weakly treated and PA (G), the vadi, is strongly emphasized. The
following example shows the characteristic features of Kamod:

1   Illustrates the correct ascent from SA (C) to RE (D).
2   The note MA tivra (F#) can only appear between two PA (G),
    where it is weakly treated.
3   This phrase shows the vakra character of GA (E) in the descend-
    ing line (E F D C).
    Also permitted is:

The upper half of the Kamod scale is identical with that of raga Kedar.
    In songs, however, the note MA tivra (F#) may also appear be-
tween DHA (A) and PA (G). In the descending line, as in raga Kedar,
the note NI komal (Bb) can occasionally appear. In such instances,
this note is used either between two DHA (A) or between DHA (A) and
PA (G). The following formula shows the important characteristics
of Kamod:

RAGA KAMOD   (Dhamar Tal)   BH, IV, 105-106

Asthayi

Antara

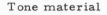

Tone material

Raga Chhayanath (Chhayanata)

This important raga is to be performed immediately after sunset, as soon as the sky has become dark. In the Rāga-Mālā of Pundarika Viṭṭhala we find the following pictorial description of Chhayanath:

> . . . Chhayanath wears a necklace of bright jewels and his head-gear is red in color. He is fair in complexion, red-eyed and sweet-tongued. Accompanied by several friends who are dressed as heroes at sunset, and holding bouquets of flowers in his hand, he makes fun of the travellers.

The vadi of this raga is PA (G); the samvadi is RE (D). Some musicians insist that the vadis should be mentioned in reverse order: vadi, RE (D), samvadi, PA (G). The note GA (E), which can be used in straight ascent, becomes vakra in descent in the phrase GA MA RE SA (E F D C). The note RE (D) is frequently approached from above, roughly from GA (E), by means of a small gliding step:

The descent from PA (G) to SA (C) can be accomplished in the following manner:

The note MA tivra (F#) is employed very infrequently, as in the ragas Kedar and Kamod. Whenever it is used, it appears between two PA (G) or assumes the function of a subtle appoggiatura leading to PA (G):

In ascent the note NI (B) is used; in descent NI komal (B♭) is preferred,

often, but not always, in the vakra phrase DHA NI komal PA (A B♭ G).
With the exception of this vakra phrase, the upper half of the Chhayanath scale is identical to those of the ragas Kedar and Kamod.

RAGA CHHAYANATH   (Dhamar Tal)   BH, IV, 131-2

Tone material

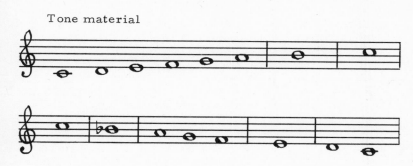

Comparison of the Auffuehrungspraxis of the Ragas
Kedar, Kamod and Chhayanath

The ascent and descent SA PA SA (C G C):

Kedar

Kamod

Chhayanath

In Kedar the note MA (F) is strong.

In Kamod the note PA (G) is strong.

In Chhayanath the ascent from SA (G) to PA (G) has to be longer and more elaborate than in the other two ragas.

The treatment and use of the note DHA (A):

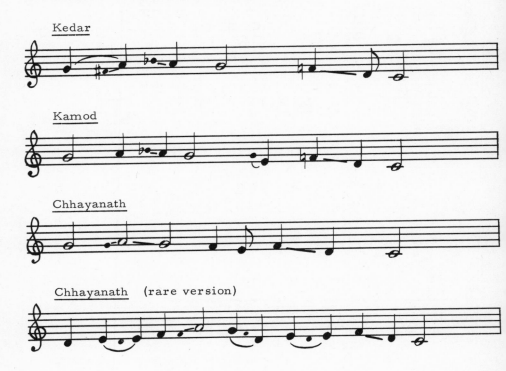

The high SA (c) is reached in all three ragas by the step PA SA (G c) without any gliding. In descent the following differences can be observed:

The gliding step SA-DHA (c-A) is accomplished in Kedar by a subtle touch of NI (B), while in ragas Kamod and Chhayanath the note NI (B) is not used in this particular glide:

Kamod

Chhayanath

The treatment and use of the notes NI komal (B♭) and NI (B):

Both notes are treated weakly in all three ragas. North Indian musicians entertain various views about the use of NI (B). Some are in favor of its use; others decline it categorically in all three ragas. A careful investigation shows that NI (B), if in use, is slightly more emphasized in raga Chhayanath than in the other two ragas. If NI (B) in Chhayanath appears in ascent, it is used in the vakra phrase NI DHA SA (B A c).

NI komal (B♭) appears in all three ragas as a weakly treated note:

Kedar

Kedar

Kedar   (in some rare instances)

Chhayanath

Raga Hamir (Hamira)

Hamir is an important raga belonging to the Kalyan thata. In Somanātha's work Rāga-Vibodha[29] this raga is listed as one of the primary ragas. Hamir has a serious, bellicose character, and its melodies are often associated with storms, thunder, and battles. They have to be performed at night.

The vadi of this raga is DHA (A); the samvadi is GA (E). One of the first rules a student learns when studying Hamir is to avoid in the ascending line the sequence MA PA (F G). Only when MA tivra (F#) appears may PA (G) follow in ascent.

   or

Another characteristic of this raga is the so-called "Hamir DHA." As we are dealing with a stormy, warlike rasa, the vadi, the note DHA (A), is intoned sharp and energetically. Usually it is approached from the next higher NI (B) by means of a small descending glide:

In ascent the note DHA (A) is followed by the high SA (c) in the sequence NI DHA SA (B A c):

   or

The entire ascending Hamir scale is:

or

Both foregoing scale examples show that the note RE (D) is touched
only very lightly. We must add that in many instances this note is
totally avoided in ascent.

There are numerous musicians who ignore the vakra passage
NI DHA SA (B A c) and perform instead DHA (NI) SA (A [B] c). This
latter progression is incorrect, but at the present time it is so frequently employed that we have to accept it as a habitual exception.

The descending line of Hamir is:

In descent the note DHA (A) is not microtonally raised. The note NI
komal (B♭) appears only between two DHA (A) or between DHA (A)
and PA (G). The note MA tivra (F#) is avoided in descent, and the
vakra phrase GA MA RE SA (E F D C) gains considerably in importance.

RAGA HAMIR   (Tivra Tal)   BH, III, 92-93

Asthayi

Antara

Tone material

Raga Shuddh-sarang

This raga actually belongs to the Kafi thata (C D Eb F G A Bb
c),[30] and should be presented later. The reason for mentioning it
here is that it avoids the Kafi note GA komal (Eb) and uses the notes
NI (B) and MA tivra (F#), which create, particularly in ascent, a
very strong link with the Kalyan family. Hence it is felt that Shuddh-
sarang may be listed among the Kalyan ragas.

Shuddh-sarang, which has to be performed at noon, is one of
Tansen's ragas. Some musicians, however, derive the word sarang[31]
from the name Sārṅgadeva, the famous thirteenth century musician-
author.

The vadi of this raga is RE (D); the samvadi is PA (G). The
note GA (E), if the Kalyan thata is taken into account, or GA komal
(Eb), if the raga is derived from the Kafi thata, is totally omitted.
The note MA tivra (F#), weakly treated, appears only in ascent, and
MA (F) is used in descent, usually linked with the lower note RE (D)
by a gliding step. The note DHA (A) appears mostly in descent,
treated weakly. NI (B) is strong in ascent and is often slightly
raised. This note is always followed (in ascent) by SA (C or c).
There are some musicians who also employ this note in descent. Pandit Bhatkhande and numerous other Indian musicians, however, use
only NI komal (Bb) in descent, invariably followed by PA (G), never
by DHA (A).

With NI (B) in descent

With NI komal (B♭) in descent

Further possibilities:
    With NI (B) in descent

With NI komal (B♭) in descent

RAGA SHUDDH-SARANG   (Ektal)   BH, VI, 127-8

Asthayi

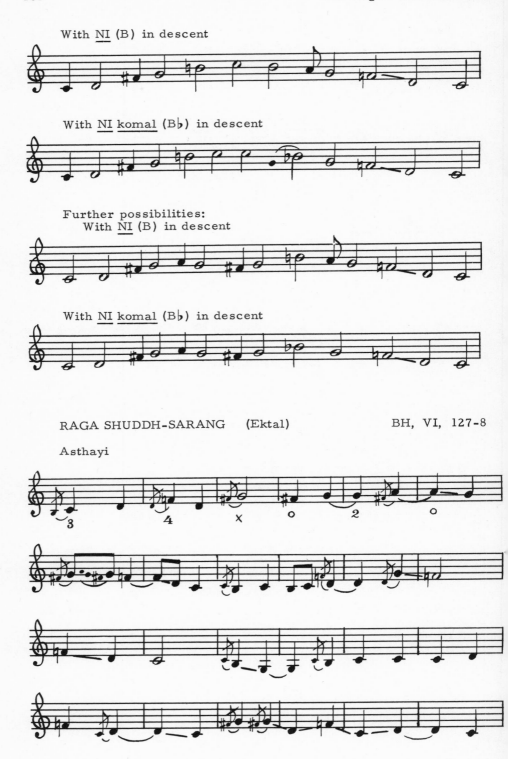

Antara

In the fifth line, measure four, we observe the note MA (F) in ascent, which is an exception. If we ignore these comparatively rare deviations which only a few musicians permit, the tone material of this raga can be shown as follows:

Raga Shyam-kalyan (Sham-kalyan, Shyama, Sham)

Shyam-kalyan has to be performed in the evening. In the Rāg-Kutūhala[32] we find the following pictorial description:

> Her body shines with the beauty of clouds; she has snatched away the picture of the figure of Kṛṣna (Ghana-śyām). The glitter of her yellow robes is full of beauty; she has decked her brow with specks of saffron. The damsel dallies in sweet smiles which raise new desires in one's heart. Such is the great melody Śyām, carrying a wreath of jewels round her neck, —a captivating beauty, —as the incarnation of Cupid. [33]

The vadi of this raga is SA (C), the samvadi, MA (F). There are some musicians who insist that the samvadi is RE (D).

Two types of Shyam-kalyan may be distinguished:

a) Shyam-kalyan with the Kamod phrase GA MA RE SA (E F D C);

b) Shyam-kalyan without this phrase, a type in which GA (E) is used very rarely.

If GA (E) is used in this raga, it appears as an exceedingly weak note, very lightly touched. For example; the famous North Indian singer Fayyaz Khan prefers to use the second type of this raga.

The notes MA (F) and MA tivra (F#) are of importance in both types. MA tivra (F#) appears in ascent and MA (F) in descent. In descent MA (F) is often linked with the next lower RE (D) by means of a gliding step. The note DHA (A) is generally avoided in ascent; in descent this note is performed in a manner very similar to that of DHA (A) in raga Deshkar. The ascending sequence RE MA tivra PA (D F# G) is important. It shows a strong relationship to a similar ascent in raga Kamod, RE PA (D G). In rare instances we observe GA MA tivra PA (E F# G) and occasionally even GA MA PA GA MA RE (E F G E F D). These two latter phrases may appear in songs, never in alaps, where the correct interpretation of the raga is of utmost importance.

The following formula summarizes our statements:

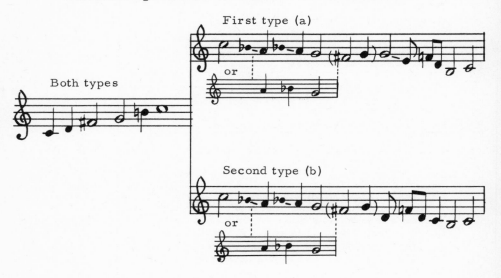

RAGA SHYAM-KALYAN   (Trital)   BH, V, 16

Asthayi

Antara

Although we have spoken of the two types of this raga, it must be added that at the present time there are many musicians who make no distinction between the two types and permit numerous liberties in the songs. In the alaps, however, musicians strictly observe the performance rules and the distinction between the two types.

Comparison of the Auffuehrungspraxis of the Ragas
Shuddh-Sarang and Shyam-Kalyan

Shuddh-sarang	Shyam-kalyan
MA tivra (F#) is weak;	MA tivra (F#) is strong;
The descent from RE (D) to SA (C) is straight: MA RE SA (F D C).	The descent from RE (D) to SA (C) is often (not always) vakra: MA RE NI SA (F D B C).

Raga Gaud-sarang (Gauda-saranga)

Gaud (or Gaur) suggests the land of sugar, the district of Gaur
in Bengal. Gaud-sarang is to be performed, like all Sarang ragas, in
the early afternoon. Pandit Bhatkhande is of the opinion that the correct performance time of this raga is the evening and that this is one
of the distinguishing marks between Gaud-sarang and the other Sarang
types.

The pictorial description in the Saṅgīta-Rāga-Kalpadruma (p. 29)
is:

> The greatest of the sages say that Saranga-gaud is fair
> in complexion, has his hair tightly bound, and delights
> in playing the vina. Sitting by the Kalpa-Vriksha
> [wishing tree] he sings in the afternoon and he has a
> voice as pleasing as that of a cuckoo.

The vadi of this raga is GA (E); the samvadi is DHA (A). Both notes
are to be treated in a vakra manner. In ascent we observe GA RE
MA GA PA (E D F E G) and in descent GA MA RE SA (E F D C).
DHA (A) in ascent appears usually in DHA PA SA (A G c) or, occasionally, in DHA PA NI DHA SA (A G B A c), and in descent we
usually find DHA NI PA DHA MA tivra PA (A B G A F# G), only very
rarely DHA PA GA (A G E). The note MA tivra (F#) usually appears
in ascent and MA (F) in descent. The upper SA (c) is generally
reached by the step PA SA (G c), only occasionally by the progression
NI DHA SA (B A c). The gliding step PA-RE (G-D) in descent is
characteristic. In a few instances we observe the appearance of the
note NI (B) either between two DHA (A) or between DHA (A) and PA
(G) or between PA and DHA. The note NI komal (B♭) is weak and is
touched only briefly.

The Gaud-sarang formula can be shown in the following:

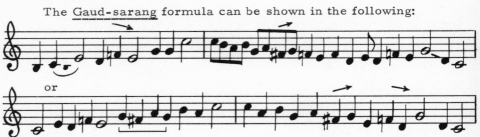

RAGA GAUD-SARANG   (Trital)   BH, IV, 135

Asthayi

Antara

The appearance of the note <u>MA</u> (F) in descent (second line, measure one, of the <u>asthayi</u>) can be considered to be an exception. Such exceptions, as we know, may occur in songs, never in <u>alaps</u>.

Tone material

<u>Raga Hindol (Hindola)</u>

Hindol, one of the famous ragas, is subordinated to the <u>Kalyan</u>
<u>thata</u>, although there are some musicians who ascribe it to the <u>Marva</u>
<u>thata</u>.[34] It is a seasonal raga which is usually performed in the
morning during the months of March and April. The word <u>hindola</u>
means "swing," and in nearly all pictorial representations of this
raga the god Krishna is shown seated on a swing. The swing hangs
on ropes which come from the sky. Krishna is surrounded by several
<u>gopis</u>, beautiful young women, who move the swing to and fro. The
god plays a cross flute, and his music delights his charming friends.
In a text by Gangadhar entitled <u>Rāga-Mālā</u> (eighteenth century)[35] we
find the following description:

> Hindola is robed in yellow, he is seated at the centre of
> the swing. The confidantes are swinging him with passion,
> singing with smiles.[36]

In the <u>Saṅgīta-Rāga-Kalpadruma</u> (p. 20) and in several other works
we find this raga described twice: once as male, once as female:

> The sages say that <u>Hindol</u> raga, gleaming with the radi-
> ance of innumerable doves flying in the sky, is highly
> amorous and moves to and fro in a slow moving swing
> in the company of women with well-shaped hips.

> The sages say that <u>Hindolika</u> is fair in complexion and
> fragrant with the smell of divine flowers. Gleaming
> like gold, and with eyes like the lotus, she has a grace-
> ful body with well-shaped hips. She holds a vina in her
> hands.

In the <u>Rāga-Sāgara</u> (3, 61) <u>Hindol</u> is described as follows:

> From my heart I pray to Hindola, fair-bodied and dressed
> in variegated patterned apparel. Adorned with ornaments
> and precious gems, fond of music of the murali, she
> devoutly worships Lord Shri Krishna, sitting with Kamala
> on a golden swing supported by braided fibres of the fig
> tree.

North Indian musicians have differing views about the <u>vadis</u> of
this raga. Some hold that the <u>vadi</u> is <u>DHA</u> (A) and the <u>samvadi</u> is <u>GA</u>
(E) and that the highly placed <u>vadi</u> serves as an indicator of the performance time, the morning. Others, however, insist that the <u>vadi</u>
is <u>GA</u> (E) and the <u>samvadi</u> is <u>DHA</u> (A), which transforms <u>Hindol</u> into
an evening raga. Nevertheless, the general view is that <u>Hindol</u> is to

Plate V. Hindola Raga

DOHA: Madhumad and Gandhari, Todi, Desi, and Bilaval, all combine to give life to Hindola.

CHAUPAYI: Various beautiful pillars are raised, which support the swing studded with precious jewels. Sitting in the swing [beside her consort], the lady-love plays the vina and the other maidens push the swing while singing a love song together. Dark clouds gather and bring rain. The lightning appears in a shaft of light, and the garden presents a beautiful view. The atmosphere is such that her love for her consort grows manifold and her heart is filled with happiness.

DOHA: The lady-love of Hindola the "Rajtarang" is sitting in the swing and sporting with her companions. There is great happiness in their hearts, and their bodies are alive with delight.

be performed in the morning. If the raga is correctly performed,
its rasa represents quiet, dignified joy.

The notes RE (D) and PA (G) are totally avoided. The fourth
degree of the scale is always MA tivra (F#) and the note NI (B) is
avoided in straight ascent. In order to reach the high SA (c) from the
lower DHA (A), the vakra feature NI DHA SA (B A c) is interpolated.

In descent two characteristic gliding steps appear: SA-DHA
(c-A), in which the note NI (B) is very lightly touched, and the step
GA-SA (E-C). The note GA (E) in descent is usually approached
from DHA (A) or MA tivra (F#).

RAGA HINDOL   (Trital)   BH, IV, 176

THE BILAVAL THATA

This thata has the largest number of subordinate ragas. Its notes
correspond to the Western medieval modus lascivus, the tonality of C
major, which, although originally avoided in the music of the church,
eventually became the most popular. It is possible that the character
of this appealing modus created a similar popularity in India. Many
centuries later, in the early 1800's, this modus, which probably had
always been popular in light songs and dances, became the basic scale
of the North Indian system of art music. Although the music of the
South employs as its basic scale the mela Kanakangi (C Db Ebb F G
Ab Bbb c), there is little doubt that the scale of the twenty-ninth mela,
Dhirashankarabharanam, which corresponds in many respects to that
of Bilaval, is and has been exceedingly popular in all types of music,
serious and light, in the temple as well as in places of gay entertain-
ment.

Raga Bilaval or Alahiya-bilaval (ancient name: Velavali)

The thata-raga Bilaval, before 1813 [37] called ragini Bilaval,
the wife of raga Hindol, must be performed in the morning. The pictorial descriptions usually deal with the female aspect, with Velavali.
In the Saṅgīta-Sāra (p. 129), for instance, we find:

> For the purpose of meeting her beloved in the trysting-
> place, she is putting on her jewels, (sitting) on her
> terrace; and she is repeatedly recalling and invoking
> her favorite deity—the god of love; her complexion is
> like the color of blue lotus. A ragini visualised as
> above, one should recognize as Velavali. [38]

In the Saṅgīta-Darpana (2, 59) and in several other works this raga
is described in the following manner:

> With a complexion radiant as a blue lotus, Velavali gives
> secret signs to her lover, and while decorating her body
> with ornaments and bright jewels she remembers her
> chosen deity, the god of love.

Plate VI. Ragini Bilaval

CHAUPAYI: The queen Bilaval is charming and beautiful. God has created her most artfully. She is so much at one with her beloved that she will not part from him even for a short while. She is deeply in love and enjoys amorous play. Her long, dark hair glistens; she has parted it in the middle of her head, and has placed a flower at the parting. Her skillful companions hold a mirror in front of her, in which she finds reflected her burgeoning youth and charm.

DOHA: Seeing her face in the mirror, she wonders at the beauty created by God and secretly marvels at it in her heart.

North Indian musicians distinguish two types of this raga:

a) the frequently performed Alahiya-bilaval (commonly called Bilaval);

b) the rarely performed Shuddha-bilaval.

Both types have the rasa of the peaceful repose of the early morning.

Raga Alahiya-bilaval, has DHA (A) as vadi and GA (E) as sam-vadi. In contrast to the raga Shuddha-bilaval, which will be discussed below, Alahiya-bilaval avoids the note MA (F) in the ascending line. The note DHA (A) is treated in the same manner as it is in raga Deshkar; that is, DHA is performed with a slight approach from, or a slight swinging out toward, NI komal (B♭), which, although essential, is not a regular note of the Bilaval scale. This remarkable vivadi can only appear in the middle octave region, never in the mandra saptaka and hardly ever in the tar saptaka, where, in any case, it would be unusually high for a singer. The note NI (B), however, can appear in ascent and descent in any octave region. The notes GA (E) and PA (G) are strong. The following example illustrates the impor-tant features of Alahiya-bilaval:

The ascending step GA PA (E G) can be executed in two ways: either with the linking and gently touched notes RE and GA (D and E), or by means of a direct glide. The correct treatment of the note DHA (A) has already been explained and is illustrated in the foregoing example.

The note <u>NI</u> (B) has to be followed by <u>SA</u> (C or c). In the descending scale, usually in the phrase <u>GA</u> <u>MA</u> <u>RE</u> <u>SA</u> the note <u>MA</u> (F) appears.

RAGA ALAHIYA-BILAVAL   (Trital)   BH, II, 91-92

Asthayi

Antara

We notice in the foregoing song example a deviation from the rule that the note MA (F) is omitted in ascent. This deviation occurs in the antara, in measures seven, fourteen, and twenty-one. This and sim- ilar irregularities have their origin in the music of the tantakars, the string players, who preferred to play the sequence D E F G (and F E D C) instead of D E G (and E F D C). Some students of these tantakars gave up string playing; they became singers and transferred the habits of string playing, simplifying complex phrases, into their vocal art. One would have to add that there are some singers who pretend to have been disciples of tantakars and adopt these habits without any justifi- cation. As I have stated before, such irregularities may occur in songs but are strictly forbidden in alaps.

Tone material

Raga Shuddha-bilaval

Shuddha-bilaval is another one of "Tansen's ragas," and is cer- tainly no more shuddha than Alahiya-bilaval. Shuddha-bilaval differs from Alahiya-bilaval in its use of the note MA (F) in the ascending scale. Another difference between the two ragas is the fact that the note NI komal (Bb), a vivadi, adds its characteristic flavor to Alahiya- bilaval, while in Shuddha-bilaval this note and its ornamental function is totally avoided.

There exists a certain similarity between Shuddha-bilaval and raga Kalyan which has caused some musicians to call Shuddha- bilaval by the name "Morning-Kalyan." The vadis of this raga are the same as those of Alahiya-bilaval, and the exact performance rules of

the two ragas were and still are the cause of excited debates among
Indian musicians. Some musicians insist that Shuddha-bilaval must
not be subordinated to the Bilaval, but that it belongs to the Khamaj
thata and that its vadis are PA (G) and RE (D).

Pandit Bhatkhande places the following song specimen among his
Alahiya-bilaval group. I cannot agree with this because the use of the
ascending MA (F) (in the third measure of lines one and four) shows
that the melody tends strongly toward Shuddha-bilaval.

RAGA SHUDDHA-BILAVAL   (Trital)   BH, II, 74

Tone material

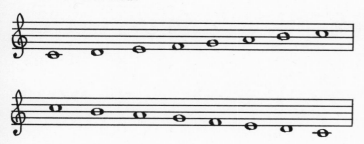

Raga Deshkar

Although its notes are similar to those of raga Bhupali (of the Kalyan thata), the treatment of the notes of Deshkar is such that nobody would subordinate this raga to the Kalyan thata. The characteristic note of Kalyan is MA tivra (F#); in ragas belonging to the Bilaval family, however, it is the vivadi NI komal (B♭), despite its extremely weak and ornamental character. The note DHA (A) of Deshkar with its subtle approach from NI komal (B♭) points distinctly toward the Bilaval group.

The vadi of this raga is DHA (A), and the samvadi is GA (E). The note PA (G) is treated very strongly; it is a vishrantishthan, a spot where melodies and phrases may be stopped or interrupted. The samvadi, GA (E), must not be treated strongly (quite in contrast to its treatment in raga Bhupali). As has already been mentioned, the vadi DHA (A) has to be approached from above, from NI komal (B♭) or even from the high SA (c). The notes MA (F) and NI (B) are totally omitted. NI komal (B♭) appears only in connection with the vadi in the form of a small ornament. The phrase PA DHA GA PA (G A E G) is characteristic. It usually appears in alaps; in songs, however, particularly in performances of recent times, it tends to be ignored.

The essential phrases of Deshkar are:

Although the note GA (E) can be used only briefly, it must be employed in order to show by its short duration the difference between
Deshkar and raga Bhupali, where this note is the vadi. Numerous
musicians of the older generation had the habit of merely teaching
their pupils melodies without telling them the names of the ragas or
pointing out any characteristic features. This method led to various
misunderstandings and errors. There exists the recording of a well-
known Indian singer which shows on its label that raga Bhupali is being
presented. This is an error which can be observed in the following
phrase:

We notice that in this particular phrase the note PA (G) is emphasized,
a note which points at the vishrantisthan of raga Deshkar. In Bhupali
this note is weakly treated and the note GA (E) requires greater emphasis. Bhupali, as we know, has a royal, dignified character, and
Deshkar is presented mostly in a rustic, cheerful manner.

RAGA DESHKAR   (Trital)   BH, IV, 244-245

Asthayi

Antara

Tone material

Raga Gunakali

There are two types of Gunakali; one belongs to the Bilaval thata, the other one to the Bhairav thata.[39]   Raga Gunakali of the Bilaval thata can be performed in two versions:

Plate VII. Ragini Gunakali

CHAUPAYI: Gunakali displays a taste for art. She is skillful, has a melodious voice, and her body is beautifully shaped. She so loses herself in thinking about her beloved that she becomes as one with him. She leaves the palace quietly and rests in the shade. An attendant follows her with a fine whisk to fan above her head. She has the grace of a golden vine. She never misses an opportunity to meet with her lover. Her body is full of joy, and her beloved seems to surprise her.

DOHA: The lady has beautiful, arresting eyes. She is also very wise. Her master, Malkaushik, is very pleasing and makes her exceedingly happy.

a) Gunakali without NI (B);

b) Gunakali with NI (B).

a) Gunakali without NI has some similarity to the raga Bhupali. It is
the use of the note MA (F), mostly in ascent, less often in descent, that
distinguishes this raga from Bhupali. Its vadi is SA (C), and the samvadi is PA (G). Despite the fact that the vadi is a low note, Gunakali
is usually performed in the morning. In order to achieve a correct
performance of this raga, it is essential to emphasize its characteristic Bilaval phrases. The note DHA (A), as in raga Bilaval, has to be
approached from above, roughly from NI komal (B♭). Although this
is an important rule, contemporary musicians do not always observe
it. Another feature is the occasional use of the note MA tivra (F♯).
Theoretically, this note is strictly forbidden in ragas of the Bilaval
family. In spite of this ban, there are some performers who touch
upon the note when intoning the samvadi (G). It is their habit to swing
out slightly from PA (G) toward MA tivra (F♯) and then return again
to the starting point.

Gunakali is rare, and no adequate song specimen can be shown.
The following phrases are important:

As I have already pointed out, the ornamenting notes NI komal (B♭)
and MA tivra (F♯) are not notated; many musicians will not even ad-
mit that these notes are in use.

b) Gunakali with NI (B)

The second version of this rare raga has various interpretations, and the characteristic phrases shown below are not necessarily the only correct ones. A remarkable distinction between the two versions of Gunakali (besides the use of NI) is the fact that the note NI komal (B♭), which in the first version appears only as a subtly touched ornament, appears in the second version, particularly in descent, as a regular note. Another distinction between the two versions is the use of MA (F) in ascent in the first version and the extremely rare use of this note in the second version. If it is used at all, it is only in descent.

RAGA GUNAKALI Bilaval Thata, Second version   BH, V, 179
(Sultal)

Asthayi

Antara

Tone material

Raga Shankara

This serious and dignified raga has to be performed at night. Its vadi is GA (E), and the samvadi is NI (B). There are some musicians who state that the vadi is NI (B) and the samvadi GA (E). As Shankara is a night raga, one can assume that the former vadi disposition is the correct one. The tone material of Shankara is nearly the same as that of Bilaval. The difference can be found in Shankara in the total omission of the note MA (F) and in treating the notes DHA (A) and RE (D) very weakly. The ornamenting NI komal (B♭) of Bilaval is not used in Shankara. The note DHA (A) appears only in the ascending phrase NI DHA SA (B A c). In some fast tans this rule is relaxed and DHA (A) may appear in direct ascent or even in descent as, for instance, in SA NI DHA PA (c B A G). Although it is not an outspoken rule, the note RE (D) is frequently omitted in ascent. The following are the important Shankara phrases:

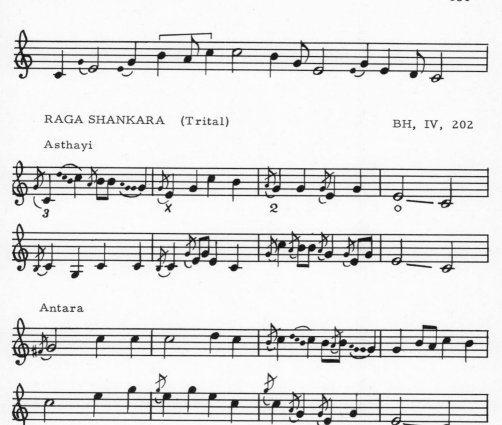

RAGA SHANKARA   (Trital)   BH, IV, 202

Asthayi

Antara

In the foregoing song specimen we observe several times the characteristic phrase NI DHA SA (B A c) and, in contrast to the rule, DHA
(A) in descent (A G) (first line, bars one and three; second line, bar
three; third line, bar three; and fourth line, bar three). Such deviations from the rule may appear in songs only.

     Another deviation from the performance rules can be observed
in the use of the strictly forbidden note MA tivra (F#). Although this
note is notated only once (third line, bar one), it appears also in the
three-note ornament before the last quarter of the first bar of the
first line and, in the same form, again in the third bar of the third
line. This ornament, notated as A G G, is nearly always simplified
and interpreted as A G F#.

The note RE (D), usually hidden in the gliding step GA-SA (E-C)
(first, second and fourth lines, bar four), is notated in a three-note
ornament of the first bar of the first line and in the third bar of the
third line.

Tone material

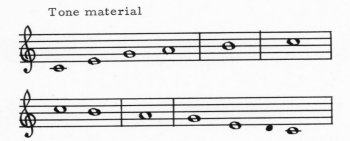

Raga Shankarakaran

This obscure and little-known raga can be ascribed to the Bilaval
thata. Although Indian musicians mention its name occasionally, I had
only one opportunity during my fourteen-year stay in India to hear
this raga and was unable to find an adequate song specimen. This report on Shankarakaran is based only on this single hearing and does
not claim to be comprehensive.

It seems that this raga is a derivative or a variant of raga
Shankara, in which the note MA (F) is used. Raga Shankarakaran has
the same vadis as Shankara and emphasizes the note PA (G). The note
MA (F) appears in vakra form in the phrase MA GA PA (F E G).

The ornament (gamak) in the second line of the foregoing example is
of interest because it employs the note NI komal (B♭). In all other

instances the note NI (B) is used. The upper SA (c) is reached, as
in raga Shankara, by the vakra phrase NI DHA SA (B A c).

Tone material

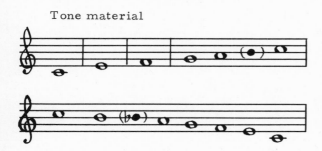

Raga Bihag (Bihaga, Behag)

This important raga, subordinated to the Bilaval thata, has to be
performed at midnight. Its rasa is a loving, thoughtful longing, combined with gentle anxiety. The vadi is GA (E), the samvadi, NI (B).
The Bihag scale employs both MA (F) and MA tivra (F#). The notes
RE (D) and DHA (A) are omitted in ascent and are weak in descent.
If the performer observes these rules, the mistaking of Yaman-kalyan
for Bihag, particularly in descent, can be avoided. The use of the
notes MA (F) and MA tivra (F#) is illustrated in the following example:

We observe that the descending scale can be continued stepwise from
the high SA (c) via MA tivra (F#) down to the vadi (E). After the
vadi the descent becomes vakra; the next note has to be MA (F), from
which the descent to the low SA (C) can be continued. The rule is that
MA (F) must appear between two GA (E). An exception to this rule is
permissible in the performance of fast tans (passages) where occasionally the following sequence can be observed:

RAGA BIHAG   (Trital)   BH, III, 177

Asthayi

Antara

Comparison of the Auffuehrungspraxis of the Ragas
Bihag and Yaman-kalyan

Bihag   Yaman-kalyan

Bihag   Yaman-kalyan

In contrast to Bihag, raga Yaman-kalyan omits frequently in ascent
the note SA (C). In Bihag the note DHA (A) is avoided in ascent and
treated weakly in descent. In Yaman-kalyan the note DHA (A) is used
in ascent and descent. The note MA tivra (F#) is weak in Bihag but
is, nevertheless, treated as a distinct note. In Yaman-kalyan this
note is usually linked by a descending gliding step with GA (E).

Raga Savani

      This raga is ascribed to the Bilaval thata. It is often called
Savani Bihag-anga ("Savani, related to Bihag") in order to distinguish
it from raga Savani-kalyan. [40] The performance rules of Savani are
not clear. Its vadis are probably PA (G) and SA (C) or, if the note
NI (B) is emphasized, GA (E) and NI (B). The strong treatment of
the note NI (B) was a characteristic in the Savani performances of the
great Aladiya Khan of Bombay and his pupils. All musicians who are
not followers of Aladiya Khan's school treat the note NI (B) in a weak
manner.

The note RE (D) appears usually only in descent in a weak form. DHA
(A), too, is used only in descent and is mostly approached from the
note MA (F) below:

Occasionally the vakra phrase NI DHA SA (B A c) is used, but it is
never employed by the pupils of Aladiya Khan. The note MA tivra
(F#), never notated, appears occasionally as a very slightly touched
ornament in the following phrase:

The vakra position of MA (F) in the descent PA MA PA GA RE SA (G
F G E D C) has been described as an important feature, but it cannot
be observed in the following song specimen.

RAGA SAVANI   (Jhaptal)   BH, V, 150

Asthayi

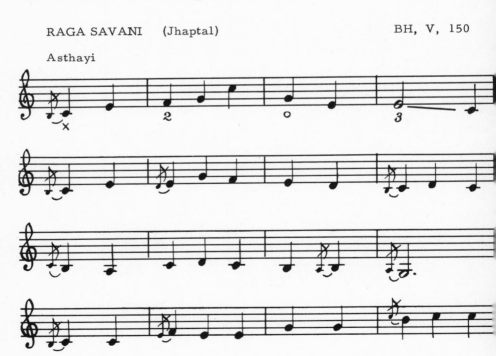

Comparison of the <u>Auffuehrungspraxis</u> of the Ragas
<u>Savani</u> (<u>Bihag-anga</u>) and <u>Savani-kalyan</u>

<u>Savani (Bihag-anga)</u>	<u>Savani-kalyan</u>
<u>MA</u> (F) is <u>vakra</u> in descent;	<u>MA</u> (F) is <u>vakra</u> in ascent and is omitted in descent;
<u>MA</u> <u>tivra</u> (F#) is part of an ornament, very slightly touched.	<u>MA</u> <u>tivra</u> (F#) is totally omitted.

Raga Nand (Nanda, Anandi)

This very rare raga with uncertain performance rules seems to be related to the Bilaval family. The following report is based upon one hearing of this raga. The singer, when asked to describe Nand, was unable (or unwilling?) to oblige. I observed both notes MA and MA tivra (F and F#) are employed; also, the notes RE (D) and NI (B) are avoided in ascent. Other features of Nand which can be observed in raga Anand-bhairav [41] are the phrases NI PA DHA MA tivra PA GA (B G A F# G E) and GA MA DHA PA RE SA (E F A G D C), and the descending step PA RE (G-D), in which the note RE (D) is approached not from PA (G) but from MA tivra (F#) or MA (F) in a gliding manner.

Tone material

Raga Bihagda (Bihagada, Begagra)

This raga should be sung or played at night. "Bihagada comes arguing and resentful and remonstrating." [42]

North Indian musicians differ in their views as to the correct
performance of this raga. Even Bhatkhande, the greatest authority of
the present century, is vague in his description of Bihagda, and the
song specimens which he uses to illustrate this raga do not tally with
the actual performance practice. The contradictions one finds may
lie in the fact that there are two types of Bihagda. We shall, therefore,
endeavor to describe them both. One type of this raga uses the notes
NI (B) and NI komal (B♭), while the other type avoids NI komal (B♭).

Bihagda with NI (B) and NI komal (B♭)

The similarity between this type and the raga Bihag is strong. It may
be of advantage, first of all, to consider the fine differences between
these two forms. Generally speaking, one can state that the curves
created by Bihag melodies are wide and long (⌒).
Bihag melodies usually begin and end with a low note, while the middle
shows this characteristic sweeping curve. Furthermore, Bihag melodies (or phrases) represent more or less uniform long waves. In
Bihagda, however, the curve of the melody is frequently interrupted
and shows a preponderance of the descending over the ascending movement (＼ ＼ ＼ ＼).

The vadis of this type of Bihagda are GA (E) and NI (B). The
note MA tivra (F♯) appears much less frequently than in Bihag, but
MA (F) is used more frequently than in Bihag. The note SA (C) is
usually approached by means of a short appoggiatura or a gliding step
from the next lower NI (B). The note RE (D) is rarely used in ascent
and is used somewhat more frequently in descent. The following
phrases are characteristic:

The foregoing example illustrates the use of the note MA tivra (F#),
a note which belongs in the Kalyan but not in the Bilaval family. However, it is just these subtle vivadis, these gently touched "wrong notes,"
which, like fine spices, contribute much to the "taste" and character
of the raga. Although this note is never notated, it has its importance,
and it usually appears in the form of a short, lightly touched ornament,
generally between two PA (G) or between PA (G) and DHA (A). The
example shows also that the note MA (F) may assume the same function as MA tivra (F#).

RAGA BIHAGDA   First type (Rupak)   BH, V, 147-8

Asthayi

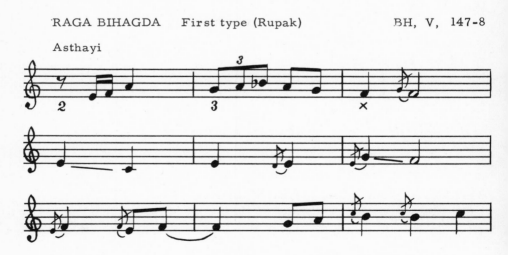

Bihagda with NI (B)

This second type of Bihagda is also called Patabihag or Patbihag.
Views concerning the performance rules of the two types of this raga
vary. Pandit Bhatkhande presents one song example which uses both
forms of NI, NI shuddha (B) and NI komal (B♭). In order to maintain

a clear distinction between the two types of Bihagda, I find it advisable to describe the second type without the note NI komal (B♭). gm

Type one

Type two

In extended form the second type will be:

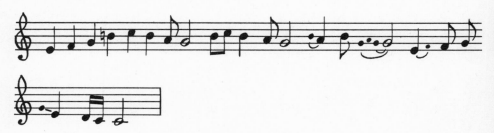

Theoretically the vadis are the same in both types. In practice,
however, this is not always the case. We observe that the note PA
(G) is often emphasized more strongly in the second type (Patabihag)
than its theoretical vadi and that the note SA (C) gains in importance
in the second type over its theoretical samvadi. We further observe
that in the second type the note DHA (A) appears in ascent only when
the melody does not exceed the next higher NI (B). If the melody aims
at the upper SA (c), the ascent is performed without the note DHA (A).

In the descending line we find a small ornament consisting of
three notes: PA DHA PA (PA) (G A G [G]). This ornament appears
only when the note DHA (A) has been used in the ascent immediately
preceding. If in the preceding ascent the melody moves to the upper
SA (c) —when, as we know, the note NI (B) is avoided—in descent a
"full-fledged" DHA (A) and the note PA (G) without the three-note
ornament can appear. This rule is carefully observed in alaps; in
songs, however, liberties are permissible. It is these rules which
clearly show the difference between Bihag and Bihagda.

No song specimen of this rarely performed raga can be found.

Tone material

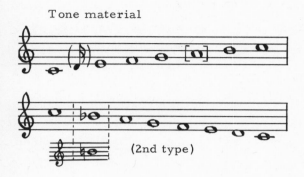

(2nd type)

Raga Maru-bihag

This rare and obscure raga can be ascribed to the Bilaval thata. Its vadis are GA (E) and NI (B). The remarkable feature of Maru-bihag is the use of the note MA tivra (F#) in ascent and descent. This predominance of MA tivra (F#) would give a musician cause to subordinate this raga to the Kalyan thata. The note MA (F) appears only in two phrases, as shown in the following example:

Tone material

Raga Kauns (Kaunsadhvani, Koshadhvani)

Kauns is another of the very rare ragas which can be subordinated to the Bilaval thata. It shows certain similarities to raga Hindol;[43]
specifically, the notes RE (D) and PA (G) are totally omitted. The
main difference can be seen in the fact that Kauns only uses the note
MA (F) and Hindol only uses MA tivra (F#). Besides the note MA
(F), there appears in Kauns a faint trace of NI komal (Bb), which is
the reason for ascribing this raga to the Bilaval group.

The vadis are GA (E) and DHA (A). The note NI (B) is avoided
in ascent, and the note MA (F) is often omitted in descent, although a
few exceptional examples show that it can be used occasionally. The
avoidance of NI (B) in ascent causes the characteristic step DHA SA
(A c). In this step the note DHA (A) is produced without an ornament.
If, however, DHA (A) in ascent is approached from above, from the
vivadi NI komal (Bb), the next higher SA (c) is produced with an
unusually long, more or less gliding appoggiatura beginning from the
low SA (C). The descent, too, shows an unusual feature: the note
DHA (A) is mostly (perhaps always) followed by the next lower GA
(E), and the two notes are linked by a gliding step.

Kauns melodies may not only be interrupted on the vadis and on
the basic SA (C), but may come to a stop on the upper SA (c).

Tone material

Raga Sohag

Neither Pandit Bhatkhande nor any of the other contemporary Indian authors mention this rare, probably recent raga. The following report is based upon a single hearing, when Sohag was performed late at night. This raga can be ascribed to the Bilaval family, although the note MA tivra (F#), which creates a link with the Kalyan thata, is frequently used. The determining factor for subordinating this raga to the Bilaval thata is the occasional use of the note NI komal (B♭) in descent.

The vadis are GA (E) and NI (B). The use of ṄI (B) and NI komal (B♭) is shown in the following example. The note DHA (A) is weak in descent.

Some musicians believe that this raga consists of phrases taken from the ragas Shankara,[44] Maru-bihag,[45] and Bihagda.[46] It is said that these more or less fixed phrases permit the performer too little freedom to improvize. This may be the reason why the rare performances of Sohag are characterized by their unusual brevity.

Tone material

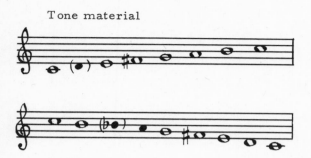

Raga Hem-kalyan

Hem-kalyan belongs to the Bilaval family and is to be performed
in a quiet and dignified manner.   Melodies in this raga usually move
in the middle and low octave regions.   The vadis are SA (C) and PA
(G).   The note NI (B) is avoided, with the one exception shown in the
song specimen below.   DHA (A) is treated weakly in alaps.   This
latter rule seems to have lost its validity, for an increasing number
of musicians tend to emphasize DHA (A) in this raga.   The note MA
tivra (F#) appears only as a very gently touched ornament.   RE (D)
is avoided in ascent; MA (F) appears very rarely in ascent and is
treated as a weak note.   Thus the ascent of the raga consists mainly
of the notes SA GA PA SA (C E G c), while all other notes between
them are weakly treated.   In descent the gliding step SA-PA (c-G) is
frequently used and is continued after PA (G) with the vakra phrase
GA MA RE SA (E F D C).

Characteristic phrases of Hem-kalyan are:

In some rare instances the note <u>NI</u> (B) may appear as an ornament, as, for instance, in the following song specimen:

RAGA HEM-KALYAN (Trital) BH, V, 49

Asthayi

Antara

Tone material

Raga Mand

This light and popular raga, which can be ascribed to the <u>Bilaval</u>
family, has its origin in the folk music of Rajputana, where its characteristic phrases appear in numerous songs and dance melodies.
<u>Mand</u> can be performed at any time. Its <u>vadis</u> are <u>SA</u> (C) and <u>PA</u> (G),

and the note MA (F) is a vishrantisthan. The notes RE (D) and DHA
(A) are weak in ascent. The note NI (B) is often performed with a
fast vibrato, a vibrato quite similar to that of a Western singer.

Pandit Bhatkhande is of the opinion that all notes of the Mand
scale have a vakra character and have to follow each other in a zigzag line:

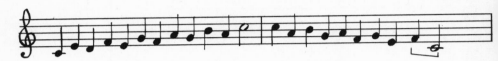

Some examples of this raga do not fully support this rule.   Important
phrases of Mand are:

RAGA MAND   (Trital)   BH, V, 189

Asthayi

Antara 1

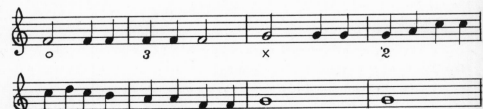

Antara 2

Tone material

Raga Mevada

This light and very popular raga can be considered as a variant
of raga <u>Mand</u>. The phrases of both ragas appear in the folk music of

Rajputana. The vadi of this raga can be MA (F) or SA (C); the samvadi has no significance in such a popular raga.

The note GA (E) is often avoided in ascent, with the exception of
the phrase GA MA (GA RE SA) (E F [E D C]).

RAGA MEVADA   (Dadra)   BH, V, 192

Asthayi

Antara 1

Antara 2

Tone material

Raga Maluha-kedar

This serious raga is performed by most musicians in the evening, but there are a few who consider it to be a morning raga. The performance rules of Maluha-kedar are somewhat uncertain. The vadis are SA (C) and MA (F). The notes RE (D) and DHA (A), occasionally even MA (F), are avoided in ascent. The note MA tivra (F#) appears at times as a very lightly touched ornament in ascent before PA (G). In a few instances this note may be hidden in the gliding step GA-PA (E-G). Some musicians avoid the note GA (E) both in ascent and descent and treat the notes RE (D) and DHA (A) weakly in ascent. The known songs in this raga, however, do not show this to be a rule. The following vakra phrases are characteristic: GA MA RE SA (E F D C), GA MA RE NI SA (E F D B C), SA MA GA PA (C F E G), and <u>SA</u> <u>NI</u> <u>RE</u> <u>SA</u> (C B D C). <u>Maluha-kedar</u> melodies usually move in the middle and lower octave regions.

RAGA MALUHA-KEDAR   (Dhamar Tal)   BH, V, 158

Asthayi

Antara

Tone material

There are a few North Indian musicians who speak of a second type of Maluha-kedar which differs from the type discussed above only by one phrase in which the note NI komal (B♭) is used: DHA NI komal PA (A B♭ G). It is probable that this phrase may have been chosen in order to show that this raga is related to the Bilaval group.

Comparison of the Auffuehrungspraxis of the Ragas
Maluha-kedar and Kedar

Maluha-kedar	Kedar
GA (E) is used;	GA (E) appears rarely;
Melodies usually move in the middle and low octave regions;	Melodies move very rarely in the low octave region;
MA tivra (F#) is rarely used and is very weak;	MA tivra (F#) and MA (F) are used;

Maluha-kedar	**Kedar**
NI (B) is strong;	NI (B) is weak and rare;
NI komal (B♭) is not used;	NI komal (B♭) can appear in the phrase MA tivra PA DHA NI komal DHA PA (F# G A B♭ A G);
Maluha-kedar uses the following Kamod phrase:	Kedar has its own typical phrase:

Comparison of the Auffuehrungspraxis of the Ragas Maluha-kedar and Kamod

Maluha-kedar	**Kamod**
MA (F) is strong;	MA (F) is weak;
NI (B) is strong;	NI (B) is weak;
Middle and low octave regions are preferred.	Middle and high octave regions are preferred.

Comparison of the <u>Auffuehrungspraxis</u> of the Ragas
<u>Maluha-kedar</u> and <u>Hem-kalyan</u>

<u>Maluha-kedar</u>	<u>Hem-kalyan</u>
Melodies often end with the note MA (F) of the low octave region;	Melodies may come to a temporary stop on the low <u>MA</u> (F), but have to move up to <u>SA</u> (C) of the middle octave region in order to come to an end;
<u>NI</u> (B) is strong;	<u>NI</u> (B) is rare and very weak;

Raga Maluha

The ragas <u>Maluha-kedar</u> and <u>Maluha</u> are often described as identical. I cannot agree with this view, because even a superficial comparison of the two ragas shows distinct differences. <u>Maluha</u> can be ascribed to the <u>Bilaval</u> family. It has the same <u>vadis</u> as <u>Maluha-kedar</u>. In <u>Maluha-kedar</u> the characteristic <u>Kamod</u> phrase <u>GA</u> <u>MA</u> <u>RE</u> <u>SA</u> (E F D C) is of some importance. This phrase does not occur in <u>Maluha</u> because the note <u>GA</u> (E) is totally omitted. Characteristic phrases of raga <u>Maluha</u> are:

The notes PA (G) and NI (B) are very weak in descent and are often covered by the gliding steps SA-DHA (C-A) or SA-PA (C-G) and DHA-MA (A-F). Although the note GA (E) is forbidden, it can be observed, never notated (and never acknowledged), as a subtle ornament between MA (F) and PA (G) in ascent. The tone material of this raga is the same as that of Maluha-kedar, if the few modifications (omission of GA and weak treatment of PA and NI in descent) are taken into consideration.

Raga Yamani-bilaval

This serious and dignified raga is performed in the morning. There are some musicians who ascribe this raga to the Kalyan thata. The vadis are SA (C) and PA (G). With one exception, which is explained below, the note MA tivra (F#) is used in ascent and MA (F) in descent. Characteristic phrases of this raga are:

RAGA YAMANI-BILAVAL   (Trital)   BH, V, 54

Asthayi

Antara

We observe that in this second type the note MA tivra (F#) appears only in descent between PA (G) and GA (E), while MA (F) is used between two GA (E).

Another interpretation of this raga classifies it as a second type of Yamani-bilaval. It avoids the note MA (F) (or MA tivra [F#]) in ascent and uses both notes in descent, with a typical Bilaval phrase in which the note NI komal (Bb) is used:

We observe that in this second type the note MA tivra (F#) appears only in descent between PA (G) and GA (E), while MA (F) is used between two GA (E).

Tone material

Raga Devgiri-bilaval

This raga has to be performed in the morning. Its vadi is SA (C), although some musicians insist that it is DHA (A); and the samvadi is PA (G).

The notes GA (E) and DHA (A) are rarely (and weakly) used in descent. MA tivra (F#) can appear (usually not notated) as a subtle and gently touched ornament before PA (G). A frequent use of this note would bring Devgiri-bilaval too close to the raga Yamani-bilaval. The note DHA (A) is approached lightly from above, from the note NI komal (Bb), as it is in Alahiya-bilaval. Melodies of Devgiri-bilaval move mostly in the middle and lower octave regions. Characteristic phrases of this raga are:

RAGA DEVGIRI-BILAVAL   (Tilvada)   BH, V, 66

Asthayi

Antara

Tone material

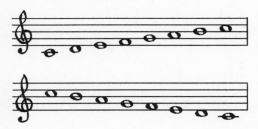

Comparison of the <u>Auffuehrungspraxis</u> of the Ragas <u>Yamani-bilaval</u> and <u>Devgiri-bilaval</u>

<u>Yamani-bilaval</u>   <u>Devgiri-bilaval</u>

Both ragas employ elements of <u>Bilaval</u> and <u>Yaman</u>;

Yamani-bilaval	Devgiri-bilaval
The low octave region is rarely used;	The low octave region is frequently used;
<u>MA</u> <u>tivra</u> (F#) is strong;	<u>MA</u> <u>tivra</u> (F#) appears rarely, and only as a weak ornament;
<u>GA</u> (E) is strong in descent;	<u>GA</u> (E) and <u>DHA</u> (A) are weak in descent;
<u>DHA</u> (A) appears after or before <u>NI</u> (B).	<u>DHA</u> (A) can be approached from <u>NI</u> <u>komal</u> (B♭).

Raga Odav-devgiri

This raga, a rare form of Devgiri-bilaval, is subordinated to the Bilaval thata. The name odav indicates that the scale of this raga is pentatonic; the notes MA (F) and NI (B) are totally omitted.

Odav-devgiri is to be performed in the morning. Its vadi is either SA (C) or DHA (A), and the samvadi, equally vague, has been described as PA (G). The note DHA (A) is treated in this raga in the same manner as it is in raga Deshkar; that is to say, it is approached from the next higher NI komal (Bb).

The similarity between the ragas Odav-devgiri and Deshkar is striking. The difference lies mainly in the cautious handling of the note GA (E), which in Odav-devgiri appears strongly in a typical Bilaval phrase but in Deshkar is weak.

Odav-devgiri

Deshkar

RAGA ODAV-DEVGIRI   (Sultal)   BH, V, 76

Asthayi

Antara

Tone material

Raga Shukla-bilaval

This serious and infrequently performed raga is subordinated to the Bilaval thata and is to be sung or played in the morning. Its vadis are MA (F) and SA (C). Musicians tend to emphasize the vadi in this raga more than in most other ragas. This practice can be observed in alaps—rarely, however, in songs.

Pandit Bhatkhande assumes that Shukla-bilaval represents a combination of elements taken from the ragas Kedar and Bilaval. I feel, however, that Shukla-bilaval could be better described as a mixture of elements taken from the ragas Gaud-mallar[47] and Bilaval.

The note GA (E) appears often with a slight turn downward toward RE (D) and back again, in the same manner as it is performed in raga Alahiya-bilaval (Bilaval): E [D] E. The vadi (F) is of great importance and phrases and melodies have to dwell frequently on this note. In addition, there are numerous phrases containing the vadi which are characteristic: GA MA RE SA (E F D C), MA GA RE SA (F E D C), and their frequent combination, MA GA MA RE SA (F E F D C). Both forms of NI are used, komal (B♭) and shuddha (B). NI komal (B♭) usually appears in conjunction with DHA (A) in descent, as shown below:

RAGA SHUKLA-BILAVAL   (Jhaptal)   BH, V, 103

Asthayi

Antara

The note NI komal (B♭) is omitted in fast-moving passages (tanas), and GA (E) is at times emphasized for a little while in order to puzzle the listener.   If the note GA (E) is stressed, it is followed by the note MA (F).

Tone material

Raga Kukubh-bilaval (Kukubh, Kukubha, Kakubh)

Kukubh-bilaval or simply Kukubh may derive its name from the ancient town of Kukuva, well-known during the Gupta period and located in the region of present Bihar.   Kukubh has been described with various rasas, some of contradictory character.   Often we read that Kukubh is assigned to Yama Daivatah, the god of Death.   N. A. Willard, however, in his "Treatise on the Music of Hindustan" describes the raga as follows:

Plate VIII. Ragini Kukubha

CHAUPAYI: The lady Kukubha is unhappy because she is separated from her beloved. She has left her palace with all its comforts and lives in the forest, which is thick with trees and undergrowth. She writes a letter to her beloved, her eyes overflowing with tears. Monkeys can be heard chattering as they play in the forest. There is a lovely pond nearby, which abounds in beautiful lotus blossoms. There are countless peacocks, cuckoos, and other birds chirping and singing, but the lady is so engrossed in thoughts of her lover that she has even forgotten to take care of herself. She appears to be in an imagined embrace with her lover.

DOHA: She is lost entirely in thoughts of her lover; her eyes are impatient to see him. Her spirit survives in her body; she does not die, although the grief and separation are unbearable.

Coocubh [wife, ragini of raga Malkauns] . . . .
The revels of the preceding night have rendered her
countenance pale, her eyes though naturally sparkling
are drowsy from want of sleep: the garlands of
chumpa flowers with which she had decorated herself
lie scattered about, and her dress is discomposed;
but yet she seems to loathe the light of the dawn,
and would fain convince her lover that the morn has
not yet blushed.[48]

Kukubh has to be performed in the morning. The vadis are MA
(F) and SA (C), and RE (D) is a vishrantisthan. Both forms of
the note NI are in use, NI komal (Bb) and NI shuddha (B). The
performance rules are unclear. There is one rule which prescribes
the frequent use of the steps SA PA (C G) and SA MA (C F).
These steps are in use, but they do not appear frequently in the
known song melodies.

One form of Kukubh may be observed in a simple, Hindu religious
song which still can be heard in and around Bombay, particularly in
the Babulnath and Bhuleshwar temples. This melody, called arti, can
be notated as follows:

Two types of Kukubh can be distinguished:
a) Kukubh, as a combination of elements taken from the ragas
    Jayjayvanti[49] and Alahiya-bilaval;
b) Kukubh, as a combination of elements taken from the ragas
    Jhinjhoti[50] and Alahiya-bilaval. This type of Kukubh comes
    close to raga Bihag; it is very rare, and no distinct material
    can be shown.
The first type is in general use; its characteristic phrases are:

The note NI komal (B♭), which appears only in descent, is always
preceded or followed by a DHA (A).

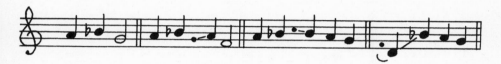

In ascent the note MA (F) (the vadi!) is very weak. GA (E) occasionally
may be observed with a slight vibrato. When the ascending line reaches
the shuddha form of NI (B), it performs a slight detour back to DHA
(A), whereupon it moves smoothly via NI (B) to the upper SA (c).

RAGA KUKUBH-BILAVAL   (Jhaptal)   BH, V, 116

Asthayi

Antara

Tone material

Raga Nath (Nata)

This raga has to be performed at night. N. A. Willard describes its pictorial representation in the following manner:

This young maiden prefers the career of glory to that of pleasure. She is adorned with jewels, and has clothed herself in men's attire, and being mounted upon a furious

Plate IX. Nata Ragini

CHAUPAYI: The lady Nata is particularly charming. She appears dramatically mounted on a handsome steed and goes into battle against Viraha (who personifies the separation of lovers), and strikes out with her sword. Inspired by her lover's great affection for her, she is brilliant and valorous. Immediately the sword descends the enemy is killed. Seeing this heroic fight, Viraha flees for his life and hurries to obey the commands of the king. Seeing this, Bhairava is greatly pleased and happy.

DOHA: The lady Nata performed a miraculous deed and was ever alert to carry out the wishes of her master. She defeated Viraha in battle and he is exceedingly ashamed of his defeat.

[See "Note on Plates," p. xii.]

steed, Minerva-like engages in battle, with those of the
opposite sex. Her countenance is flushed with the ardours
and fatigues of such an undertaking.[51]

Raga Nath is rare and even experienced musicians can mistake it for
raga Chhayanath.[52] The performance rules are not utterly clear. The
vadis of this raga are MA (F) and SA (C). The note RE (D) is rarely
used; if it appears, it is employed before or after GA (E) and in the
phrases SA RE SA (C D C) and MA RE SA (F D C). The note GA (E)
has vakra character in descent: GA MA RE SA (E F D C). The note
DHA (A), too, appears in the vakra phrases DHA NI PA (A B G), DHA
NI komal PA (A B♭ G), and also in DHA NI komal DHA PA (A B♭ A G).
The note NI (B), if used, appears mainly in ascent and NI komal (B♭)
in descent. There are many musicians who avoid NI (B) in ascent,
but the rule concerning its use is not clear.

RAGA NATH   (Jhaptal)   BH, V, 129

Asthayi

Antara

In the antara of the foregoing song example, the note PA (G) coin-
cides twice with the sam.   This can cause considerable confusion
because certain phrases of raga Chhayanath will move exactly in
the same manner.   In Chhayanath the note MA (F) should be
lightly treated and PA has to be strong.   Furthermore, the rare
appearance of MA tivra (F#) in Chhayanath would eventually remove all doubts whether raga Nath or raga Chhayanath is being
performed.   In Nath there has to be a strong MA (F) and a complete absence of MA tivra (F#).

If the note PA (G) is stressed in raga Nath, a certain similarity to raga Bilaval can be noticed.   It may be of use to compare here a characteristic Nath phrase with a similar one of raga
Bilaval in order to illustrate the use of the notes MA (F) and PA
(G) and the descending phrases before the low SA (C) in both
ragas:

Nath   Bilaval

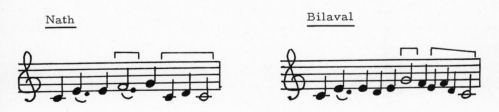

Tone material

Nath can be combined with a number of other ragas, as can be observed, for instance, in Nath-bihag, Nath-kamod, Kedar-nath, etc.

Raga Shuddha-nath

This very rare raga can be subordinated to the Bilaval thata. As far as we know, it is only performed by the pupils of the deceased Aladiya Khan of Bombay. There exist no reliable descriptions of its performance rules, and no song examples are available. After one hearing of this raga, the following phrases appear to be important:

The stressed notes, probably the vadis, are MA (F) and SA (C). The note PA (G) is treated weakly, and GA (E), another weak note, appears here not in vakra but in straight form in ascent. RE (D) is used in ascent more frequently than in raga Nath. The singer at the one occasion I had of hearing this raga, tended to stop his phrases and melodies not only on the vadis but also on the note RE (D). It is difficult to state whether this feature and the occasional octave step SA SA (C c) represent characteristics of Shuddha-nath. The Nath phrase SA RE SA (C D C) is used and may be the element which provides the Nath relationship of this raga.

Tone material

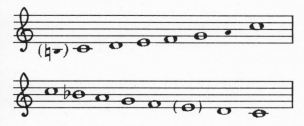

Raga Nath-narayan (Nattanarayana)

Nath-narayan has a fierce, bellicose character. Pictorial descriptions generally portray the raga as a fierce warrior riding into battle.[53]

The vadis are the same as those in raga Nath. Nath-narayan differs from Nath in the strong treatment of the note DHA (A) in descent, the avoidance of NI (B), and the predominance of PA (G) over MA (F), an unusually weak vadi.

The difference between the ragas Nath-narayan and Narayani[54] lies in the use of the note NI (B). In the former raga this note is avoided, in the latter it is avoided in ascent but used in descent.

Characteristic phrases of Nath-narayan are:

RAGA NATH-NARAYAN   (Jhaptal)   BH, V, 131

Asthayi

Antara

Tone material

Raga Nath-bilaval

This raga has to be performed in the morning. It represents a combination of elements taken from the ragas Nath and Bilaval. The combination is usually achieved in such a manner that Nath passages occur in the lower tetrachord and Bilaval passages in the upper. The vadis of this raga are the same as those in Nath and in Nath-narayan. In ascent the note NI (B) is used, while in descent (with very rare exceptions) the note NI komal (B♭) is employed. Some musicians insist that the phrase PA-RE SA RE SA (G-D C D C) is characteristic of this raga. It must be added, however, that there are several song melodies in Nath-narayan in which this phrase does not occur.

RAGA NATH-BILAVAL   (Jhaptal)   BH, V, 134

Asthayi

Antara

Tone material

Comparison of the Auffuehrungspraxis of the Ragas
Shukla-bilaval and Nath-bilaval

Before continuing the review of ragas of the Bilaval family, it may be of some value to compare a few characteristics of the ragas Shukla-bilaval and Nath-bilaval. Both possess the same tone material, the same vadis, and, to some extent, the same Bilaval features. The small but essential differences between the two ragas are:

Shukla-bilaval	Nath-bilaval
The occasional gliding step from the upper SA (c) to either MA (F) or GA (E) is long drawn:	The descent from the upper SA (c) is executed partly vakra, partly stepwise, but always moving in small intervals:

A jumping away from MA (F) in an upward direction occurs comparatively often;	A jumping away from MA (F) does not occur;
In ascent the note PA (G) is usually not used immediately after MA (F),	PA (G) follows the note MA (F) in ascent; only occasionally can we observe the

Shukla-bilaval

although there is no strict
rule which forbids this
sequence:

Nath-bilaval

interpolation of a very weak
GA (E) as an ornamental
feature:

In fast passages appear:

Raga Pahadi

This light and popular raga can be subordinated to the Bilaval
thata. Numerous folk melodies sung and played by the farmers in the
Punjab are based on, or resemble, the Pahadi scale. It rarely happens that serious art songs, khyals or other forms, are performed in
Pahadi. The light character of this raga makes it possible to perform
it at any time during the day or night. Pahadi and a few other light
ragas such as raga Pilu[55] or raga Jhinjhoti,[56] are often performed a
fourth higher than other, more serious ragas. Many contemporary
musicians of the North call the tuning a fourth higher of the tanbura
and tabla by the ancient term MA-grama (MA-scale, F-scale), which
has little in common with the MA-grama of the medieval Sanskrit
theorists. One cannot speak here of a regrouping of śrutis but only of
a simple process of transposition. In short, the note SA, which up to
now has been represented (arbitrarily) by the note C, must now be
transcribed a fourth higher, to F.

The reason for this transposition is that instrumentalists believe
that a higher melody will convey a fresher and brighter mood. This
view is not foreign to Western string players, particularly amateurs,
who occasionally tune their instruments a little higher in order to

achieve an especially brilliant effect. Serious modern Indian musicians reject this popular "MA-grama" and insist that even Pahadi
melodies should be performed in a normal SA (C)-mode. Despite the
objection, there are innumerable amateur village, and even city, musicians who transpose the Pahadi raga to F. We shall therefore
present this raga in the popular "MA-grama." The vadi is SA (F!)
and the hardly noticed samvadi is PA (C!). The notes MA (B♭!) and
NI (E!), although used occasionally, are very weak.

RAGA PAHADI   (Dipchandi)   BH, V, 185

Asthayi

Antara

Tone material

Raga Sarparda

This "recent" raga of Islamic origin[57] belongs to the Bilaval thata. Its character is serious and dignified. Sarparda has to be performed in the morning. The vadi is SA (C); the samvadi is PA (G). The notes GA (E) and DHA (A) are strong. NI (B) appears in ascent and NI komal (B♭) in descent.

Although Sarparda may have been of foreign origin, Indian theorists consider it to be the result of a combination of phrases taken from the ragas Alahiya-bilaval, Bihag, and Goud (the Goud phrase is supposed to be a concluding feature in Sarparda melodies). The phrases are:

Alahiya-bilaval

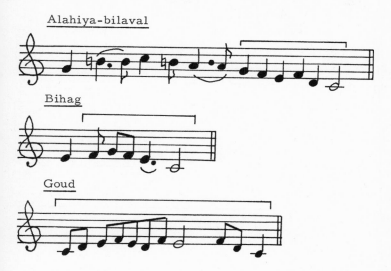

Bihag

Goud

In the creation of Sarparda some individual Sarparda phrases are
linked with the phrases of the three ragas listed above. The individual
Sarparda phrases are:

I   II   III

Each of these individual Sarparda phrases, if extended by the notes
MA (F) and GA (E), can be linked with phrases of Alahiya-bilaval,
Bihag, and Goud in the following manner:

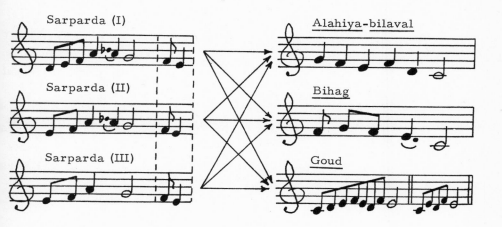

Sarparda (I)   Alahiya-bilaval

Sarparda (II)   Bihag

Sarparda (III)   Goud

RAGA SARPARDA   (Ektal)   BH, V, 48

The linking of the phrases is not always as distinct as shown above. The alaps usually offer a clearer picture than do the songs. A cursory analysis of the foregoing song melody shows the following:

Line	Measures	Characteristics
2.	1-6	Individual Sarparda material;
3.	2-3	Bihag material; MA (F) appears in ascent;
3.	4-6	Bilaval material;
4.	1-6	Bilaval material;
5.	1-6	Bilaval material;
6.	1-6	Bihag material (MA, F, in ascent).

The Goud phrase does not appear in this song. The choice of the
phrases is, of course, left to the discretion of the performer, who has
the liberty to avoid one or the other.

Tone material

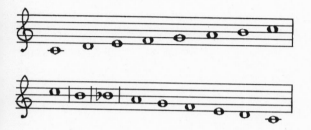

Raga Durga (Bilaval)

North Indian art music distinguishes two types of raga Durga:
one subordinated to the Bilaval thata and the other ascribed to the
Khamaj family.[58]

Durga (Bilaval), not one of the heavy and serious ragas, has a
pleasant, friendly, but by no means light-hearted, character and is
usually performed at night. Some musicians set its performance time
in the late morning. Its vadis are MA (F) and SA (C). The note DHA
(A) is strong. PA (G), which appears mostly in ascent, leads either
directly or via some grace notes (MA [F] and PA [G]) to DHA (A).
The notes GA (E) and NI (B) are avoided. The note GA (E) can appear
in the form of a subtly touched ornament but never as a full-fledged
note. In ascent we frequently observe the vakra passage MA RE PA
MA (F D G F), but in fast passages a straight ascending motion
is permissible. In descent we observe the two characteristic
gliding steps SA-DHA (c-A) and MA-RE (F-D). In addition, the
sequence SA RE DHA SA (C D A C) is characteristic of this
type of Durga.

In tanas

A song specimen of this type of <u>Durga</u>, in which the performance rules are not strictly observed, has been already shown in Chapter I, pp. 31-35. Below appears another specimen which illustrates the use of the ornamenting note GA (E).

RAGA DURGA (Bilaval That)   (Trital)   BH, V, 167

Asthayi

Antara

Tone material

Raga Gorakh-kalyan

This comparatively recent raga is not mentioned by any of the well-known contemporary North Indian theorists. Despite its lack of "official recognition," however, Gorakh-kalyan was very popular during the years 1930-45.

This raga is not related to Kalyan. It belongs to the Bilaval thata and is to be performed at night. Its vadis are MA (F) and NI komal (B♭). The ascending scale of this raga is the same as that of raga Durga (Bilaval). In descent the note NI komal (B♭) appears, mostly between two DHA (A). The note PA (G) is weak. There are musicians who avoid this note entirely in ascent. The numerous subtle ornaments, particularly on DHA (A), and the descending step MA RE (F D) are characteristic:

We are unable to present a suitable song specimen of this raga. Musicians who have invented a song in Gorakh-kalyan value it like a precious treasure, and they are usually unwilling to show and explain it to competitive fellow musicians.

Tone material

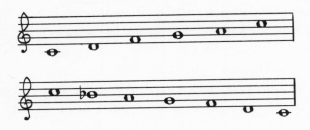

Raga Jaladhara-kedar

This rare raga belongs to the Bilaval family and has to be performed at night. Its tone material and vadis are the same as those in raga Durga (Bilaval). The difference between Durga (Bilaval) and Jaladhara-kedar lies mainly in the treatment of the note PA (G): this note is treated weakly in Durga and strongly (mainly in ascent) in Jaladhara-kedar. The emphasis on PA (G) has led some musicians to consider it, and not MA (F), as vadi. In ascent we observe that MA (F), before it leads to PA (G), is provided with a tiny gliding step back to RE (D). In short, Jaladhara-kedar has the same gliding steps as Durga (Bilaval): SA-DHA (c-A), MA-RE (F-D), and two more gliding steps which end on PA (G): DHA-PA (A-G), and less frequently RE-PA (D-G). Characteristic phrases of this raga are:

The similarity of Jaladhara-kedar to the raga Shuddh-mallar[59] is of
interest.   A comparison of these two ragas will be made later.[60]

RAGA JALADHARA-KEDAR   (Jhaptal)   BH, V, 162

Asthayi

Antara

In the foregoing song specimen (second line, measure three; third line, measure one; sixth line, measure one) we notice that the notes SA (C) and MA (F) are approached from the officially forbidden notes NI (B) and GA (E), respectively. Both "appoggiaturas" are only gently touched. In searching for indications of a link between Jaladhara-kedar and raga Kedar, we could mention this vivadi NI (B), a trace of which can appear in songs but never in alaps.

There exists a second type of Jaladhara-kedar which may show a more distinct relationship with the Kalyan family by occasionally using the notes MA tivra (F#) and NI (B). It is difficult to say whether there is a distinct second type of this raga, or whether we are only concerned with a variant of the original in which the higher notes tend slightly toward Kalyan and the lower toward Kedar. The following song specimen shows this "second type" of Jaladhara-kedar, rather freely handled:

RAGA JALADHARA-KEDAR (Second type) (Jhaptal)   BH, V, 163

Asthayi

Antara

Tone material

Raga Dipak (Bilaval)

There exist two types of Dipak, one belonging to the Bilaval and
another to the Purvi thata.[61] The pictorial representation and the
alleged magical effect of this raga have been mentioned in Chapter I.
N. A. Willard's description of Dipak is:

> The flame which the ancient musicians are said to have
> kindled by the performance of this rag, is depicted in
> his fiery countenance and red vestments. A string of
> large pearls is thrown round his neck, and he is mounted
> on a furious elephant accompanied by several women. He
> is also represented in a different form.[62]

The magic power ascribed to this raga, if rendered faultlessly, is the
creation of fire. As Dipak is to be performed in the evening, a time
when the lamps are lit, the chance of having a fire in the house is, of
course, greater than at other times. There are numerous musicians
and theorists who shy away from describing Dipak or even from
mentioning its name.

Plate X. Raga Dipak

DOHA: Kanada, Dhanashri, Bhairavi, Basant (Vasant), and Des are all engaged in dalliance with raga Dipak.

CHAUPAYI: Dipak is dancing, and he presents a delightful spectacle. His forehead is lighted by the flame of a bright lamp. He lives in a fine palace and leads a rich life immersed in pleasure. With his female companions he enjoys amorous sport. He holds his apparel with one hand and with the other he strikes at birds; at his mere touch the air becomes surcharged with passion. He fondles his lady-love's breasts, and her affection for him increases in many ways. She feigns annoyance and blushes with shame and love. At the same time the couple hear the melodious notes of the cuckoo.

DOHA: Dipak raga presents a happy spectacle in the company of lovely young maidens who are in the prime of their maddening youth.

Dipak (Bilaval) is an old raga. Its vadi is GA (E), although
some musicians insist that it is SA (C). This ambiguity in the placing
of the vadi provides the performer with a convenient excuse when his
faultless performance creates no fire. The samvadi of this raga, as
in so many other ragas, has no practical value and is rarely mentioned.
It probably is MA (F) or PA (G). Dipak (Bilaval) melodies generally
move within the middle and low octave regions.

As in many other ragas of the Bilaval family, both NI shuddha
(B) and NI komal (B♭) are employed. The note RE (D) is avoided in
ascent. DHA (A) occasionally shows vakra treatment.

Orthodox old Indian musicians are only very rarely willing to perform
Dipak or explain its performance rules. The ancient belief in its
magical powers is still alive, if not openly admitted. This may be
one reason why there exist only a few songs in this raga. Pandit
Bhatkhande, for instance, in his large collection of songs, presents
only one example:

RAGA DIPAK (Bilaval)   (Jhumra)   BH, V, 202

Asthayi

Antara

Tone material

Raga Lachhasakh

This is a rare and somewhat obscure raga which is to be performed in the morning. The vadis are DHA (A) and GA (E). The

note <u>RE</u> (D) is avoided in ascent.   This causes a certain similarity
to raga <u>Gaud-sarang</u>.[63] Characteristic phrases of <u>Lachhasakh</u> are:

RAGA LACHHASAKH   (Jhaptal)   BH, V, 92

Asthayi

Antara

The foregoing song specimen is not particularly suitable for demon-
strating the characteristic features of Lachhasakh. It uses occasionally the note RE (D) in ascent; the note NI komal (B♭), a subtle sign
of Bilaval-relationship, is totally avoided. Such latitude is permissible
in songs but not in alaps. It is possible that some reputable musicians
and theorists equate the ragas Lachhasakh and Shukla-bilaval (e. g.,
the last song specimen of the Shukla-bilaval group in Bhatkhande's
Hindusthani Sangit Paddhati[64] is a closer representation of Lachhasakh
than of Shukla-bilaval). The difference between the two ragas is indistinct, and the performance rules of both are not clearly defined. It
can, of course, be pointed out that the vadis differ in both ragas,
although the note MA (F) also has a certain importance in raga

Lachhasakh. Another feature showing the difference between the
two ragas is the gliding steps in Shukla-bilaval, which usually are
longer than those in Lachhasakh.

Tone material

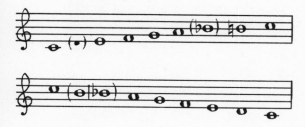

Raga Patmanjri (Patamanjari, Patmanjari, Bangal-bilaval)

There are two types of this rarely performed raga: the one
which is now under consideration belongs to the Bilaval family; the
other is ascribed to the Kafi thata.[65] Gangoly offers the following
pictorial description of Patmanjri (Phata-manjari), taken (and translated) from the Sangīta-Sāra-Samgraha by S. M. Tagore:

> Shining in the bower of a vine-plant, decked with crown
> and armlets set with sapphires, I always adore the melody
> Phata-manjari, attended with a couple of damsels on
> either side.[66]

N. A. Willard presents the following description of "Patmanjari the
wife of Hindol":

> The object now before us is oppressed with the deepest
> anguish. She sheds incessant tears, which give her a
> sad and solitary relief, the only consolation her tender
> heart will admit. The flowers hung round her neck no
> longer laugh in the bloom of freshness, the fever in her
> mind and body have withered them to sapless leaves,
> which exhale no more their wonted perfume.[67]

Patmanjri has to be performed in the morning. Its vadis are SA (C)
and PA (G). The note NI (B) is avoided in some songs; in others,
when NI (B) is used, it appears mostly in descent. RE (D) is generally approached from above, from about GA (E). These are the few

Plate XI. Ragini Patmanjari

CHAUPAYI: The embers of anger glow as her lover prepares to leave. Reminded of his affection, she feels all the more mortified. She casts her face down and is speechless, but she sheds torrents of tears, as if a large necklace had broken and caused innumerable beads to fall. Her lover thereupon addresses her sweetly and showers affection upon her and pacifies her in various ways. He assures her of his deep devotion.

DOHA: I cite the words of Lord Brahma and Lord Shiva and do not utter one word which is untrue. Oh, Lord Shiva, if you bestow blessings upon mortals, please remove the anguish of my beloved.

rules which can be stated with certainty. For the most part, the
performance rules of this raga are not well defined, and numerous
deviations and exceptions can be noted.

There exists a certain similarity between the ragas Patmanjri
and Jayjayvanti.[6][8] The difference between them lies in the use of the
note GA (E). In Jayjayvanti both GA (E) and GA komal (E♭) are in use;
in Patmanjri, however, only GA (E) is employed. Some essential
Patmanjri phrases are:

With NI (B)

Without NI (B)

RAGA PATMANJRI   (Dhamar Tal)   BH, V, 197

Asthayi

Tone material

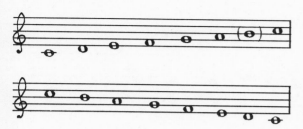

Raga Chhaya

This raga belongs to the Bilaval thata. Its vadis are PA (G) and and SA (C). Both forms of NI are in use; NI shuddha (B), weakly treated in ascent, and NI komal (B♭) in descent, mostly in the vakra phrase DHA NI komal PA (A B♭ G). The note MA (F) is weak. If we consider for a moment the importance of this note in the ragas Chhayanath[69] and Nath,[70] we recall that in Chhayanath, MA (F), although not a really strong feature, has a certain importance, and that in Nath it is strong and is the vadi.

The ascent in Chhaya is usually SA RE GA PA (C D E G). If MA (F) does appear in ascent, it is very gently touched, as can be seen in the following song specimen (first and fourth lines, measure two). The unusual emphasis accorded to MA (F) (sixth and eighth lines, measure two) is a liberty which may be found in a few songs, never in alaps.

RAGA CHHAYA   (Jhaptal)   BH, V, 173

Asthayi

Antara

Tone material

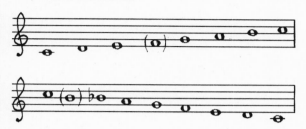

Comparison of the Auffuehrungspraxis of the Ragas
Chhaya and Chhayanath

Chhaya	Chhayanath
MA (F) is very weak;	MA (F), although not strong, has some importance;
The melody cannot stop on MA (F);	A stop of the melody on MA (F) is characteristic of Chhaya-nath and Nath;
MA tivra (F#) is not used;	MA tivra (F#) may be used occasionally;
The ascent GA PA (E G) is characteristic:	The ascent GA MA PA is possible:

rarely

Raga Chhaya-tilak

This rare raga consists of a combination of phrases taken from the ragas Chhayanath and Tilak-kamod.[71] The manner of combining the phrases is left to the performing artists. They must particularly

avoid a predominance of one phrase over the others. One of the most
frequently used combinations is the employment of one phrase from
Chhayanath and one from Tilak-kamod in the asthayi and the antara:

Asthayi
Chhayanath Phrase

Asthayi
Tilak-kamod Phrase
(X)

Antara
Chhayanath Phrase
(XX)

Antara
Tilak-kamod Phrase
(XXX)

The foregoing example shows that in the asthayi the Chhayanath phrase
is linked to the second measure of the Tilak-kamod phrase at (X):

In the antara the first measure of the Chhayanath phrase (at XX) is linked to the second measure of the Tilak-kamod phrase (beginning at XXX):

RAGA CHHAYA-TILAK   (Jhumra)   BH, V, 176

Asthayi

Antara

In the foregoing song specimen we find combinations of Chhaya-nath and Tilak-kamod phrases which differ to some degree from the ones described above. Tilak-kamod phrases can be noticed in the first line, bar two; second line, bar three; third line, bars one to four; fourth line, bars three and four. Of interest are the first two mea-sures of the antara, in which are employed Tilak-kamod phrases which in Chhaya-tilak only rarely serve as material for combinations. The tone material must be derived from the materials of the ragas Chhayanath and Tilak-kamod and may vary from one performance to the other.

Raga Hansadhvani (Hansdhvani)

This is another of the rare ragas ascribed to the Bilaval family. It has to be performed at night. Its vadi is SA (C) or GA (E), and the samvadi, hardly ever mentioned, is believed to be PA (G). The notes MA (F) and DHA (A) are totally avoided. Hansadhvani is one of the most simple ragas of North Indian art music. As far as we know, there are no elaborate performance rules or characteristic phrases, and any succession of notes within its tone material is permitted.

RAGA HANSADHVANI   (Trital)   BH, V, 200

Asthayi

Antara

Tone material

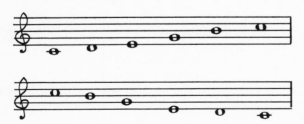

THE KHAMAJ THATA

Raga Khamaj (Khammaja, Kambhojika)

Khamaj is a thata raga. Its notes represent the material of the third largest family of North Indian ragas. Raga Khamaj is a light, popular form in which one sings numerous thumris,[72] ghazals,[73] and horis[74] but very few khyals and other serious types. In the Cattvārim-sacchata-Rāga-Nirūpanam (p. 18) this raga is pictorially described in the following manner:

> Kambhoja has a face like the bright moon and well-formed breasts like lotus buds. She is decorated with beautiful lotus flowers and wears an ornament of five flowers on her ears.

In the Rāga-Sāgara (3, 31):

> I always sincerely pray to Kambhoji who loves music, is restless and given to senuous pleasures. Resting her left cheek in the palm of her hand, she scribbles in the ground with her toes.

Even today Khamaj is still considered to be a "flirtatious" raga. It is equally popular with Hindus and Mohammedans. We have reason to assume that in the past the Khamaj scale found its way into the ch'in music of late medieval China.[75]

Khamaj is usually performed at night, but because of its light character can be sung or played at other times too. This raga has only a few performance rules. The vadis are GA (E) and NI komal (B♭). In the ascending line NI shuddha (B) appears, while in descent NI komal (B♭) is used. The notes RE (D) and DHA (A) are weak; RE (D) is frequently avoided in ascent. Although it is not a strict rule, musicians habitually omit the note PA (G) in descent. Important phrases of Khamaj are:

RAGA KHAMAJ   (Trital)   BH, II, 117

Asthayi

Antara

Tone material

Raga Tilang

This light raga has to be performed at night. Its vadis are GA
(E) and NI (B). The notes RE (D) and DHA (A) should be avoided, a
rule which is not always obeyed at the present time. RE (D) appears
occasionally in descent as a very weak and lightly touched note. DHA
(A), too, can appear in a similar manner, as shown in the following
alap example. The note NI (B) is used in ascent and NI komal (B♭)
in descent. The phrase PA GA MA GA SA (G E F E C) is important—
a Tilang performance would be incomplete without it.

RAGA TILANG   (Chautal)   BH, V, 233

Asthayi

Antara

Tone material

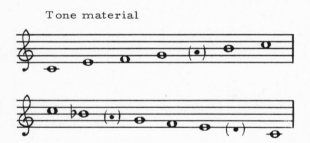

Raga Tilak-kamod

Tilak-kamod has a light character similar to raga Tilang and is
subordinated to the Khamaj thata. As far as we know, there exists
only one khyal in this raga, which was sung by the famous Fayyaz
Khan. All other songs in Tilak-kamod are light thumris or ghazals.
The vadis are RE (D) and PA (G). The note GA (E) is avoided in
ascent and is treated very lightly in descent. DHA (A) appears only
in descent and MA (F) mainly in ascent, although there are some musicians who employ the latter note in descent.

Characteristic phrases in this raga are:

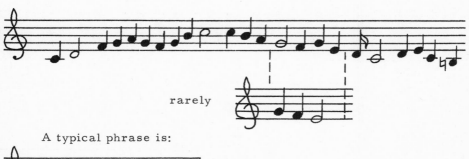

rarely

A typical phrase is:

Further <u>Tilak-kamod</u> material is:

RAGA TILAK-KAMOD   (Jhaptal)   BH, III, 294

Asthayi

Antara

Tone material

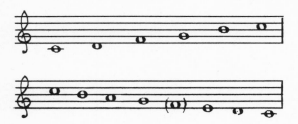

Raga Des

Des is a light raga which must not be mistaken for raga Desi
(which belongs to the Asavari thata).[76]   Raga Des is ascribed to the
Khamaj thata and has to be performed at night.   Its vadis are RE (D)
and PA (G).   There are some musicians who consider PA (G) as vadi
and RE (D) as samvadi.   As we are dealing with a light raga, this
reversal is of little consequence.   The notes GA (E) and DHA (A) are
avoided in ascent.   As so often before, NI (B) appears in ascent and
NI komal (B♭) in descent.   The note GA komal (E♭) can appear occasionally, always in connection with RE (D), as illustrated below.

Characteristic phrases of this raga are:

RAGA DES   (Dhamar Tal)   BH, III, 289

Asthayi

Antara

Tone material

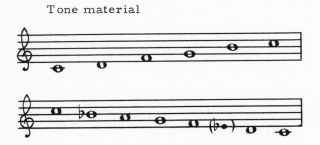

Raga Sorath

This raga is another light form belonging to the Khamaj thata. It has to be performed in the evening. Its vadi is RE (D); the samvadi is DHA (A), or, as some musicians state, MA (F). The notes GA (E) and DHA (A) are avoided in ascent. It may have been the avoidance of DHA (A) in ascent which caused the shifting of the samvadi to MA (F). In ascent appears the note NI (B) and in descent NI komal (B♭). The descending gliding step MA-RE (F-D) is essential in Sorath.

Important phrases of this raga are:

There are some musicians who insist that Sorath is nothing but raga Des with the note GA komal (E♭). This statement is erroneous because, as has already been shown, GA komal (E♭) can appear in Des, always in connection with RE (D), while in Sorath this note occurs very rarely and only in one particular phrase:

or

RAGA SORATH   (Tilvada)   BH, V, 262

Asthayi

Antara

There is a remarkable similarity between the ragas Sorath and Sur-mallar.[77] The difference lies in the vadis and in the use of the note DHA (A): in Sorath this note is comparatively strong in descent, while in Sur-mallar it is weak.

Tone material

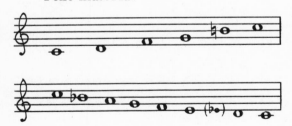

Raga Durga (Khamaj)

     This raga belongs to the Khamaj thata. Another raga Durga, ascribed to the Bilaval family, has been discussed before.[78] Durga (Khamaj) is to be performed at night. Its vadis are GA (E) and NI

(B). The notes RE (D) and PA (G) are totally omitted. NI (B) is used in ascent and NI komal (B♭) in descent. The gliding step DHA-MA (A-F) in descent is typical of this raga. Other than this step, Durga (Khamaj) has no characteristic phrases.

RAGA DURGA (KHAMAJ THATA)   (Chautal)   BH, V, 237

Tone material

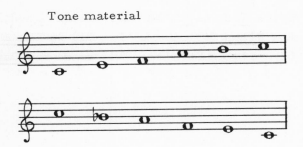

Raga Rageshri

This rare and serious raga is ascribed to the Khamaj thata. It has to be performed at night. The vadis are GA (E) and NI (B). The note RE (D) is very weak and appears only in descent. As usual, NI (B) is used in ascent and NI komal (Bb) in descent. According to the rules, the note PA (G) is to be omitted. In practice, however, it does appear as a gently touched ornamental note between two DHA (A).

The characteristic phrases of this raga are:

RAGA RAGESHRI   (Jhaptal)   BH, V, 241

Asthayi

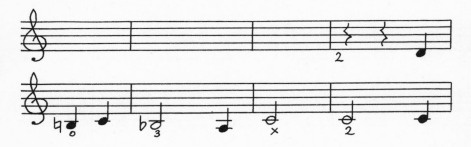

Antara

The similarity between this raga and raga <u>Durga</u> (<u>Khamaj</u>) is remarkable. The difference between the two ragas lies in the use of the note <u>RE</u> (D), which is used in descent in <u>Rageshri</u> and avoided in <u>Durga</u> (<u>Khamaj</u>). Another difference is the gliding step <u>DHA-MA</u> (A-F) in <u>Durga</u> (<u>Khamaj</u>), which does not appear in this form in <u>Rageshri</u>.

There is a slight similarity between Rageshri and raga Bageshri.[7]
The differences are clearly noticeable.

Tone material

Raga Patarageshri

This very rare raga belongs to the Khamaj thata. Its vadis are
GA (E) and NI (B). Despite the strong similarity between Patarageshri and Rageshri, there are a few points which show the difference
between the two ragas. In Patarageshri the note PA (G) is used in
ascent; DHA (A) is totally omitted. The notes PA (G) in ascent and
RE (D) in descent are weak.

I know of no appropriate song specimen in this raga.

Tone material

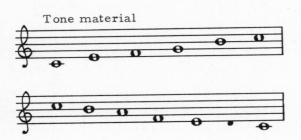

Raga Khambavati

This important raga is to be performed at night. N. A. Willard offers the following pictorial description of it:

> Cumbhavutee (wife of Malkos) . . . This wanton beauty, neglectful of care, studies her own enjoyment: she is constantly immersed in music and dancing: mirth and pleasure are her constant attendants.[80]

The vadis of this raga are GA (E) and NI (B).

There are three types of Khambavati:

a) The type in which both vadis are omitted (!) in ascent:

Pandit Bhatkhande mentions only this first type, although the song examples shown in his work represent the second or a combination of first and second types.

b) Khambavati which becomes similar to raga Khamaj, where the note RE (D) is avoided in ascent and where, of course, both vadis are in use:

c) Khambavati as performed by Aladiya Khan and his pupils. In this form the similarity to Rageshri is stressed—the note PA (G) is totally avoided:

The first two types have the same descent; in the third type, as already mentioned, the note PA (G) is avoided.

Plate XII. Ragini Khambavati

CHAUPAYI: The queen Khambavati is so wonderfully blessed that Lord Brahma recounts anecdotes to her. He has created her with such care that she is indeed a treasure house of beauty and grace. Lord Kamdeva is shamed before her divine, dazzling beauty, and Lord Brahma, seated on the lotus flower, forgets to recite the Vedas. Khambavati talks so enchantingly that one's mind becomes confused and even the daily rituals of sacred worship are forgotten. The trees and plants offer her sweet and fragrant blossoms.

DOHA: Kamdeva is shamed by the beauty of Khambavati, burnt up and reduced to ashes. Discerning eyes are charmed by the beauty of Khambavati.

Descent with PA (G)

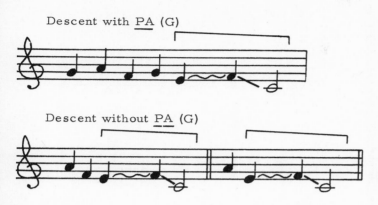

Descent without PA (G)

The phrase shown in the preceding example shows the only difference between the third type of Khambavati and Rageshri. The second and third types of Khambavati avoid the note RE (D); raga Rageshri, however, uses it.

RAGA KHAMBAVATI   (Trital)   BH, V, 222

Asthayi

Antara

Tone material

First type

Second type

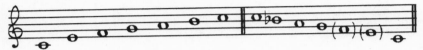

Third type

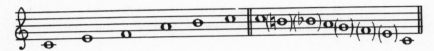

Raga Gara

Gara is a light raga which is ascribed to the Khamaj family. It
is to be performed at night and usually serves as a basis for thumris
and ghazals. Its vadis are GA (E) and NI (B) or, as some musicians
state, GA (E) and DHA (A). Raga Gara has very few performance
rules. Its melodies move mainly in the middle and lower octave
regions. The notes GA (E) and NI (B) usually appear in ascent and
their komal forms, GA komal (Eb) and NI komal (Bb), in descent, a
rule which at the present time is not always observed. Some important Gara phrases are:

The exclamation marks show the use of NI komal (Bb) in ascent and
GA shuddha (E) in descent.

Gara is often described as a combination of phrases taken from
the ragas Jhinjhoti,[81] Pilu,[82] and Khamaj. Even a cursory investigation shows that this is not always accurate, because musicians can
take numerous liberties in ragas of so light a character as Gara. If
one looked, it would be possible to detect in a lively Gara performance
many phrases from ragas other than the ones listed.

RAGA GARA   (Dhamar Tal)   BH, V, 253

Tone material

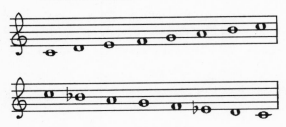

Raga Jhinjhoti

Jhinjhoti is used in both light and serious music. Whenever this
raga is applied to light music, musicians are inclined to perform it in
the "MA-grama."[83]   Our description of Jhinjhoti is based upon the
"SA-grama, " the C mode, the material of its serious aspect.

While Jhinjhoti can be performed at any time, it is heard most
frequently at night. Its vadi is GA (E); the samvadi, DHA (A), occasionally also NI (B). In ascent from SA (C) to MA (F), either RE
(D) or GA (E) is avoided, producing the ascending sequence SA RE
MA (C D F) or SA GA MA (C E F). Only in very rare instances can
we observe an ascent in which both RE (D) and GA (E) are employed
in succession. As in numerous other ragas, NI (B) appears in ascent
and NI komal (B♭) in descent. There are a few exceptions, however,
when NI (B) is avoided in ascent and replaced by NI komal (B♭).

The resemblance between Jhinjhoti and Khambavati is striking.
The difference between the two ragas lies in the descent; in Khambavati the succession GA MA SA (E F C) is preferred, while in Jhinjhoti
the straight line MA GA RE SA (F E D C) is used. Another difference
can be found in the ranges employed—Khamaj melodies generally
move in the middle and upper octave regions; Jhinjhoti melodies prefer the middle and lower regions. There exists a certain similarity
between Jhinjhoti and raga Tilang.[84]   The difference is easily observed
because Tilang avoids the notes DHA (A) and RE (D) in descent and
Jhinjhoti does not.

Some characteristic <u>Jhinjhoti</u> phrases are:

RAGA JHINJHOTI   (Dadra)   BH, V, 207

Asthayi

Antara

Tone material

Raga Narayani

This rare raga is subordinated to the Khamaj thata and is to be performed at night. Its vadis are RE (D) and PA (G). The note GA (E) is totally omitted. NI (B) appears rarely, usually only in ascent in the low octave, hardly ever in the middle octave region. In descent NI komal (B♭) is employed.

Characteristic phrases of Narayani are:

Melodies in this raga usually begin with the upper <u>SA</u> (c) in descending lines.

RAGA NARAYANI   (Sultal)   BH, V, 273

Asthayi

Antara

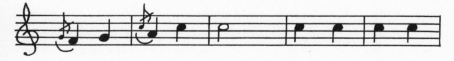

Tone material

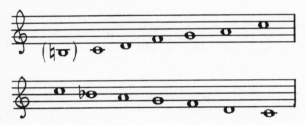

Raga Jayjayvanti

This important and often-performed raga is considered by musicians to be a friendly, loveable, and somewhat romantic raga which is to be sung or played at night. In the Saṅgīta-Rāga-Kalpadruma (p. 33) we find the following pictorial description, which has been quoted from numerous earlier works:

> Buxom and comely, with eyes like a gazelle's, her golden skin fragrant with divine flowers, Jayjayvanti is the consort of Megha-raga, god of rains. Drunken, playing upon a lute, she carols like a Kokila.[85]

The scale of this raga, which can employ GA (E) and GA komal (E♭), NI (B) and NI komal (B♭), represents a border phenomenon between the Khamaj and Kafi thatas. The vadis of Jayjayvanti are RE (D) and PA (G).

One can distinguish two types of this raga:

a) Jayjayvanti, Sorath-anga, the older type, resembling raga Sorath;

b) Jayjayvanti, Bageshri-anga, a type presumed to be of recent
    origin, resembling raga Bageshri.

Both forms of GA and NI are employed in both types. GA komal (E♭)
usually appears between two RE (D):

a) Jayjayvanti, Sorath-anga

    This type is considered to be the true Jayjayvanti. Its ascending
scale usually avoids the note DHA (A), and thus produces the Sorath
ascent (SA RE) MA PA NI SA ([C D] F G B c):

Of interest is the treatment of the vadi, RE (D), when it is followed by
GA (E). In such instances RE (D) is taken slightly high and is approached from GA komal (E♭), usually twice, by small short descending gliding steps. This is followed by GA shuddha (E), which is
reached from the preceding RE (D) by means of a short ascending
gliding step.

    The note DHA (A) appears only in descent, with the one exception
shown above: DHA (A) can be used in the phrase NI SA DHA NI komal
RE SA (B c A B♭ d c). If an ascending melodic line leads (more or
less) stepwise up to the note DHA (A), then, as can be expected,
this note becomes a turning point and represents the beginning of
a descent:

If, however, an ascending line aims at a note higher than DHA (A),
then the Sorath ascent (without DHA) becomes manifest:

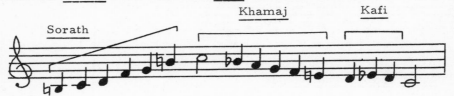

The preceding example shows Jayjayvanti to consist of Sorath material
and a short Kafi[86] phrase. Two ascents are possible, one with GA
(E) and another without it. NI (B) appears in ascent (Sorath) and NI
komal (B♭) in descent (Khamaj). The combination of Khamaj elements
with the short Kafi phrase produces GA (E) and GA komal (E♭) in
descent: MA GA RE GA komal RE SA (F E D E♭ D C).

b) Jayjayvanti, Bageshri-anga

    This allegedly recent type is rare. It differs from the first type
in the form of its ascent:

The descent is the same as that of the first type:

The following song specimen represents the first type of <u>Jayjayvanti</u>:

RAGA JAYJAYVANTI   (Jhaptal)   BH, IV, 275

Asthayi

Antara

Tone material

THE BHAIRAV THATA

Raga Bhairav (Bhairava, Bhairau, Bhairaon, Bhairo)

Bhairav is a thata raga. Its notes represent the material of the fourth family of North Indian ragas.

The heavenly palace on Mount Kailasa where Shiva and his spouse Parvati dwell is guarded by three giants (Bhairava, Bhima, and Darshana). The awe-inspiring Bhairava, also believed to be one of the incarnations of Shiva, is represented by this raga. The pictorial aspect of raga Bhairav is described in numerous Sanskrit and other works. In the Rāga-Sāgara (third section, Madras MS) we find:

> Contemplation of Bhairava: The sea of notes and microtones, with the nectar of all varieties of rhythms and time measures, the fulfilment of the desire of the worship of Siva, with the body always besmeared with ashes, decked with matted locks, with the shine of the young moon on the head, with skulls as decorations, I adore Bhairava, the skilful Dancer.[87]

In the Rāga-Māla by Mesakarna, Bhairav is described as follows:

> White in complexion, clad in white, carrying the crescent and the horn and wearing a garland, Bhairava is born from the mouth of Siva, and carries the poison on his neck, and his eyes are red. He [also] carries the trident, the skull, and the lotus, and wears jewelled pendants on his two ears and matted locks. This [melody] is sung by the gods in the morning in Autumn.[88]

In the Rāg-Kutūhala by Rādhā Krsna[89] we read:

> On his matted locks the Ganges sparkle and play [sic]; his large forehead is clasped by snakes; his three eyes offer emancipation from all woes; and round his face the earpendants dangle; his body, smeared with ashes, carries ornaments provided by snakes; and his hands carry the trident, and the drum which he beats; it is the incomparable picture of Sada-Siva [a gracious aspect of the God]. The melody of Bhairava shines as a great masterpiece [picture].[90]

Bhairav today still represents awesome grandeur, horror, fright, but also a certain mood of melancholy and even tender

Plate XIII. Raga Bhairaon

DOHA: Malashri and Bhairavi, Patmanjari and Lalit performed many deeds which endeared them to Bhairaon.

CHAUPAYI: The lady adorns Bhairaon with ornaments, and a charming beauty sits by his side. He is filled with love and extends his hands to embrace his beloved. His feeling of love increases, and his eyes become transfixed. Her body is aglow with the fire of love; she gives her heart to him. There is a luxurious bed in the palace, and on this the lady-love enjoys divine happiness.

DOHA: Having given away her heart in love, her eyes are fixed upon his face and his image sinks deep down and is preserved within her heart.

adoration.[91] This very important raga has to be performed in the
early morning, before sunrise. Its <u>vadi</u> is <u>DHA</u> <u>komal</u> (A♭), and the
<u>samvadi</u> is <u>RE</u> <u>komal</u> (D♭). Some musicians state that the compara-
tively high position of the <u>vadi</u> demands a greater emphasis on the
notes of the <u>uttaranga</u> (the upper half of the scale C-c) than on the
notes of the <u>purvanga</u> (the lower half of the scale). In practice no
such emphasis can be observed.

     Each of the two <u>vadis</u> is performed with a slow, rather wide
vibrato which extends roughly across the interval of a semitone:

The upper limit of the vibrato is not clearly defined; some singers
extend this heavy, slow oscillation beyond the note D (or A). The
vibrato can begin either with the basic note (D♭ or A♭) or, in certain
instances, with the upper vibrato limit, approximately D or A. If
D♭ (or A♭) is the highest note of a melodic curve, for instance in C
D♭ C   (or in F G A♭ G), the vibrato begins on the scale note D♭ (or
A♭). If, however, D♭ (or A♭) is not the highest note and is followed
by one or more notes in the same direction, for instance in C D♭ E
(or in F G A♭ B c); the vibrato is started from above, that is, roughly
from D (or A):

In descent the vibrato always starts from above with the note which
constitutes the upper vibrato limit (D or A). The following examples
show the use of the Bhairav vibrato in ascent and descent:

With the exception of the two heavy vibratos, Bhairav has no
characteristic phrases or vakra steps.

It is remarkable that the treatment of the notes DHA komal (A♭)
and NI (B) in nearly all evening ragas differs from that in morning
ragas such as Bhairav.

In morning ragas: NI (B) is weak,
                    DHA komal (A♭) is strong;
In evening ragas: NI (B) is strong,
                    DHA komal (A♭) is weak.

Bhairav Thata

RAGA BHAIRAV   (Dhamar Tal)   BH, II, 224

Asthayi

Antara

Tone material

Raga Gunkari (Gunakari, Gunakali, Gunakiri, Gunakriya)

Gunkari, often called Gunakali, belongs to the Bhairav thata.
A raga with the same name belonging to the Bilaval family was
discussed above on pages 125 f.   Pictorially, this raga is described in the Cattvārimsacchata-Rāga-Nirūpanam (p. 15) in the
following manner:

> Consort of the Kaushik raga (Malkouns) Gunakriya is
> mysterious in her movements, smeared with gorochan
> (a special pigment drawn from cowdung), she is chaste
> and virtuous and much loved by the cowherds.

In the Sangīta-Darpana (2, 56) and several other works:

> Gunakiri is widely known as the grief-stricken lady with
> a downcast face because her lover has gone away to a
> distant land. Her lotus red eyes are full of sorrow, her
> hair loose and dishevelled and her body soiled.

In the Rāga-Sāgara (3, 23):

> I meditate on Gundakriya who has a vina on her left.
> She is dressed in pleasing yellow, has finely shaped
> hips and plays in the garden among sandal trees.

The Gunkari of the Bhairav thata is a rare raga which is performed in
the morning. Its vadis are DHA komal (Ab) and RE komal (Db). Some
musicians reverse them and describe RE komal (Db) as vadi and DHA
komal (Ab) as samvadi. The notes GA (E) and NI (B) are theoretically totally avoided; in practice, however, although never or very
rarely notated, they appear as subtle appoggiaturas before the two
vadis, GA (E) before RE komal and NI (B) before DHA komal (Ab).
The note MA (F) is very weak. If this rule were not observed, the
similarity between Gunkari and raga Jogiya[92] would be too great.

We observe the same heavy vibrato on RE komal (Db) in this
raga as is found in raga Bhairav. The vibrato on DHA komal (Ab) is
always started from above, irrespective of whether or not the note is
the highest point in the curve.

RAGA GUNAKARI   (Tivra Tal)   BH, V, 320

Asthayi

Antara

The preceding song specimen shows some irregularities which deserve
our attention. The note <u>NI</u> <u>komal</u> (B♭), a note foreign to this raga,
appears as a notated appoggiatura before <u>DHA</u> <u>komal</u> (A♭) in the third
line, bar two, and in the sixth line, bar four. This <u>NI</u> <u>komal</u> (B♭) is
nothing but an indication that the vibrato on <u>DHA</u> <u>komal</u> (A♭) must be
started from above, from approximately <u>NI</u> <u>komal</u> (B♭).

Of interest are the approaches of the vibrato of the note <u>RE</u>
<u>komal</u> (D♭) in the fifth line, bar two, and a similar one leading to <u>DHA</u>
<u>komal</u> (A♭) in the sixth and seventh lines, both in bar one. These
notated "appoggiaturas," which indicate the wrong direction of the
vibrato beginnings, can be explained in the following manner: in the
fifth line, bar one, the approach of the vibrato on <u>RE</u> <u>komal</u> (D♭) from
<u>SA</u> (C) is correct because <u>RE</u> <u>komal</u> (D♭) is the highest note in the
curve. The ornamenting and theoretically forbidden <u>GA</u> (E) in the
fifth line, bar two, which again approaches <u>RE</u> <u>komal</u> (D♭), is nothing
but an endeavor to create some variety in the direction of the
approaches. This procedure of approaching the same note once from
below and then from above, although not fully correct, can be observed
frequently in Indian art music. Usually the approach of the vibrato is
not notated, and the performing musician can allow himself the freedom of different approaches of the vibratos if his artistic taste demands
variety. A similar instance can be observed in the sixth line, bar one.
Two bars before, in the fifth line, bar five, the correct approach of
the <u>DHA</u> <u>komal</u> (A♭) —from above—is indicated. In the sixth line, bar
one, however, the vibrato on the same note is started from below,
from <u>PA</u> (G). The same procedure can be observed in the seventh
line, bar one. These liberties and deviations from the rule are permitted in songs; in <u>alaps</u>, however, they are not allowed.

Tone material

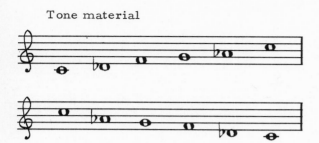

Raga Jogiya

This serious raga, representing quiet contemplation and adoration, is to be performed in the early morning when the first glimmer
of light becomes visible in the sky. Its vadis are MA (F) and SA (C).
The notes RE komal (D♭) and DHA komal (A♭) are performed without
the Bhairav vibrato. When DHA komal (A♭) is held as a long note, it
is often performed with a fast vibrato which resembles the vibrato of
a Western singer. The note GA (E) is totally avoided. Some musicians also avoid the note NI (B); others employ it only in descent. NI
komal (B♭), a note foreign to the Bhairav family, can be employed in
one of the characteristic phrases shown below. In some instances,
PA (G) is avoided in descent, a feature which cannot be described as
a rule.

Characteristic phrases of Jogiya are:

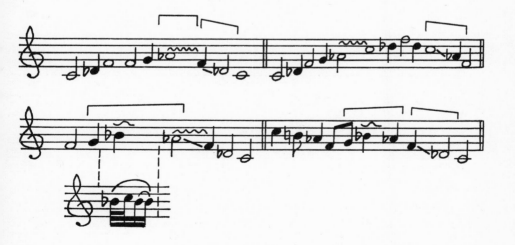

In a gramophone recording of this raga made by Abdul Karim Khan,
the note <u>GA</u> (E) is used. Also, <u>PA</u> (G) appears in descent:

This version of <u>Jogiya</u>, created by the greatest singer of India's recent
past, represents a remarkable modification of <u>Jogiya</u>. Abdul Karim
Khan's celebrated pupil, Gangubai, does not follow her master in the
<u>Auffuehrungspraxis</u> of this raga and performs <u>Jogiya</u> without the note
<u>GA</u> (E).

RAGA JOGIYA   (Chautal)   BH, V, 326

Tone material

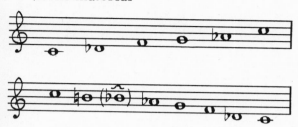

Raga Ramkali (Ramakali, Ramakri)

This raga is ascribed to the Bhairav thata and is to be performed in the morning after sunrise. Its pictorial description in the Cattvārim-sacchata-Rāga-Nirūpanam (p. 10) is:

> The wise men say that Ramakri holds a vina in her hands and is seated on a mountain top. She is a fairy with face and body like a lotus and is inaccessible to the Kinnars and the Yakshas, the demi-gods.

In the Saṅgīta-Darpana (2, 60) we read:

> Ramakali is dressed in robes of blue and adorned with ornaments of bright gold. Although proud, she is grace-fully sweet when in company with her lover.

In the Rāga-Sāgara (3, 18) we find:

> We always worship the goddess Ramakriya, reddish blue in complexion like the jambu fruit, seated in a heroic posture holding bow and arrow.

There are four different types of raga (formerly ragini) Ramkali. All four have the vadi PA (G) or DHA komal (Ab) and the samvadi SA (C) or RE komal (Db). The four types are:

a) A very rare type in which the notes MA (F) and NI (B) are avoided in ascent.

b) A type in which all notes of the Bhairav scale are employed. The difference between the two ragas lies in the fact that Bhairav melodies move generally in the middle and low octave regions, while Ramkali melodies of the second type move in the middle and upper octave regions.

c) A type in which the notes MA (F), MA tivra (F#) and NI (B), NI komal (Bb) are used.

d) A very rare type in which GA (E) and GA komal (E♭) are employed.

The most frequent type is the third one. In this type it is of importance
for the performer to move as quickly as possible from SA (C) up to
PA (G) and into the upper half of the scale:

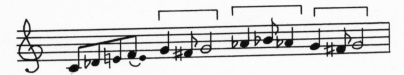

The preceding example shows that the note MA tivra (F#) often stands
between two PA (G) and that NI komal (B♭) appears mostly between
two DHA komal (A♭). It is a rare event if NI komal (B♭) is preceded
by the note MA (F).

The following example shows a typical Ramkali (third type)
descent:

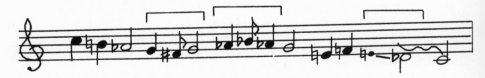

The vibrato on RE komal (D♭) is performed in the same manner as it
is in raga Bhairav.

RAGA RAMKALI   (Trital)   BH, IV, 305

Asthayi

The preceding song specimen shows a remarkable exception. The note RE komal (D♭) is avoided in ascent in the middle octave region. This is caused by the use of the favored sequences SA GA MA GA (C E F E) and SA GA MA PA (C E F G), which does not represent a characteristic feature of this raga.

Tone material

Raga Kalingra (Kalingda)

Kalingra has to be performed in the morning. There are some contradictory views concerning the vadis of this raga. Some believe that the vadis are DHA komal (Ab) and GA (E); others speak of the vadis PA (G) and SA (C); a third group maintains that the vadis are MA (F) and GA (E)!

Because of the comparatively light character of this raga, the vadis have no particular significance. Superficially viewed, one could say that Kalingra is a light version of raga Bhairav. A closer inspection of the raga shows, however, that it has no strong and weak notes, that all notes of the scale have the same importance, and that the Bhairav vibratos on RE komal (Db) and DHA komal (Ab) are avoided. Some musicians of the older generation try to emphasize to some degree the note GA (E), while others seem to place more importance on the upper notes of the scale than on the lower notes; but neither procedure can be considered characteristic. The phrase GA RE komal GA RE komal (E Db E Db) can appear frequently, but this, too, does not represent a typical feature.

RAGA KALINGRA   (Dadra Tal)   BH, III, 333

Asthayi

Antara

Tone material

Raga Bibhas (Vibhasa, Vibhas)

There are three types of Bibhas; one belongs to the Bhairav thata, a second to the Purvi thata,[93] and a third to the Marva thata.[94] The present discussion deals with the first type. Bibhas has to be performed in the morning. Although it does not possess the light and flirtatious character of raga Kalingra, it is not nearly as serious and heavy as raga Bhairav. Many of the older Indian musicians believe that Bibhas, if correctly performed, creates magic. It is impossible to ascertain exactly which magical powers are ascribed to this raga, because each of the old musicians has his own confusing and different view about them.

The vadi is DHA komal (Ab) and the samvadi is either GA (E) or RE komal (Db). The scale of this raga is approximately the same as that of raga Bhairav, but here the notes MA (F) and NI (B) are omitted. The notes RE komal (Db) and DHA komal (Ab) are taken slightly high in ascent. In descent no microtonal alterations are noticeable.

Some musicians perform the notes RE komal (Db) and DHA komal (Ab) with a vibrato which differs considerably from the Bhairav vibrato. The Bibhas vibrato has a short duration and oscillates within a narrower interval than that of Bhairav. The following example tries to compare the vibratos of the ragas Bibhas and Bhairav:

Bibhas (Bhairav Type)

Bhairav

RAGA BIBHAS (BHAIRAV THATA)   (Chautal)   BH, V, 342

Asthayi

Antara

Tone material

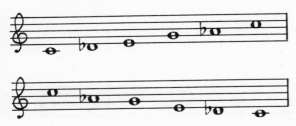

Raga Ahir-bhairav

This raga consists of a combination of phrases taken from the ragas Bhairav and Kafi.[95] The manner of combining the phrases is left to the performing musician. In the purvanga, the lower tetrachord of the scale, Bhairav phrases usually appear, while in the uttaranga, the upper tetrachord, Kafi material is employed.

The vadis of Ahir-bhairav are MA (F) and SA (C). The note RE komal (D♭) is performed with the characteristic Bhairav vibrato. The notes DHA (A) and NI komal (B♭), taken from the Kafi scale, are, of course, quite different from the corresponding Bhairav notes.

There are various methods employed in the combination of Bhairav and Kafi materials. In addition to the method mentioned above, we find that occasionally the note NI shuddha (B) is used in the low octave region in order to emphasize the Bhairav character. At times the asthayi of a khyal employs exclusively Bhairav material,

while the <u>antara</u> is based upon <u>Kafi</u> notes, including even a <u>RE</u> shuddha
(D); a method which can be observed in the following song specimen:

RAGA AHIR-BHAIRAV   (Adachautal)   BH, V, 293

Asthayi

Antara

It would be futile to establish the scale of <u>Ahir-bhairav</u> because it is
subject to change from one performance to the other. However, it is
always some combination of the <u>Bhairav</u> and <u>Kafi</u> notes.

Raga Gauri (Gaudī)

    Raga (formerly ragini) <u>Gauri</u> has to be performed in the evening.
Another raga with the same name is ascribed to <u>Purvi</u> family.[96]

In a Sangīta-Mālā of an anonymous author, written during the middle of the eighteenth century, we find the following pictorial description of Gauri:

> Gaudī rāgini: The fair damsel has defeated the cuckoo
> by the flourish of her word surpassing nectar; she has
> decked her ears with new sprays of mango-blossoms,
> having a complexion like the beautiful blue cloud, her
> handsome body is robed in white silk; her lotus-face
> subdues the pride of the Moon, (for) the creator used
> all his skill and art in creating her form with great
> care; her grace and beauty are attractive alike to the
> eyes and the mind; (its structure is) Sa ri ga ma pa dha
> ni, with ṣadja as its initial note. Gaudika is sung at
> the end of the day in autumn.[97]

Of some interest is the description of this raga by N. A. Willard:

> Gouree [wife of Malkos] . . . This very young brunette
> had adopted the blossom of the mangoe for her ornament.
> She is endeavouring to sing her favorite melody, but is so
> infatuated and intoxicated as to be hardly able to proceed
> with it.[98]

The vadis of Gauri are RE komal (D♭) and PA (G). The notes GA (E) and DHA komal (A♭) are avoided in ascent. Occasionally the step RE komal PA (D♭ G) can be observed in ascent. It is performed in the same manner as it is in Shri raga.[99] RE komal (D♭) is occasionally performed with the Bhairav vibrato.

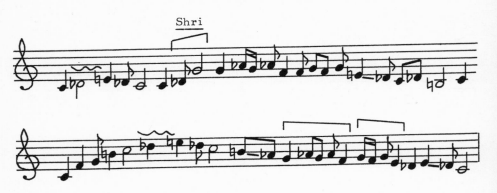

All forms of Gauri treat the low NI (B) equally heavily; phrases and melodies may come to a stop on this note.

The note <u>RE</u> <u>komal</u> (D♭) can have the <u>Bhairav</u> vibrato. <u>DHA</u> <u>komal</u>
(A♭), however, cannot have a vibrato.

RAGA GAURI   (Chautal)   BH, V, 354

Asthayi

Antara

Tone material

Comparison of the Auffuehrungspraxis of the Ragas
Gauri and Bhairav

Gauri

GA (E) and DHA komal (A♭)
    are avoided in ascent;

RE komal (D♭) is usually a
    short note and is weak;

DHA komal (A♭) is performed
    without a vibrato;

The step RE komal-PA (D♭-G)
is important.

Bhairav

GA (E) and DHA komal (A♭) are
    used in ascent;

RE komal (D♭) is often a long
    note and is strong;

DHA komal (A♭) is performed
    with the characteristic
    Bhairav vibrato.

Raga Bangal-bhairav (Bengal-bhairav, Bangala, Bangali)

    Bangal-bhairav, a rare raga, is to be performed before sunrise.
In the Cattvārimasacchata-Rāga-Nirūpaṇam (p. 18) this pictorial
description is offered:

Bangali is dark in complexion and dressed in black. Bold
and determined, she is desirous of pleasures and plays of
love. Big-breasted and holding the lute in her hands, she
is fond of flowers.

In the Saṅgita-Darpana (2, 49):

Bright and fair like the sun, large eyed, with her long
hair tightly bound, Bangali is holding the shining trident
in her left hand. With white ashes smeared on her body
she carries a bamboo basket filled with flowers tied to
her waist.

In the Rāga-Sāgara (3, 25):

I always remember Bangala, the greatest of the ragas,
who worships at the feet of Lord Shiva. His locks,
blue-black, the color of bees, are finely stringed on
the sides. He holds a sword in his hand and is
beautiful like the red rose. He is widely cherished
by the people.

N. A. Willard describes it in the following manner:

Bungal, (ragini), the wife of Bhairav . . . . A joginee
or female mendicant or devotee. Her face is sprinkled
over with ashes; her body is stained with marks of
ground sandal; and her forehead streaked with musk.
Her clotted hair is tied in a knot; a yellow saree
conceals her bosom; she holds a lotus in her right
hand, and a triple dart in her left. This Raginee,
although the native of foreign and distant land, appears in the costume properest for a wife of Bhyron
[Bhairav].[100]

The vadis of this raga are DHA komal (Ab) and RE komal (Db). The
note NI (B) is totally avoided. GA (E) is vakra in descent; melodies
cannot progress from GA (E) to RE komal (Db) but have to move via
MA (F): PA MA GA MA RE komal SA (G F E F Db C). Both RE
komal (Db) and DHA komal (Ab) are performed with the Bhairav
vibrato.

RAGA BANGAL-BHAIRAV   (Trital)   BH, V, 279

Although according to the performance rules the note NI (B) is forbidden, we find this note in the preceding song specimen. It occurs
as a short appoggiatura before DHA komal (A♭) (first line, bars one
and four; third line, bars one, three, and four; fourth line, bars one
and three). This appoggiatura is nothing but an indication of the approach of the Bhairav vibrato on the vadi. A second form of NI (B)
represents another ornament, a gentle veering of the note SA (C) to
NI (B) and returning to SA (C) (third line, bars two and four; fourth
line, bar two). These deviations from the rule denote subtle ornaments in which NI (B) cannot be considered as a full-fledged note of
the scale. They may appear in songs but never in alaps.

Tone material

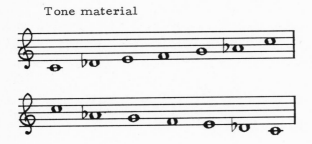

Raga Anand-bhairav

Anand-bhairav has to be performed in the morning. It represents a combination of phrases taken from either Bhairav and
Bilaval or Bhairav and Nanda.[101] This ambiguity creates two types
of Anand-bhairav. The vadis of both types are MA (F) and SA (C).
This is an example of the type which utilizes Bhairav and Bilaval
material:

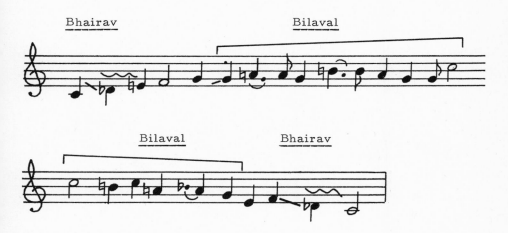

The second type, using phrases from Bhairav and Nanda, is interesting.
The Nanda scale is here slightly modified, as we find mostly the note
MA (F) and not MA tivra (F#). The combination of Bhairav and modified Nanda can be made in three different ways:
    a) the note DHA (A) is used exclusively;
    b) the note DHA komal (Ab) is used exclusively;
    c) DHA (A) is used in ascent and DHA komal (Ab) in descent.
These three variants are not always clearly apparent. In order to
achieve a clear description, they are here shown separated from each
other. The lower half of the scale usually uses Bhairav notes, while
the upper half is characterized more by its frequent zigzag steps than
its relationship to Nanda.

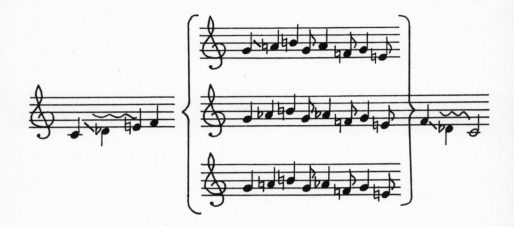

The three "Nanda variants" shown above are often, particularly in the antaras, replaced by Bhairav phrases.

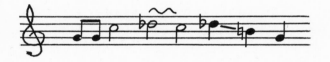

RAGA ANAND-BHAIRAV   (Jhaptal)   BH, V, 282

Asthayi

Antara

The preceding song specimen represents the first type of Anand-
bhairav. Bilaval material appears only in the third line and in the
last two bars of the seventh line; the rest is Bhairav. The combining
of Bhairav and Bilaval or Bhairav and Nanda materials is left to the
performing artists, who probably alter it from one performance to
the next. Therefore it is impossible to set up unambiguous tone
material. One would have to postulate two scales, one of Bhairav
and one of Bilaval (or Nanda), from which notes can be selected for
each separate performance.

Raga Prabhat (Prabhat-bhairav)

Prabhat is performed in the morning in a slow and dignified
manner. Its vadis are MA (F) and SA (C). The Prabhat scale is the
same as the scale of raga Bhairav, but it introduces occasionally,
besides MA (F), the note MA tivra (F#). This MA tivra (F#) usually
appears between two MA (F) or between GA (E) and MA (F), a procedure which reminds us of raga Lalit. [102] The notes RE komal (Db)
and DHA komal (Ab) are performed with the characteristic Bhairav
vibrato. The notes RE komal (Db) and PA (G) are infrequently used

in ascent. This latter feature cannot be called a rule; nevertheless,
it can be observed in the majority of the known songs in this raga.

RAGA PRABHAT   (Trital)   BH, V, 304

Asthayi

Antara

Tone material

Raga Saurashtra-bhairav (Saurashtra-tank)

This rare raga must not be mistaken for the raga Tanki (Shri-tank).[103] It belongs to the Bhairav thata and is to be performed in the morning. North Indian musicians have differing views about the performance rules of this raga. Some insist that the note PA (G) be totally omitted, while others use it. The vadis are MA (F) and SA (C). The notes RE komal (Db) and DHA komal (Ab) are performed with the Bhairav vibrato. The Saurashtra-tank scale employs both forms of DHA, DHA komal (Ab) and DHA shuddha (A). The notes DHA komal (Ab) and PA (G) always appear in succession in the middle octave range, both in ascent and descent. The note DHA (A), however, excludes a preceding or succeeding PA (G), but it demands both in ascent and descent a preceding or succeeding MA (F). This rule is shown below in the shape of a formula.

<u>In ascent</u>   <u>In descent</u>

Either: F A (without G)   Either: A F (without G)

Or: G A♭ (with or without a   Or: A♭ G (with or without a
         preceding F)   succeeding F)

RAGA SAURASHTRA-BHAIRAV   (Tivra Tal)   BH, V, 287

Asthayi

Antara

Tone material

Raga Shiva-bhairav (Shiv-bhairav, Shivmat-bhairav)

Shiva-bhairav is a morning raga ascribed to the Bhairav thata. Its vadis are DHA komal (A♭) and RE komal (D♭). Shiva-bhairav consists of the regular Bhairav material, to which are added two characteristic phrases. In one of these phrases the note GA komal (E♭) appears, in the other, NI komal (B♭). Both of these foreign notes are intoned slightly low in this raga.

The characteristic Bhairav vibrato on RE komal (D♭) is avoided only in such instances when RE komal (D♭) is preceded by the micro-tonally low-altered GA komal (E♭). Similar, but not treated quite as strictly, is the performance of DHA komal (A♭) when it is preceded by the low-altered NI komal (B♭). These two low-altered notes appear only in descent. In ascent only GA (E) and NI (B), the normal notes of the Bhairav scale, are used.

RAGA SHIVA-BHAIRAV   (Dhamar Tal)   BH, V, 298

Asthayi

Antara

Tone material

Raga Jivan-bhairav (Asavari-bhairav)

This rare raga is similar to Shiva-bhairav and, as the name shows, belongs to the Bhairav family. Occasionally it is called Asavari-bhairav because a characteristic phrase added to the basic Bhairav material strongly resembles raga Asavari.[104] The phrase is a descending sequence of GA komal RE komal RE komal SA (Eb Db Db C). Some musicians call Jivan-bhairav just a prakar of Bhairav (a type of Bhairav), not recognizing its independent existence. The vadis are MA (F) and SA (C). The note GA shuddha (E) is avoided in descent; in its place stands the already mentioned Asavari phrase with GA komal (Eb).

The difference between Jivan-bhairav and Shiva-bhairav becomes
clear if we consider the lower halves of their descending scales:

Raga Dutiya-bhairav

As far as we know, this very rare raga was performed only by
Aladiya Khan Saheb of Bombay. It is most likely that the raga was
his creation. Very little is known concerning its performance rules;
even the vadis are only vaguely indicated. One can assume that the
vadis are MA (F) and SA (C), as they are in numerous other ragas
of the Bhairav family. The note RE komal (Db) is avoided in ascent
and appears in descent in the characteristic phrase shown below.
This phrase causes a vakra descent between GA (E) and SA (C):

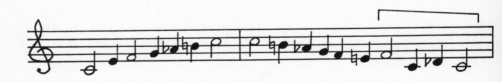

Raga Meghranjani

North Indian musicians have various views about the performance
rules of Meghranjani. The vadis are MA (F) and SA (C). The notes
PA (G) and DHA komal (Ab) are totally avoided, although some musicians reject this rule. The wide interval between the upper SA (c)
or NI (B) and MA (F) is generally bridged by a long gliding step. The

note RE komal (D♭) is performed without the Bhairav vibrato. Of
interest is the occasional appearance of the note MA tivra (F#),
usually between two MA (F), or between GA (E) and MA (F) (or MA
and GA).

It is uncertain whether the avoidance of the note SA (C) in ascent can
be considered to be a rule. It can be observed in the succeeding song
specimen:

RAGA MEGHRANJANI   (Jhaptal)   BH, V, 315

Asthayi

Antara

Tone material

Raga Devranjani

The vadis of this rare raga are SA (C) and MA (F). The notes RE komal (D♭) and GA (E) are totally avoided. NI komal (B♭) appear in one characteristic phrase; this note has the same position and intonation as it does in raga Shiva-bhairav.[105] In ascent the note NI shuddha (B) is treated very weakly. It occurs more in the form of a subtle appoggiatura than in the form of a full-fledged note.

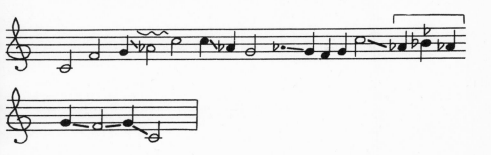

RAGA DEVRANJANI (Jhaptal) BH, V, 331

Asthayi

Antara

Tone material

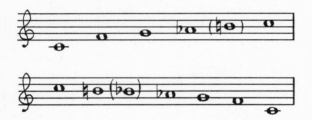

Raga Lalit-pancham

Lalit-pancham, ascribed to the Bhairav thata, is performed
after midnight. Its vadis are MA (F) and SA (C). The note MA (F)
assumes a special importance in many ragas which are sung or played
late at night. The note PA (G) is avoided in ascent. The occasional
use of the note MA tivra (F#) indicates the relationship with the ragas
Lalit [106] and Pancham. [107] The note GA (E) appears occasionally in
descent in a "pseudo" vakra formation: GA MA GA RE komal (E F E
Db) or GA MA tivra GA RE komal (E F# E Db). The note RE komal
(Db) is often avoided in ascent; hence the progressions SA GA MA (C
E F) and the simple SA MA (C F) are now considered to be characteristic features of Lalit-pancham.

RAGA LALIT-PANCHAM   (Trital)   BH, V, 307

Asthayi

Antara

Tone material

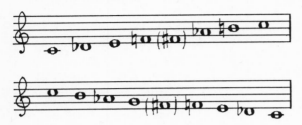

Raga Jangula

The performance rules of this rare raga are somewhat obscure and subject to argument among musicians. The vadis are MA (F) and SA (C). The lower half of the Jangula scale usually contains only Bhairav material. The upper half uses in addition to DHA komal (Ab), DHA shuddha (A), and in addition to NI (B), NI komal (Bb). These added notes, DHA (A) and NI komal (Bb), always appear in the characteristic phrase DHA NI komal PA (A Bb G), as shown below. This phrase shows some similarity, mostly in descent, to raga Anand-bhairav (or to raga Nand). In Anand-bhairav, however, the note DHA (A) (or, in some instances also DHA komal [Ab]) is not only used in the above stated phrase but may appear in other combinations.

It may be advisable to refer once more to the song specimen of raga Anand-bhairav (p. 258). We observe that there is no noteworthy difference between Anand-bhairav and Jangula. However, if we consider the alap examples of both ragas, we notice that the note DHA (A) (or DHA komal [Ab]) is used more frequently in Anand-bhairav than in Jangula.

RAGA JANGULA   (Ektal)   BH, V, 359

Asthayi

Antara

Tone material

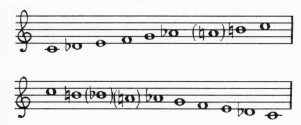

Raga Zhilaf (Zilaf, Shilaf)

There are two types of this raga, one belonging to the Bhairav
thata and the other to the Asavari thata.[108]   The first type will be
considered here. Zhilaf and raga Sarparda,[109] perhaps to some

degree raga Kafi,[110] and several other ragas are believed to be of
Persian origin. Zhilaf is to be performed in the late morning. Its
vadi is DHA komal (A♭) and the samvadi is usually described as SA
(C). There are some musicians who prefer the note GA (E) as
samvadi. The notes RE komal (D♭) and NI (B) are avoided. The latter
note (NI), however, may occasionally appear as a very weak and
gently touched ornament. The vadi is performed with the characteristic Bhairav vibrato.

RAGA ZHILAF   (Jhaptal)   BH, V, 348

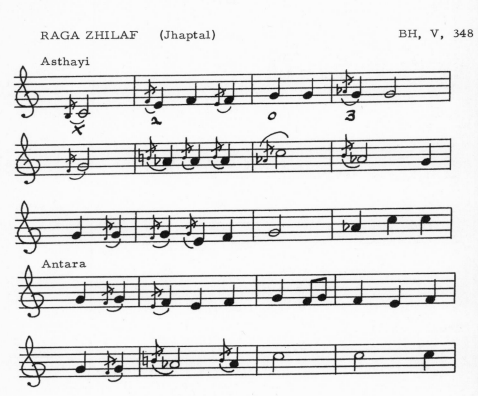

Pandit Bhatkhande mentions another version of the first (Bhairav) type of this raga, in which the notes RE komal (Db) and NI (B) are used. One Zhilaf song which I had the opportunity to hear contained not only these two notes but also DHA komal (Ab) and DHA (A). This shows how far the views concerning the performance rules of this raga diverge. However, it must be stated that the alap example and the song specimen shown above represent the prevailing Auffuehrungs-praxis of the first type of Zhilaf. If, for instance, the note RE komal (Db) is used too frequently, the similarity with raga Bhairav becomes disturbing. It rests with the performing musician to treat this "dangerous" note in such a manner that there is still a noticeable difference between the two ragas. One method would be to use the note RE komal (Db) only in descent and to avoid it in ascent. Unfortunately, there are several songs in Zhilaf in which this note appears in both ascent and descent, and the listener has the impression that he is hearing a badly performed raga Bhairav.

Tone material

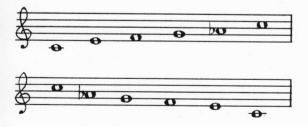

Raga Suryakauns

This very rare raga can be ascribed to the <u>Bhairav</u> <u>thata</u>. As far as we know, there was only one singer who performed <u>Suryakauns</u> in public, the great Abdul Karim Khan. Very little is known about its performance rules except that the notes <u>RE</u> <u>komal</u> (Db) and <u>PA</u> (G) are totally avoided. The scanty material of this raga is:

The preceding example shows that the note <u>NI</u> <u>komal</u> (Bb), a foreign note in the <u>Bhairav</u> family, is used both in ascent and descent. The note <u>DHA</u> <u>komal</u> (Ab) is occasionally performed with the <u>Bhairav</u> vibrato, one of the few features which creates a relationship between <u>Suryakauns</u> and <u>Bhairav</u>.

THE PURVI THATA

Raga Purvi (Puravi, Purvika)

Purvi is a thata raga. Its notes represent the material of the fifth family of North Indian ragas.

The raga Purvi has a deeply serious, quiet and somewhat mysterious character, and is to be performed at the time of sunset. The Rāga-Kalpadruma (p. 23) gives this pictorial description:

Charming and beautiful, scantily dressed, lotus-eyed Puravi appears at the end of the day. Idle and sleepy, she suffers from the pangs of separation and dreams only of her lover.

In the Cattvārimsacchata-Rāga-Nirūpanam (p. 8) we read:

Master of archery, seated on an elephant and dressed in white, Purvika has a splendid body and is served by all the different varnas [musical sounds].

In the Rāga-Sāgara (3, 49):

I remember Purvika dressed in a garment woven with threads of gold. Fair and charming like the moon, she holds a cup of wine and a parrot in her hands and she is served by women who are graceful and lively like the young deer. The head of her lover rests in her lap.

The vadis of this raga are GA (E) and NI (B). Phrases and melodies can be interrupted or stopped on the vadi GA (E), on SA (C), and occasionally also on PA (G). Frequent interruptions on PA (G) are not advisable because they would alter the character of the raga and create a close similarity with the raga Puria-dhanashri.[111]

The ascending Purvi scale (C Db E F# G Ab B c) is often modified in such a manner that the notes SA (C) and PA (G) are avoided (B Db E F# Ab B c). This modified form of the scale can be observed frequently in fast tanas. The foreign note MA (F) may appear occasionally in the form of an ornament between two GA (E). This MA (F) is at times performed in such a way that its intonation changes toward MA tivra (F#) and then quickly returns to MA (F), from where the

melodic line proceeds to the succeeding GA (E). The treatment of
the note MA (F) can be illustrated in this way: E F F# F E.

The antaras of Purvi melodies frequently contain in their first measures these notes:

Some musicians treat the note DHA komal (A♭) in a manner similar
to their treatment of the note MA (F). .We observe a slight veering
toward DHA (A) and a return to DHA komal (A♭): A♭ A A♭. This
turn, however, occurs only in a few rare instances.

RAGA PURVI   (Jhaptal)   BH, II, 228

Asthayi

Antara

Tone material

Shri Raga

One does not speak of "raga Shri" but always of Shri raga. It
is one of the most important and famous ragas of northern India and

 राग श्री राग ॥ ३८ ॥ दोहा पंचम और कोदास सुएा तीजा सेत मलार, श्रत्र राग श्री राग सुष्ट
सुनि पंचम में द्वार ॥ चोपई श्री राग राज श्ररधबी लिखे रागहि मुनते राग श्रध्रि हि मे रागही
में सब दीन जिहि हरमन में दकथुक होन जाही ॥ जात तें बलान त रंगा मान्य रंग जय
उमडी गंगा ॥ गुनि क्षाप एु एु एु नपावे तान क्रमान नारद सी घरबे ॥ सुघर रस संगि सी
तिनि विज्ञाने मन कु उचित राज मन माने ॥ दोहा ॥ सुर गं धा न गति तान की ॥ तो बनेद
सब त्रंग ॥ एबातें निनी पाठ्र ॥ श्रा रा गप रस संगः ॥ ३८ ॥

Plate XIV. Raga Shri-rag

DOHA: After listening to Pancham and Kedar and Set-mallar, listen to Shri-rag, Asavari, Bhim, Pancham, and Kedar.

CHAUPAYI: Shri Shri-rag is majestic and royal in appearance, and you perceive his image upon listening to this raga. He spends the whole day in merriment and love, and it is difficult to describe his secret pleasures inside the palace. An ascending string of tans is poured forth from the musical instruments, as if the river Ganga had risen in a flood. Even the skilled ones cannot comprehend the mysteries of this raga, and the outlines of the tans can be shown or taught only by the sage Narada. The notes SA, DHA, RI, SA, GA are the components of this raga, the form of which is very pleasing and satisfying to kings.

DOHA: SA, RI, GA, DHA, NI is the pattern of movement of this raga, and its components vary according to the sentiments they carry. One comprehends these matters only when one knows Shri-rag well.

is now subordinated to the Purvi thata. It is to be performed at sunset.
Popley assumes that Shri raga was created by Hrdaya Nārāyaṇa Deva,
Rajah of Gadā Desa, and that it is mentioned for the first time in the
Hrdayaprakāsa.[112] This seems to be an error, because the raga name
Shri already appears in the Rāga-Sāgara, a work which was written
probably even before the time of Nārada and Dattila. Its pictorial
representation is described in the Saṅgīta-Darpana (2, 70):

> Shri raga impressive and majestic like a king, with features
> like the god of love himself, has his ears adorned with tender
> leaves and is dressed in red.

In the Rāga-Sāgara (3, 9) we find:

> I always sincerely pray to Shri raga who is seated on his
> throne in a heroic posture; one of his hands rests on the
> head of a tiger. The precious stones set on his head-
> gear are all sparkling in the sun. Lovely women surround
> him on both sides.

Shri is not only a raga of the sunset; it can also be performed
during the rainy period (June to September) and during November and
December. Its character is mysterious, gentle, and often depicts the
meditation of love and the nostalgic and prayerful mood of early
evening. The vadis of this raga are RE komal (Db) and PA (G). The
notes GA (E) and DHA komal (Ab) are avoided in ascent. A characteristic feature of Shri raga is a particular vibrato performed on the note
RE komal (Db):

The Shri vibrato is rendered slowly, but not as heavily as that
of raga Bhairav. It begins with the note SA (C), swings at first downward toward NI (B) as if trying to gain a preparatory start, moves via
SA (C) to RE komal (Db) and then oscillates twice or thrice between
RE komal (Db) and GA komal (Eb), or even between RE komal and GA
(E). The vibrato ends with RE komal. A further characteristic of
this raga is the sudden "turning away" from the last note of the vibrato
and the immediate intoning, without gliding or appoggiatura, of the
succeeding note.

In fast <u>tanas</u> the note <u>DHA komal</u> (A♭) appears in the ascending line:
D♭ F# G A♭ B c. In <u>alaps</u>, however, where the faultless representation of <u>Shri</u> is of utmost importance, the notes <u>DHA komal</u> (A♭) and
<u>GA</u> (E) are strictly avoided in ascent.

SHRI RAGA   (Jhaptal)   BH, III, 356

Asthayi

Antara

Tone material

Raga Puria-dhanashri

This raga belongs to the Purvi thata. Its vadis are PA (G) and
RE komal (D♭). Although the vadi (PA) stands in the upper tetrachord
of the scale, usually a sign of a morning performance time, Puria-
dhanashri is always sung or played in the evening.   The Puria-
dhanashri material comes very close to that of raga Purvi.   The difference between the two ragas lies in the treatment of the note PA (G);
in Puria-dhanashri this note is the vadi and is treated strongly, while

in Purvi it is weak. We also observe that the note MA (F), which occasionally may appear in Purvi as a slight ornament, is totally avoided in Puria-dhanashri. The step GA PA (E G) has to be used frequently. Further performance rules are the same as in raga Purvi.

RAGA PURIA-DHANASHRI   (Trital)   BH, IV, 336

Asthayi

Antara

Tone material

Raga Vasant (Vasanta, Vasanti, Basant)

Vasant (in Bengal: Basant) is a famous and frequently performed raga. The Sanskrit word vasanta means the brilliant season of spring. The great majority of theorists consider Vasanta to be a male raga. In a few works, however, for instance in the Rāga-Kalpadruma (p. 20) and in the Saṅgīta-Darpana (2, 71), the name is Vasanti, the female form of Vasanta. Several pictorial descriptions of this raga are offered. In the Rāga-Kalpadruma (p. 20) and several other works we find:

> Vasantika, beautiful like the blue lotus, wears earrings
> made of mango blossoms and the knot of her hair at the
> top is adorned with the tail-feathers of the peacock. Lovely
> and graceful, her beauty is enhanced by the glistening black
> bees circling around her.

In the Rāga-Sāgara (3, 17) we read:

> I bear constantly in my heart the image of Vasanta, sur-
> rounded by cuckoos, parrots, and the shari birds, dancing
> in the garden of love in the company of several lovely
> women.

Raga Vasant is subordinated to the Purvi thata and is performed in slow tempo and late at night, particularly in the spring. Its character is gentle loveliness and quiet joy. Its vadi is the high SA (c), and the samvadi is PA (G). Vasant melodies, similar to those of raga Sohani,[113] usually begin with the high SA (c) or move quickly up to it, and then descend slowly to lower regions. They end by returning to the high vadi. Similar to raga Purvi, both forms of the note MA are employed, MA (F) and MA tivra (F#). The use of these two notes will be illustrated below in several alap excerpts. Before considering

Plate XV. Ragini Basant

CHAUPAYI: Basant is exceedingly pleasant and is with someone very lovely and satisfying. The spring season has begun, and lovely maidens in male attire are singing with abandon, and other companions are playing musical instruments. The mango grove has flowered with a splash of enchanting color, spreading enrapturing fragrance in the air, and the bees are humming. There is a soft, sweet-smelling breeze, and it is pleasantly raining. The women are dallying with their lovers, and the companions are singing melodiously. The words of their songs are cleverly composed.

DOHA: Basant, the abode of happiness, is trying to capture the heart of her lover Dipak, while singing and dancing rapturously in thickly shaded arcades.

the appearances of these two notes, we will consider the descending scale of Vasant with which melodies begin.

The gliding step NI-DHA komal (B-A♭) does not represent a fixed rule, but it is frequently employed. It may either be used or avoided, according to the taste of the performer. The phrase MA tivra GA MA tivra GA (F# E F# E), however, is characteristic of this raga. The succession of notes MA tivra GA (F# E) is always performed twice in a row. This rule applies to alaps. In songs it is also possible to observe the two notes in a single feature. The last four notes of the descending scale, MA tivra GA RE komal SA (F# E D♭ C), have to be performed in comparatively quick succession. In slow tempo this sequence is not permitted.

The ascending scale differs at several points from the descending form:

It begins with the characteristic gliding step SA-MA (C-F) and shows that in the ascending line the notes RE komal (D♭) and GA (E) are generally avoided. The important note MA (F) is usually performed twice in succession. When repeated it is approached from above from approximately MA tivra (F#), by means of a tiny gliding step. The note MA (F), after being stated twice, veers slightly toward GA (E) and then is followed by MA tivra (F#) and DHA komal (A♭). The note

PA (G) is avoided in ascent. The continuation toward the upper SA (c) after DHA komal (A♭) can be performed in three different forms, as shown in the preceding example.

Of interest is the intonation of the note DHA komal (A♭). If it is preceded (in descent) by a note which is higher, for instance by NI (B), it shows no alteration. If, however, DHA komal (A♭) represents the highest point in a melodic curve, or if it is succeeded by higher notes, it is often altered slightly high.

Toward the beginning of antaras (usually in the first or second measures) we frequently find the phrase:

which again shows the avoidance of PA (G) in ascent. This phrase (with or without the microtonal alteration of DHA komal) can be observed in numerous ragas of the Purvi family.

RAGA VASANT   (Trital)   BH, IV, 390

Asthayi

Antara

Tone material

Raga Paraj

This raga must be performed at night. It has the same tone
material and the same vadis as raga Vasant. Therefore, in order to
describe Paraj it is advisable to compare it with Vasant. Both Vasant
and Paraj melodies begin with the high SA (c). The Vasant descent is
characterized by gliding steps, for instance NI-DHA komal (B-A♭);

the Paraj descent avoids these gliding steps. It is possible that now
and then a Vasant descent is performed without the above mentioned
gliding step. In such instances the similarity between the two ragas,
particularly in the upper half of the scale, becomes so pronounced
that misunderstandings can easily arise. Thus, it is recommended
that the descending gliding steps be used in Vasant if for no other
reason than to avoid confusion with Paraj. Vasant phrases, with the
exception of the last four descending notes, are performed in a slow
and dignified manner, while Paraj phrases demand a quicker speed and
lighter treatment.

The note NI (B) has no particular significance in Vasant. In
Paraj, however, this note becomes important and almost assumes the
function of the vadi; phrases and melodies in raga Paraj can always be
interrupted on this note. The characteristic Vasant formula

does not appear in Paraj. The note MA tivra (F#) is weaker in Paraj
than in Vasant. The note MA (F), which has a particular position in
Vasant, appears in Paraj usually between two GA (E):

The characteristic gliding step in the ascending scale of Vasant, SA-
MA (C-F), is not employed in Paraj. In Paraj the ascending step SA
GA (C E) is usually performed without any gliding. The note RE
komal (D♭) is usually avoided in the Paraj ascent, as it is in raga
Vasant. Some musicians state that RE komal (D♭) has to be totally
omitted in the Paraj ascent. They are in error—RE komal (D♭) can
be found occasionally in ascent, particularly in the upper octave region.

A comparatively distinct difference between the two ragas can
be found in the use of the note PA (G) in the Paraj ascent. This note

is always avoided in the <u>Vasant</u> ascent. But even this rule has been
ignored, because there are some musicians who constantly avoid <u>PA</u>
(G) in the <u>Paraj</u> ascent and thus create too strong a similarity with
<u>Vasant</u>.

The preceding example illustrates the use of <u>PA</u> (G) in the ascent and
descent of <u>Paraj</u> between the notes <u>MA</u> <u>tivra</u> (F#) and <u>DHA</u> <u>komal</u> (A♭),
and vice versa; it further shows that <u>PA</u> (G) is avoided in <u>Paraj</u> only
when an extended and direct ascent toward the high <u>SA</u> (c) is intended
(F# A♭ B c).

RAGA PARAJ   (Shikar Tal, $\frac{6+6+2+3}{4}$)   BH, IV, 429

Asthayi

Antara

Tone material

Raga Dipak

The first of the Dipak types has already been described as a member of the Bilaval family. [114] The type of Dipak under considera-tion here belongs to the Purvi thata. The pictorial representation generally concerns Dipak irrespective of its thata classification. One description, similar to that of the first type of raga Dipak and published in an anonymous text in a Gujarati journal, Suvarna-Mālā,[115] is as follows:

> Mounted on an elephant, surrounded by a bevy of young
> damsels, with gaits of elephants, his complexion is rosy,
> his robes are scarlet, he carries garlands made of pearls.
> His dress is beautiful, his hair disheveled, he sings in
> auspicious words like the bee in a grove, such is Dipaka to
> be understood.[116]

Dipak is an ancient raga which, as Chapter I has mentioned, is said to produce fire if correctly rendered. The belief in its magic power is still so strong, particularly with musicians of the older generation, that many performers shy away from singing it; hence it can be heard only very rarely. Some of the old musicians even avoid mentioning its name. The performance rules are few and at times contradictory.

The vadis are SA (C) and PA (G). The note RE komal (Db) is avoided in ascent and NI (B), DHA komal (Ab), and MA tivra (F#) are avoided in descent. Melodies of this type of Dipak usually begin in the same manner as those of the ragas Vasant and Paraj, with the high SA (c). Characteristic phrases are:

The descent shows the important gliding steps SA-PA (c-G) and PA-GA (G-E) which cause the avoidance of the already mentioned three notes NI (B), DHA komal (Ab), and MA tivra (F#). The note RE komal (Db) is treated weakly in descent.

The ascent of this raga frequently shows the characteristic
vakra progressions MA tivra DHA komal PA (F# A♭ G) and NI RE
komal SA (B d♭ c).

RAGA DIPAK   (Jhaptal)   BH, V, 409

Asthayi

Antara

The phrase PA DHA komal PA (second line, bars three and four) of
the preceding song specimen is a deviation from the rule. The correct
progression is MA tivra DHA komal PA (F# Ab G).

Tone material

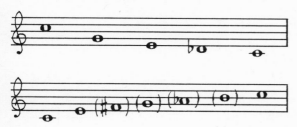

Raga Gauri (Gaudī)

There are two types of Gauri; the one which has already been
discussed[117] belongs to the Bhairav family, and the one under consideration now belongs to the Purvi thata. The raga is to be performed
in the evening.

The vadis of this second type of Gauri are RE komal (Db) and
PA (G). The note NI (B), particularly in the middle octave region,
usually appears between two DHA komal (Ab). The note RE komal
(Db) is treated in the same manner as in Shri raga.[118]

Gauri (ascribed to the Purvi thata) can be performed in three
different ways.

a) Gauri with MA tivra (F#) and DHA komal (Ab):

b) Gauri with MA shuddha (F), MA tivra (F#), and DHA komal
(A♭). The only difference between the first and second forms
of this (second) type of raga Gauri lies in the occasional use of
the note MA (F):

c) Gauri with MA (F), MA tivra (F#), DHA komal (A♭), and
DHA shuddha (A). This third form can also be called raga
Shubri-gauri and is more rare than the first two forms.
The notes DHA komal (A♭) and DHA (A) are of comparatively little importance here. The attention of the listener
is attracted by the note PA (G), the samvadi, which is
stronger in this form than in the other two. Raga Shubri-
gauri uses as a characteristic feature the following Anand-
bhairav [119] phrase:

either

or

RAGA GAURI   (Form a)   (Trital)   BH, V, 367

Asthayi

Antara

RAGA GAURI   (Form b)   (Trital)   BH, V, 366

Asthayi

Antara

There was no possibility of obtaining an adequate song specimen of the third form.

It is remarkable that in the preceding song specimen (form b) the note PA (G), the samvadi (!), is totally omitted. It is impossible to state with any degree of certainty whether this remarkable avoidance of PA (G) represents a rule or only a whim of the singer, or, perhaps, an unusual attitude of Pandit Bhatkhande, who notated this melody in the conventional notation of North India.

Tone material

a)

b)

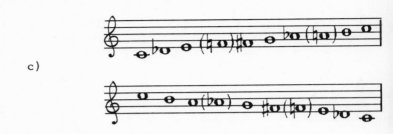

c)

Raga Bibhas (Vibhas)

There are three types of this raga. One belongs to the Bhairav thata;[120] a second type, which is under consideration here, is ascribed to the Purvi thata; and a third type, which will be presented later,[121] belongs to the Marva family. Although the performance time of this raga is subject to dispute, the majority of musicians tend to consider Bibhas as a morning raga.

The vadis are DHA komal (A♭) and RE komal (D♭). The note PA (G) is very strong. The notes NI (B) and MA tivra (F#) usually appear only in descent. Occasionally we do find MA tivra (F#) in a vakra phrase which employs this note in a pseudo ascent: PA MA tivra DHA komal PA (G F# A♭ G). The note MA (F) is totally avoided

The following Purvi phrases with NI (B) and MA tivra (F#) are frequently used in descent:

Characteristic Bibhas phrases are:

An abbreviated and somewhat superficial description of this raga would state that it represents a combination of a modified <u>Bhairav</u> scale in ascent; that is, <u>Bhairav</u> without <u>MA</u> (F) or <u>NI</u> (B) and often without <u>RE komal</u> (D♭); and the <u>Purvi</u> scale without <u>MA</u> (F) in descent.

RAGA BIBHAS   (Jhaptal)   BH, V, 391

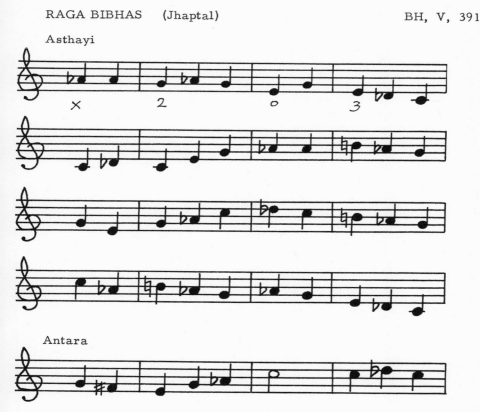

Tone material

Raga Malvi (Malava)

This little known raga belongs to the <u>Purvi thata</u> and is to be performed in the evening. In the <u>Rāga-Sāgara</u> the following pictorial description of this raga can be found:

> With his hands on the two breasts of a beautiful damsel, with his beautiful cheeks shining with swinging ear-pendants, kissing fervently the faces [sic] of the young damsel, I am [thus] contemplating in my heart—the melody of Malava.[122]

The <u>vadis</u> are <u>RE</u> <u>komal</u> (Db) and <u>PA</u> (G). It is remarkable that the <u>vadi</u> is avoided in ascent; the note <u>NI</u> (B), too, is omitted in the ascending line.

    <u>Malvi</u> melodies usually begin (like ragas <u>Vasant</u>, <u>Paraj</u>, and others) with the upper <u>SA</u> (c), and thus show at the beginning of a piece a descending movement.

The note <u>RE komal</u> (D♭) is often performed with the <u>Shri</u> vibrato.[123] Its intonation is "slightly low." Although there is no strict rule, the note <u>DHA komal</u> (A♭) is frequently avoided in descent.

    The notes <u>RE komal</u> (D♭), <u>PA</u> (G), and <u>NI</u> (B) are avoided in ascent in the majority of known songs. In descent the note <u>NI</u> (B) is weak, but the notes <u>PA</u> (G) and <u>RE komal</u> (D♭) are strong. <u>PA</u> (G) in descent is often linked to the lower <u>GA</u> (E) by means of a gliding step.

       RAGA MALVI   (Trital)   BH, V, 388

       Asthayi

Antara

Tone material

Raga Triveni

This raga belongs to the Purvi family and is to be performed in the evening. Its vadis are RE komal (Db) and PA (G). The note MA (F) is totally avoided. This omission, which actually concerns the note MA tivra (F#) because MA (F) does not appear in the Purvi scale, suffices to create a clear distinction between Triveni and Bibhas (Purvi thata). The notes DHA komal (Ab) and NI (B) are rarely used in ascent. RE komal (Db) is performed with the characteristic Shri vibrato, and DHA komal (Ab), too, is usually rendered with a small vibrato.

The following song specimen is the only one known to North Indian musicians. If a singer is asked to perform raga <u>Triveni</u>, one can expect that he will use this melody.

RAGA TRIVENI   (Jhaptal)   BH, V, 377

Asthayi

Tone material

Raga Tanki (Shritank)

Tanki is usually performed in the evening. Its vadis are PA (G) and RE komal (D♭). RE komal (D♭) is performed with the Shri vibrato. The notes MA tivra (F#) and DHA komal (A♭) are generally avoided in ascent, and MA tivra (F#) is weak in descent.

RAGA TANKI   (Trital)   BH, V, 383

Asthayi

Antara

Tone material

Comparison of the Auffuehrungspraxis of the Ragas
Malvi, Triveni, and Tanki

Malvi:	Triveni	Tanki
The vadi is RE komal (D♭);	The vadi is RE komal (D♭);	The vadi is PA (G);
RE komal (D♭) is avoided in ascent;	RE komal (D♭) is used in ascent;	RE komal (D♭) is used in ascent;
MA tivra (F#) appears in ascent and descent;	MA tivra (F#) rarely appears in ascent;	MA tivra (F#) is avoided in ascent;
DHA komal (A♭) is avoided in ascent;	DHA komal (A♭) rarely appears in ascent.	DHA komal (A♭) is avoided in ascent.
Malvi melodies begin with the upper SA (c).		

Raga Rewa

This rare raga is to be performed in the evening. Its <u>vadis</u> are
<u>GA</u> (E) and <u>DHA</u> <u>komal</u> (A♭). The notes <u>RE</u> <u>komal</u> (D♭) and <u>DHA</u>
<u>komal</u> (A♭) are performed without any vibrato and are weak. The
notes <u>MA</u> (F), <u>MA</u> <u>tivra</u> (F♯), and <u>NI</u> (B) are totally avoided, whereby
the steps <u>GA</u> <u>PA</u> (E G), <u>PA</u> <u>SA</u> (G c), <u>SA</u> <u>DHA</u> <u>komal</u> (c A♭), and <u>PA</u>
<u>GA</u> (G E) gain importance and assume characteristic features.

The <u>asthayi</u> of <u>Rewa</u> <u>khyals</u> roughly follows these lines:

The <u>antara</u> can be:

or

RAGA REWA   (Sultal)   BH, V, 394

Antara

Opinions concerning the correct Auffuehrungspraxis of this raga differ
considerably. One well-known Bombay musician insisted that only
the following version was the true form of raga Rewa:

In this second version Rewa has the vadis RE komal (D♭) and PA (G).
The notes RE komal (D♭) and DHA komal (A♭) are performed with
vibratos, particularly the former note, which requires the Shri
vibrato. In addition, the note MA tivra (F#) is used lightly but distinctly in descent.

This version of raga Rewa has a certain similarity with raga
Bibhas (Purvi thata). The difference between the two ragas lies
mainly in the vadis.

Tone material, first version

Tone material, second version

Raga Jetashri (Jetshri)

This raga is to be performed in the evening. Its <u>vadis</u> are <u>GA</u>
(E) and <u>NI</u> (B) or, according to some musicians, <u>PA</u> (G) and <u>SA</u> (C).
The notes <u>RE komal</u> (D♭) and <u>DHA komal</u> (A♭) are avoided in ascent
and are treated weakly in descent, where they are performed without
any vibrato. The <u>Vasant</u> phrase <u>MA</u> tivra <u>GA</u> <u>MA</u> tivra <u>GA</u> (F♯ E F♯
E) is characteristic also for <u>Jetashri</u>, and should appear several
times in every song of this raga.

RAGA JETASHRI   (Trital)   BH, V, 399

Raga Hansnarayani (Hansnarayni)

   Hansnarayani comes from the music of the South. A comparison
of the scales of this raga and the southern Hamsanayarani leaves little
doubt. It is possible, however, that the raga originated in the North
and was brought to the South. Whichever way the raga traveled, the
two scales are closely related. With the exception of the descending
NI (B in the North, Bb in the South) the notes are identical.   The
performance time of this raga is vague. Its vadis are SA (C) and PA
(G). The note DHA komal (Ab) is to be totally avoided.   Despite

this rule, there are some musicians who use it and several other
liberties which, being the individual modifications of each performer,
need not be listed.

The low note NI (B) always leads in ascent to RE komal (D♭),
whereby the note SA (C) loses some of its importance. The ascent
between PA (G) and the upper SA (c) is mostly performed by means of
a jump, thus avoiding the notes DHA komal (A♭) and NI (B). The note
PA (G), apart from the above mentioned jump, appears mainly in
descent, although its use in ascent is not strictly forbidden. SA (C)
always follows RE komal (D♭) in descent.

Hansnarayani employs a few characteristic ornaments (gamakas)
which have to be performed very lightly and in fast tempo:

The gliding step RE komal-SA (d♭-c) is frequently used.

RAGA HANSNARAYANI   (Trital)   BH, V, 413

Asthayi

Antara

Tone material

Raga Manohar

This little known raga, which is believed to be of recent origin (late nineteenth or early twentieth century), can be ascribed to the Purvi thata. Its vadis are GA (E) and DHA komal (A♭). The notes RE komal (D♭), PA (G), and NI (B) are rarely used in ascent. This causes the vakra phrase PA MA tivra DHA komal SA (G F♯ A♭ c). If the descending line aims at a note lower than SA (C), the step RE komal NI (D♭ B) is used, never RE komal SA NI (D♭ C B). If, however, the melody aims at the lower SA (C), the step RE komal SA (D♭ C) becomes permissible.

RAGA MANOHAR   (Trital)   BH, V, 415

Asthayi

Antara

Tone material

THE MARVA THATA

The scale of this thata is, like the scales of all other thatas, heptatonic, and represents the material of the sixth family of North Indian ragas. This thata contains the note PA (G), which is avoided in the scale of raga Marva.

Raga Marva (Marava)

Raga (formerly ragini) Marva is the raga of sunset. Some writers describe its character as quiet and contemplative, representing gentle love, while others speak of passionate emotions. The over-all mood of Marva is that of the sunset in India, where the night approaches much faster than in northern latitudes. This onrushing darkness awakens in many observers a feeling of anxiety and solemn expectation. In the Rāga-Māla by Puṇḍarika Viṭṭhala we find the following pictorial description:

> The kings at war always worship Maravi, whose face shines like the moon and who has long tresses of hair. With moist eyes, faintly smiling, she is adorned skillfully with sweet smelling flowers of different varieties. Her complexion gleams like gold; she is attired in red and her eyes are like those of a fawn. She is the elder sister of Mewar. In Marva NI and GA are sharp, SA is the graha and amsa, and RI and DHA are the nyasa.

In the Rāga-Sāgara (3, 37) we read:

> I think of Marava, standing by the side of the three-eyed Lord Shiva beneath a mango tree. She holds the wheel of a chariot on which are painted pictures [representing esoteric scenes].

Whenever Marva is conceived of as the expression of quiet, tender love, both its vadis, RE komal (Db) and DHA (A), are intoned slightly low:

315

When the performer feels that <u>Marva</u> represents the mood of anxiety
and solemn expectation of sunset, both <u>vadis</u> are rendered with a
certain "pompous sheen" ("like elephants") in which no microtonal
low-alterations occur. The different intonations of the <u>vadis</u> depend
entirely on the emotional attitudes of the performers. At the present
time most Indian musicians pay no attention to these problems. An
examination of live and recorded performances of this raga shows a
glimpse of the road along which future Indian music will travel—away
from microtonal alterations.

In ragas such as <u>Marva</u> in which neither the pure fourth nor fifth
are employed, the accompanying <u>tanbura</u> has to be tuned to:

This tuning shows that in raga <u>Marva</u> (in contrast to the scale of the
<u>Marva</u> <u>thata</u>) neither <u>MA</u> (F) nor <u>PA</u> (G) are employed; hence the
first string of the tanbura has to produce the note <u>NI</u> (B).

The <u>vadis</u> and the note <u>MA</u> <u>tivra</u> (F#) have to be treated very
strongly. As already stated, the note <u>PA</u> (G) is totally avoided. The
note <u>GA</u> (E) has to precede <u>MA</u> <u>tivra</u> (F#) in ascent and <u>RE</u> <u>komal</u> (D♭)
in descent. <u>GA</u> (E) has to be handled with some caution; if it is used
as a long held note, the similarity of <u>Marva</u> with raga <u>Puria</u>[124] becomes
too pronounced.

The note NI (B) in ascent does not lead to SA (C or c) but to RE komal (D♭ or d♭), and in its very rare appearances in descent it leads to DHA (A). If the upper SA (c) is aimed at in ascent, the note NI (B) has to be avoided. In such instances the note DHA (A), which precedes SA (c), has to be rendered in the following manner:

A similar procedure can be observed in descent. If the upper SA (c) is followed by a succession of descending notes, the note NI (B) is generally avoided and the step SA DHA (c A) becomes prominent.

The descending gliding step RE komal-SA (D♭-C) must always be performed slowly and heavily.

RAGA MARVA   (Trital)   BH, II, 276

Asthayi

Antara

In the preceding song specimen, two deviations from the performance rules can be found. One is the step SA NI (C B) in the first and third lines, bars four and one, respectively; second line, bars two and three; and third line, bars two and three. The other is the step SA RE komal (c d♭) in the third and fourth lines, bars four and one, respectively. Such liberties may be taken in songs, never in alaps.

Tone material

Raga Puria (Puriya, Purya)

This raga is to be performed in the evening. Its mood is love and peace. Although this raga is a pronounced, quiet type, there are none of the microtonal low-alterations in its scale which generally appear in other ragas of similar character. The vadis are GA (E) and NI (B). The note PA (G) is totally avoided. The notes RE komal (D♭), MA tivra (F#), and DHA (A) are weak. The steps NI-RE komal (B-D♭ or B-d♭) in ascent and MA tivra-GA (F#-E) in descent are usually performed by means of glides.

Puria melodies generally move within the ranges of the middle

and low octaves. If the performing artist emphasizes the notes of the
upper octave region too much, there is danger that the Puria
character will become distorted and a disturbing similarity with raga
Sohani [125] be created.

In the preceding phrases of Puria it can be seen that the note SA (C)
in ascent is hidden by the gliding step NI-RE komal (B-D♭ or B-d♭).
The upper SA (c) can be reached in ascent from NI (B) only by a vakra
movement via DHA (A), performed as it is in the Marva ascent.
Phrases and melodies may often be interrupted on the low NI (B) or
DHA (A).

    The difference between the ragas Puria and Marva lies mainly
in the vadis.

RAGA PURIA   (Dhamar Tal)   BH, IV, 475

Asthayi

Tone material

Raga Sohani

This raga has a tender, loving mood. The opinions concerning its performance time differ considerably. Some musicians consider Sohani as a morning raga and rest their argument upon the fact that its vadi is placed in the upper tetrachord of the scale. Other musicians, however, insist that Sohani be performed after midnight and long before the first glimmer of daylight. My experience shows that the night performance time is much preferred to the first one and that Sohani is usually performed at about four o'clock in the morning, two hours before the Indian sunrise.

The Sohani scale is the same as that of the ragas Marva and Puria. The vadis are DHA (A) and GA (E), and the note PA (G) is totally avoided. Like Marva and Puria melodies, Sohani melodies usually begin with the high SA (c) and move from there in a descending line. Toward the end of the song they return to the high SA (c). The subsequent Sohani song specimen shows that its melody, although not beginning with the high SA (c), moves already during the first measure into the prescribed high range, from where it gradually descends. In descent Sohani melodies move only rarely below SA (C) of the middle octave region. The note GA (E), occasionally also MA tivra (F#), is usually the lowest point of the melodic line.

The differences between the ragas Sohani, Marva, and Puria can be observed in various aspects. The most notable ones are the ascents of the three ragas, particularly from DHA (A) to the high SA (c).

Marva and Puria avoid one note here or show vakra steps; e.g., in
Marva the progressions MA tivra DHA SA (F# A c) or MA tivra DHA
NI RE komal (F# A B d♭), and in Puria the progressions NI DHA SA
(B A c) or NI RE komal SA (B d♭ c). In Sohani, however, straight
progressions are used both in ascent and descent, e.g. in MA tivra
DHA NI SA (F# A B c), SA RE komal SA (c d♭ c), but also in SA RE
komal NI (c d♭ B) and SA NI DHA (c B A), and so forth. Other distinguishing features among the three ragas can be found in their vadis
and in the ranges of their melodies. Marva melodies usually frequent
the middle, Puria the middle and lower, and Sohani the upper and
middle, octave regions.

RAGA SOHANI   (Dhamar Tal)   BH, III, 435

Asthayi

Antara

Tone material

Raga Lalit (Lalita, Lalat)

Lalit is generally ascribed to the Marva thata, but there are
some musicians who place this raga in the Bhairav family. Lalit(a)
is represented pictorially in numerous works.

In the Cattvārimsacchata-Rāga-Nirūpanam (p. 14):

Lalit is a yogi, loving and affectionate, fair complexioned,
with matted hair, body anointed with divine fragrances and
holding the stag [by the hind legs].

The "holding of the stag by the hind legs" requires a few words of
explanation. It refers to the legend in which Shankar was performing
a "Yagna" to which all gods were invited. The moon (a stag), seated
on his traditional mount, tried to escape. Lord Shiva quickly caught
hold of the hind legs of the fleeing stag and stopped the moon from
escaping. The stag, being active and restless, symbolizes the human
mind and its desires. The holding of the stag signifies concentration
of mind and complete self-control.

In the same work (p. 13) Lalita is described as a female:

Lalita is a pretty young maiden, shining gold in her complexion. She holds a vina, and a cuckoo perches on her
lotus-like hand. Seated beneath the kalpa-taru [a tree
which fulfills all wishes] with her breasts highly adorned,
she is exceedingly amorous.

In the Rāga-Sāgara (3, 7):

Lalita, the mother goddess of music holds a vina and a book
in her hands. With beautiful eyes like red lotuses, she is
charmingly playful and speaks happily in a soft voice.

The following description is taken from a raga-mala text in Hindi by
Deo Kavi,[126] entitled Rag-Ratnakar (p. 10):

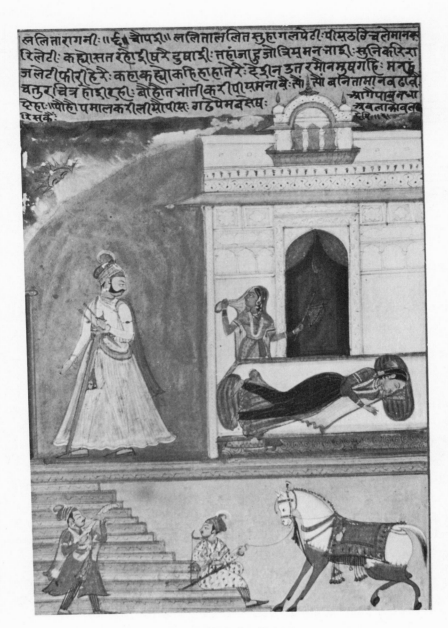

ललितारागनी ॥ई॥ चोपद॥ ललितालित सुहगलयेटी पसठठ चिलोमानक
रिलोटी कहासत रहाईधरे दुघाटी तहाजाद्दुजो त्रिम मन जाडी सुनिकरिस
जलेटीफोरी हेरे कहक हाकिहिहाते रे देशीन उतरमोनमुघगहि मन्
चतुरचित्रहाइरुह बोहित जोतीकरो प्रमना बैं तो सो बनितामानवढले
देहाः पोहो प मालकरीलिशेपिसे गठपेमबसम्   आगैंपाबाल नभा
प्रिसदेँ   अवलाआवल

Plate XVI. Lalita Ragini

CHAUPAYI: The beautiful Lalita is with her lord and lover. When the lord decides to leave, she lies down on her bed in a mood of injured pride. She straightens her gown and tells him to go to his mistress. Her lover is wounded, and he holds her mute face in his hands. She becomes motionless like a picture. The lord showers affection upon her and tries to please her in various ways, but the lady Lalita continues to show her anger.

DOHA: Her lover is about to leave, but his love for the lady is so deep and true that he cannot move. This is the strength of "abalah" [the one who is weak and without strength].

Lalita is of a delicate frame of golden complexion, she
wears ornaments and robes made of gold; coming out of
her chamber in a spring morning, she waits, her mind
full of the expectation of her love. . . . Dressed in
yellow, she carries a garland of fresh campaka flower,
mingled with blossoms of mango and aśoka; she has decked
her complexion of gold with ornaments of gold; her voice
is mistaken for the song of the cuckoo on spring mornings.
The Moon leaving the celestial abode (and assuming the
form of her face) has secured the rare ambrosia of her
sweet and juicy lips. Lalita is seeking union with her beloved (alternately—the melody seeks the notes DHA, NI,
SA, GA, and MA) and coming out of her abode is looking
out for him. [127]

Raga (formerly ragini) Lalita, "the wife of Hindol, " is to be
performed in the very early morning. Its vadis are MA (F) and the
upper SA (c). The Lalit scale is closely related to the scales of the
three preceding ragas, with the exception that Lalit employs the note
MA (F) in addition to MA tivra (F#). This is one of the very few
ragas in which the succession MA MA tivra (F F#) is permitted. The
notes MA tivra (F#) and RE komal (D♭) are weak. The performance
of the note DHA (A) was and still is the subject of stormy arguments
among North Indian musicians. Some use this note without attempting
any alteration of it. Others, particularly those belonging to the
Gwalior school, among them the now deceased singer Abdul Karim
Khan, intone this note so low that it can be described as DHA komal
(A♭). Another group of musicians, including Fayyaz Khan, intones
the note in such a manner that it stands between DHA (A) and DHA
komal (A♭). Similar to the ragas Marva and Puria, the ascent of
Lalit avoids the note SA (C) if the melody moves upward from NI (B)
via RE komal (D♭). If, however, the ascent moves from or through
DHA (A), the next higher note has to be SA (c). In descent the note
SA (C) is normally reached from RE komal (D♭).

In order to indicate the varied intonations of the note DHA (A)
in the following alap fragments, it will be notated in a manner which
corresponds to Fayyaz Khan's intonation, a DHA komal (A^{+}♭) altered
slightly high. In the subsequent song specimen, however, this note
will be notated as DHA (A) in its shuddha form.

One frequently used <u>Lalit</u> phrase is:

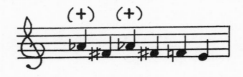

RAGA LALIT   (Dhamar Tal)   BH, IV, 516

Tone Material

Raga Bibhas (Vibhasa)

This type of <u>Bibhas</u> belongs to the <u>Marva thata</u>. There are two other types of <u>Bibhas</u>, which are ascribed to the <u>Bhairav</u> and <u>Purvi</u> <u>thatas</u>, respectively.[128] Its pictorial representation is described in the <u>Sangīta-Rāga-Kalpadruma</u> (p. 30) as follows:

> At the break of dawn when the cocks crow, raga Vibhasa
> is handsome and lovely like Kamadeva, the god of love.
> He is of fair complexion, exceedingly graceful and dressed
> in spotless white. He is courageous, self-possessed and
> spirited. His fine locks brush against his soft cheeks.

The <u>Sangīta-Darpana</u> (2, 136) offers only the laconic comment that Vibhasa is just like <u>Lalit</u>.

<u>Bibhas</u> (<u>Marva</u>) is a mixture of <u>Bibhas</u> (<u>Bhairav</u>) and raga <u>Marva</u>. The <u>vadis</u> are <u>DHA</u> (A) and <u>GA</u> (E). The <u>Bhairav</u> notes of the scale are <u>SA</u> (C), <u>RE komal</u> (D♭), <u>GA</u> (E), and <u>PA</u> (G). The <u>Marva</u> notes are <u>MA tivra</u> (F#), <u>DHA</u> (A), and <u>NI</u> (B). The note <u>MA</u> (F) is totally avoided. <u>PA</u> (G) appears only in ascent after <u>GA</u> (E), never after <u>MA tivra</u> (F#). Despite this rule, it can be observed that a quick succession of <u>MA tivra PA</u> (F# G) may occur in the form of a subtle appoggiatura. If <u>MA tivra</u> (F#) is not used as a grace note but as a fully valued note in ascent, it cannot be succeeded by <u>PA</u> (G) but rather by <u>DHA</u> (A). The note <u>DHA</u> (A) is often treated in the same manner as it is in raga <u>Deshkar</u>.[129] As the notes of the lower half of the scale are taken from the <u>Bhairav</u> scale, it can be noted that <u>RE komal</u> (D♭) in descent is performed with the characteristic <u>Bhairav</u> vibrato. The remarkable feature of <u>RE komal</u> (D♭) in this form of

Plate XVII. Ragini Bibhas

CHAUPAYI: As Megh-mallar starts his amorous play, Bibhas reciprocates passionately by tightly embracing Megha. The lover has bow and arrows in his hands and is about to begin the play of love. As he affectionately touches her breasts, her body stretches in aching love. Both players of the game are strong, dexterous, and deft. The match is quite equal, and the battle ends without either of the contenders being defeated.

DOHA: Listen to the story of this sport of love where the beloved is happy in the company of her lover, and there is much laughter and merriment. The whole atmosphere is surcharged with love and passion.

<u>Bibhas</u> is that in spite of the <u>Bhairav</u> vibrato, it is here intoned slightly
high, or at least higher than the note altered microtonally low in raga
<u>Bhairav</u>.[130]

RAGA BIBHAS (Marva Thata)   (Adachautal)   BH, VI, 38

Asthayi

Antara

Tone material

Raga Pancham (Hindol-pancham)

   This raga belongs to the Marva family. The following description quoted from the work of Bhāva-bhatta (Anūpa-Saṅgīta-Vilāsa,
p. 142) refers to Panchama (Bhinna-panchama):

> Of yellow complexion, with hairs of russet hue, he strikes
> great terror in his enemies in battles, taller than the tallest,
> he carries strings of skulls on his breast, incessantly loud
> and terrific laughters emanate from his throat to resound
> in the skies, —Bhinna-pañcama has thus been indicated by
> the learned.[131]

Musicians distinguish two types of Pancham, one in which the note PA
(G) is totally avoided, and a second one in which this note is used.
Raga Pancham, often described as a summertime form, is usually
performed late after midnight. As in raga Lalit, the notes MA and
MA tivra (F and F#) are employed.

   The vadis are MA (F) and SA (C). The note RE komal (Db) is
avoided in ascent. There are some musicians who state that RE komal
(Db) has to be avoided totally. This method, particularly in the first
type of this raga, creates too strong a similarity with raga Hindol.[132]
The use of both forms of the note MA (shuddha and tivra, F and F#)

Plate XVIII. Pancham Ragini

CHAUPAYI: There is a comfortable, fine bed in the unusually beautiful house. Ragini
Pancham dallies with her lover. She is charming, fascinatingly beautiful, and endowed
with all the graces. She is always with her lover, day and night, and does not leave him
for an instant. She is so beautiful that even the god of love grows pale in her presence.
Talented skilled musicians sing her praise in sweet, melodious voices, and expert women
play dexterously on musical instruments. The king is charmed with the music and dis-
tributes precious gifts. Those learned in the arts feel jubilant and are happy.

DOHA: As Pancham appears, everyone's eyes are magnetized by the beauty of her form.
Lord Kamdeva feels shy in her presence, and that is the reason why he is called "anang"
[without body or form].

allows two ways of ascent. If MA tivra (F#) is used, the sequence
SA GA MA tivra (C E F#) is preferred. If MA (F) is used, the char-
acteristic step SA MA (C F) is generally preferred; however, SA GA
MA (C E F) may be observed in some instances and very rarely even
RE komal MA (D♭ F) may be found.

   First type (without PA):

The following song specimen represents the first type of Pancham,
in which the notes PA (G) and RE komal (D♭) are totally avoided and
the note NI (B) is avoided in ascent and treated weakly in descent:

   RAGA PANCHAM   (Jhaptal) First type   BH, VI, 42

Antara

The following song specimen represents a second form of the first type of this raga. The note <u>PA</u> (G) is totally avoided but <u>RE komal</u> (D♭) is employed:

RAGA PANCHAM   (Dhamar Tal)   BH, VI, 48

Asthayi

Antara

Sanchari

If the descending phrase or melody comes to a stop on the note SA (C), the step RE komal SA (Db C) is permissible. If, however, a descent which progresses below SA (C) is planned, the note SA (C) is usually avoided and NI (B) is used. Although this rule is clearly defined, there are musicians who ignore it (cf. the next song specimen, fourth line, bars two and three).

In a few exceptional instances the note PA (G) is used, which gives the raga a different character. It is remarkable that this raga performed with the note PA (G) has no separate name of its own, for numerous ragas which differ from each other in much less detail are distinguished by specific names.

The note MA (F) deserves a few additional remarks. It appears not only after SA (C) in ascent but also in phrases such as GA MA GA (E F E) or RE komal MA MA tivra (Db F F#). The note MA tivra

(F#) in ascent is followed mostly by DHA (A), occasionally also by NI (B), very rarely by the upper SA (c). Only in very rare instances can one observe the succession MA tivra PA (F# G).

The note NI (B) appears both in ascent and descent in the second type of this raga. In this type the note MA (F) appears only in a few instances.

RAGA PANCHAM   (Sultal) Second type   BH, VI, 44

Tone material

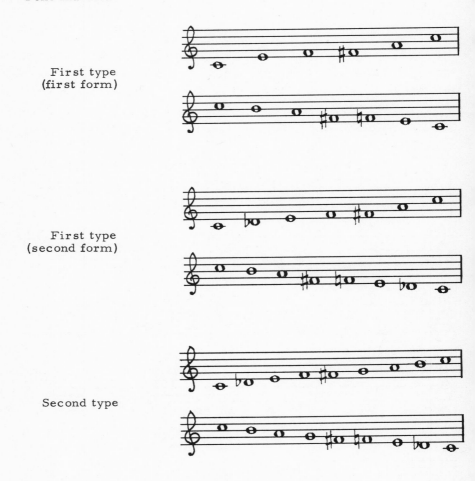

First type
(first form)

First type
(second form)

Second type

Raga Maligaura

    This rare raga is to be performed in the evening. Its vadis are
RE komal (D♭) and PA (G). Maligaura melodies usually move within
the middle and lower octave ranges. The raga combines elements
taken from Shri raga[133] and raga Puria.[134] Theoretically there are
three types of Maligaura:
    a) Maligaura with DHA (A), a type used mostly by the pupils of
        Aladiya Khan of Bombay;
    b) Maligaura with DHA komal (A♭);

c) <u>Maligaura</u> with both forms of <u>DHA</u>, <u>shuddha</u> and <u>komal</u> (A and
   A♭).

In order to simplify the following explanations, the scales of <u>Shri</u> raga
and raga <u>Puria</u> are shown here.

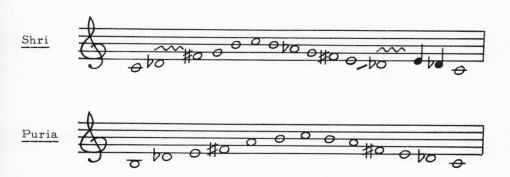

Shri

Puria

<u>Shri</u> characteristics become noticeable in <u>Maligaura</u> if the notes <u>PA</u>
(G), <u>RE komal</u> (D♭) with vibrato, and <u>DHA komal</u> (A♭) are used.
<u>Puria</u> characteristics arise if the notes <u>GA</u> (E) and <u>DHA</u> (A), or the
phrases <u>NI RE komal SA</u> (B D♭ C) and <u>NI RE komal NI</u> (B D♭ B) are
stressed. In practice the combination of the two ragas is not quite
as simple as placing the two elements in succession, because the constituent features cannot be clearly separated. The reason is that <u>Shri</u>
and <u>Puria</u> elements partly overlap.

Here are some <u>alap</u> examples in which the elements of <u>Shri</u> and
<u>Puria</u> are purposely kept apart as much as possible:

As has been implied before, the essential method in performing this and similar compound ragas is to see that neither one nor the other of the constituent elements gains undue predominance. Only in very rare instances can one observe a great artist juggling this dangerous predominance without harming the raga.

The interpretation of the note <u>DHA</u> <u>komal</u> (A♭), a <u>Shri</u> feature, deserves attention. Although there are numerous musicians who intone this note as A♭, there are some who apply to it a slight microtonally high-alteration in ascent.

Whenever the note <u>DHA</u> (A) is used in its <u>shuddha</u> form, and when the inner balance between the two constituent ragas is disturbed, the raga is often called not <u>Maligaura</u> but <u>Gaura</u>.

The following song specimen is anything but an ideal combination of <u>Shri</u> and <u>Puria</u>. The combination is simplified by using the note DHA <u>komal</u> (A♭) in the <u>asthayi</u> and <u>DHA</u> (A) in the <u>antara</u>.

RAGA MALIGAURA   (Trital)   BH, VI, 11

Asthayi

Antara

Tone material

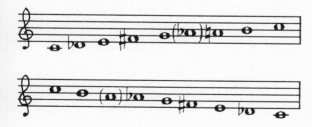

Raga Purba (Purbya)

This rare and somewhat obscure raga is to be performed in the evening. It represents a combination of elements taken from the ragas Purvi,[135] Puria,[136] and Marva. The vadis of this raga are usually described as GA (E) and NI (B). There are some musicians who do not agree with this vadi disposition. The main difference between Purba and Maligaura lies in the use of the note PA (G): Purba avoids it; Maligaura uses it.

Purba melodies move mostly within the middle and low octave regions. Occasionally the note DHA komal (A♭) is used besides DHA (A). The former note is usually microtonally high. The combination of Purvi, Puria, and Marva elements can be made in the following manner:

A graphic representation concerning the combination of these elements is shown in the following diagram:

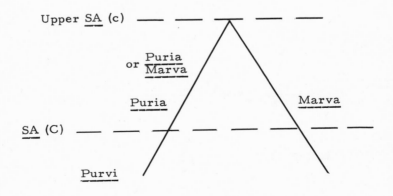

There are a few musicians who insist that the Purba scale has to include the note PA (G). In such regrettable instances the similarity
between Purba and Maligaura becomes so strong that the two ragas
can hardly be distinguished from each other.

RAGA PURBA   (Trital)   BH, VI, 4

Asthayi

Antara

Tone material

Raga Purvakalyan

This rare raga has the vadis RE komal (D♭) and DHA (A).
Purvakalyan represents a combination of elements taken from the

ragas <u>Marva</u> and <u>Kalyan</u>.[137]   <u>Purvakalyan</u> usually employs <u>Marva</u>
notes in the lower, and <u>Kalyan</u> notes in the upper, tetrachords of the
scale. <u>Kalyan</u> appears here with the note <u>PA</u> (G).

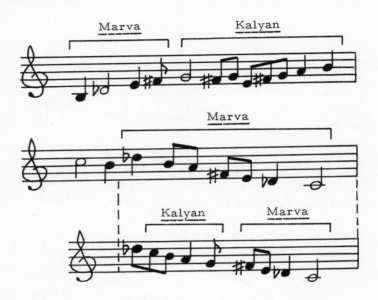

This rule applies to the ascending line. In descent there are two possibilities: either only notes of the <u>Marva</u> scale are used or, similar
to the ascent, <u>Kalyan</u> elements appear in the upper, and <u>Marva</u> elements in the lower, tetrachords.

RAGA PURVAKALYAN   (Ektal)   BH, VI, 8

Asthayi

Antara

Tone material

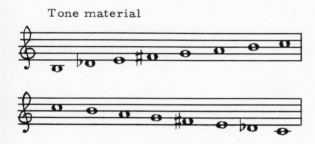

Raga Jait (Jayat, Jet)

This raga, which must not be mistaken for Jayat-kalyan,[138] is
to be performed in the evening. Its vadis are PA (G) and SA (C). One
can distinguish two types of Jait, the second of which can again be sub-
divided into two different forms.

The first type has the following scale:

The notes GA (E) and DHA (A) are strong and almost assume the
functions of vishrantisthans. Of importance are the descending gliding
steps SA-PA (c-G), PA-GA (G-E), and GA-RE komal-SA (E-D♭-C),
and the ascending step GA-PA (E-G).

The note RE komal (D♭) is weak.

    The second type of this raga adds the note MA tivra (F#) to the scale, which emphasizes its relationship with raga Marva. Like the Auffuehrungspraxis of Marva, the note MA tivra (F#) in ascent is not succeeded by PA (G) but by DHA (A). In this second type, too, the note RE komal (D♭) is weak, unlike its treatment in raga Marva.

    In a second form of the second type of raga Jait, the note DHA komal (A♭) is added to the scale, a note which may appear either between two MA tivra (F#), two PA (G), or between MA tivra and PA. In this form the note RE shuddha (D) also appears occasionally in the high octave region.

In this latter form the typical <u>Marva</u> step <u>MA</u> <u>tivra</u> <u>DHA</u> (F# A) is occasionally replaced by <u>MA</u> <u>tivra</u> <u>PA</u> <u>DHA</u> (F# G A).

The following song specimen represents the second form of the
second type of this raga.

RAGA JAIT   (Jhaptal)   BH, VI, 24

Asthayi

Antara

Tone material

First type

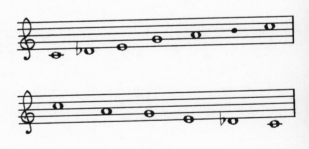

Second type
(first form)

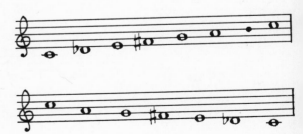

Second type
(second form)

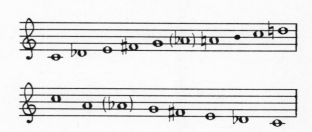

Raga Varati (Barari, Berari)

This raga is to be performed in the evening. A Bengali theorist,
Radha Mohan Sen, published in 1881 a rag-mala text in which he describes Varati as follows:

> Barari: Barari is the second ragini (of Bhairava), a young
> damsel, who makes the four quarters effulgent with her
> radiance. Her tresses are new clouds—her robes are
> white: the flowers of the Wishing Tree are her pendants
> for the ears. Her face is the Moon without the marks
> (spots) of the deer. The "beauty" has golden bracelets
> on her wrists. The breadth of her waist is very narrow,
> her navel is deep like a lake, and her breasts are firm.
> The fragrance of her body is fascinating: the blind bees
> mistake it as that of lotuses. In a pleasant mood she
> smiles and indulges in pleasantries with her beloved.
> The damsel shines as a full-toned melody, the string of
> notes being SA, RI, GA, MA, PA, DHA, NI: Her home
> is the note SA; she should be sung at the end of the day.[139]

The vadis of this rare raga are GA (E) and DHA (A). The note
RE komal (Db) is strong and is performed with a fast vibrato. MA
tivra (F#) plays an unimportant role and is weak. The scale of this
raga is that of Marva with the important additional note PA (G).

RAGA VARATI   (Chautal)   BH, IV, 29

Asthayi

Antara

Tone material

The similarity between the ragas Varati and Purva-kalyan[140] is remarkable. The difference between the two ragas lies in the use of the note PA (G) in descent. In Varati this note is strong, in Purva-kalyan it is weak.

Varati

Purva-kalyan

Raga Bhatiyar (Bhatyar, Bhatihar)

This raga is to be performed late after midnight. Its vadis are
MA (F) and SA (C). Some musicians consider the note MA tivra (F#)
as vadi because both MA shuddha (F) and MA tivra (F#) are of considerable importance in this raga. MA (F) generally appears in
descent and MA tivra (F#) in ascent. The notes RE komal (Db) and
PA (G) are used only in descent. NI (B) is weak in ascent and is often
used in descent in the vakra phrase DHA NI PA (A B G). If in descent
the melodic line reaches the note GA (E), it usually turns upward
again, either to MA tivra (F#) or straight to PA (G). If continued,
the ascent could be MA tivra DHA SA (F# A c). The descent leading
to SA (C) is usually MA RE komal SA (F Db C) or, if GA (E) is used,
PA GA RE komal SA (G E Db C). The second form of descent occurs
much more frequently than the one containing the step MA RE komal
(F Db). The appearance of MA (F) warrants a succeeding GA (E),
from where another ascent generally occurs.

RAGA BHATIYAR   (Tilvada)   BH, VI, 53

Asthayi

Tone material

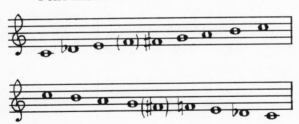

Some Indian musicians speak of three other rare types of this raga:

a) Bhatiyar which uses all notes in their shuddha form and thus
    becomes a member of the Bilaval thata. This type resembles
    raga Bhankar.[141] The difference between the two ragas lies in

the treatment of the notes MA (F) and PA (G). In Bhatiyar
the note MA (F) is strong and PA (G) is of much lesser importance, while in Bhankar PA (G) is strong and MA (F) weak.
The scale of this rare type of Bhatiyar is:

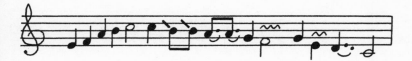

b) Bhatiyar with DHA komal (A♭) instead of DHA (A), using all
other notes in their shuddha form. This type can be ascribed to
the Bhairav thata.

c) Bhatiyar with NI komal (B♭), using all other notes in their
shuddha form. This type can be ascribed to the Khamaj thata:

In all three types the notes GA (E) and RE (D) are performed with a
short fast vibrato.

Raga Bhankar (Bhakhar, Bhikhar)

This very rare raga is to be performed late after midnight.
Bhankar is believed to be comparatively recent. Its vadis are PA
(G) and SA (C). Both forms of MA, MA shuddha (F) and MA tivra
(F#), are used, which distinguishes between this raga and raga Bib-
has (Marva thata).[142] The note MA (F) is much weaker than in raga
Bhatiyar and usually appears only as an insignificant, slightly touched
ornamental feature. However, PA (G), the vadi, is very prominent.

RAGA BHANKAR   (Tivra Tal)   BH, VI, 58

Asthayi

Antara

Tone material

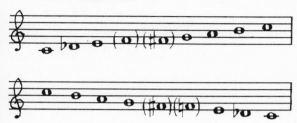

Raga Lalita-gauri

This rare raga can be assigned to the Marva family. Its performance time and performance rules are indistinct. Lalita-gauri consists of the basic Gauri (Purvi thata)[143] material to which are added
the Lalit notes MA (F) and MA tivra (F#). The vadis cannot be determined with certainty; it is possible that the vadis of Gauri (Purvi thata)
play some role in this raga.

The interruption or dwelling on the note NI (B) and the Shri vibrato on
RE komal (Db) are characteristic. Also of importance is the Lalit
phrase MA MA tivra MA (F F# F). Notes which are higher than PA
(G) are treated in the following manner:

The preceding example shows that both forms of DHA, shuddha (A)
and komal (A♭), are in use. Usually we find the shuddha form in
ascent and the komal form in descent, a habit which, in the preceding
example is not always carried out. Steps such as MA tivra DHA komal
MA tivra SA (F# A♭ F# c) or MA tivra DHA MA tivra SA (F# A F# c)
are permitted.

The following song specimen is not particularly suited for the
representation of Lalita-gauri, but it is the only one available. Pandit
Bhatkhande, too, expresses his doubts about this song; he mentions
that its melody stands very close to the raga Bhatiyar. He adds, however, that the famous Ashikali Khan Saheb of Jaipur insists that the
song represents Lalita-gauri.

RAGA LALITA-GAURI   (Dhamar Tal)   BH, VI, 67

Tone material

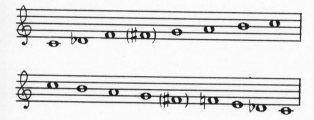

Raga Sazgiri (Sazagiri)

This rare raga is to be performed in the evening. Its vadi is GA (E); the samvadi is occasionally described as NI (B). Melodies in this raga move mainly in the middle and low octave regions. Sazgiri employs both MA (F) and MA tivra (F#), and DHA komal (Ab) and DHA (A). When listening to a Sazgiri performance, one usually has the impression that a combination of elements taken from the ragas Puria[144] and Purvi[145] is being presented.

The step NI RE komal (B Db) in ascent from the low to the middle octave region is characteristic. In ascent between the middle and high octave regions either NI RE komal (B db) or, avoiding NI (B), PA SA (G c) or DHA SA (A c) are employed. In descent there are no specific rules; progressions such as SA NI MA tivra (c B F#), SA NI DHA komal PA (c B Ab G), and, in the low octave region, NI DHA MA tivra (B A F#) are in use.

The last phrase in the preceding example, PA-DHA-GA (G-A-E), shows how the weak PA (G) of Purvi is linked with the Puria step DHA GA (A E).

RAGA SAZGIRI   (Ektal)   BH, VI, 63

Asthayi

Antara

Tone material

THE KAFI THATA

The scale of this <u>thata</u> represents the material of the seventh family of North Indian ragas.

Raga Kafi

Raga <u>Kafi</u> is believed to have been created at the time of the Islamic invasions into India. It is possible that it was imported by the Mohammedans, but there is no reliable support for this theory. Since the scale is simple and well liked, one could also assume that both Indians and Mohammedans knew it before the two cultures met. One example showing the widespread use of <u>Kafi</u>, perhaps somewhat far-fetched, is a melody of a Chinese philosopher of the Sung dynasty (960-1279), transcribed by Laurence Picken in the first volume of the <u>New</u> <u>Oxford</u> <u>History</u> <u>of</u> <u>Music</u> (p. 109):[146]

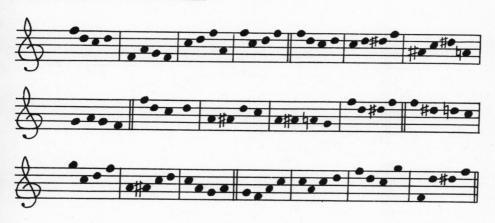

It is a well-known fact that musicians, musical instruments, and melodies were imported into China from the West, particularly from Tibet, India, and, without doubt, from the Mohammedan peoples. If we replace in the preceding song melody all A#'s with B♭ and all D#'s with E♭, we have a tone material which represents the scale C D E♭ F G A B♭ c, the scale of <u>Kafi</u>.

The North Indian <u>Kafi</u> is a light and very popular raga. It is difficult to find serious pieces in this raga; mainly <u>thumris</u>, <u>horis</u>, <u>ghazals</u>, and other light forms appear. This raga is to be performed during the second quarter of the night. The following pictorial description is taken from the <u>Rāga-Sāgara</u> (3, 33), where the raga is called by its old name, <u>Kāpikā</u>:

> In the lotus of my heart I cherish Kapika, the inspirer
> of Kandeva (god of Love) who surpasses even Lakshmi,
> the goddess of fortune. Fair and beautiful, dressed in
> blue garments and adorned with various ornaments, she
> is very fond of parrots. Living in a house whitewashed
> with lime, she is exceedingly amorous and playfully sits
> in the lap of her lover.

The scale of raga <u>Kafi</u>, in contrast to that of the <u>thata</u>, shows various modifications which can be expected in a light raga. The use of <u>GA</u> and <u>GA komal</u> (E and E♭), and <u>NI</u> and <u>NI komal</u> (B and B♭) is frequent. The <u>vadis</u> are <u>PA</u> (G) and <u>SA</u> (C). The note <u>PA</u> (G) is very strong and represents something like the "center" of the melody. Besides this strong emphasis on the <u>vadi</u>, raga <u>Kafi</u> has no significant performance rules. Characteristic phrases of this raga are:

The use of the two forms of <u>GA</u>, <u>shuddha</u> (E) and <u>komal</u> (E♭), and of the two forms of <u>NI</u>, is shown in the following:

Usually the shuddha note appears in ascent and the komal in descent.
The note DHA komal (A♭) may appear as a substitute for DHA (A) both
in ascent and descent.

RAGA KAFI   (Trital)   BH, II, 318

Asthayi

Antara

Tone material

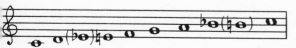

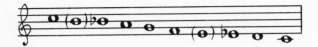

There are some musicians who not only use both forms of GA (E) and
NI (B), but also employ DHA (A) and DHA komal (A♭). In such instances the raga is called Nilambari.[147]

Raga Bhimpalasi (Bhimpalashri)

Bhimpalasi is to be performed in the afternoon. It is a light
raga which is to be rendered in slow tempo in a quiet, peaceful, and
tender mood. The Sangīta-Rāga-Kalpadrumā (p. 22) offers the following pictorial description:

> The greatest of the sages say that Bhimpalashri is fair,
> delicate and charming and is the embodiment of art. With
> eyes like lotus, she is divinely fragrant. Holding a vina,
> she sings with a husky voice.

The vadis of this raga are MA (F) and SA (C). The note PA (G) is a
vishrantisthan. The notes RE (D) and DHA (A) are avoided in ascent.
Melodies in this raga often begin with the low NI komal (B♭), occasionally also with PA (G). The notes GA komal (E♭) and NI komal (B♭)
are usually intoned slightly sharp if used in the ascending line. In descent no microtonal alterations can be observed. Some notes of the
Bhimpalasi scale are approached in the following manner:

If the same note is repeated, two possibilities of approach can be observed:

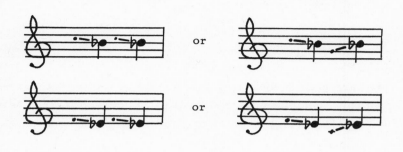

RAGA BHIMPALASI   (Trital)   BH, III, 558

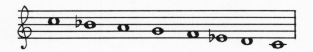

Raga Dhani

This rare raga is often described as "Bhimpalasi without the note DHA (A)." This definition appears to be correct at first, superficial hearing. A careful investigation, however, does not uphold it. The vadis of this raga, quite different from those of Bhimpalasi, are GA komal (E♭) and NI komal (B♭). The note DHA (A) is totally avoided. According to Pandit Bhatkhande (VI, 103), the note RE (D) is to be omitted, a rule which in contemporary practice is not observed. RE (D) does appear, usually in descent as a weakly treated note. The vadis are performed with a light vibrato which always begins with the next higher note.

RAGA DHANI   (Trital)   BH, VI, 104

Asthayi

Antara

Tone material

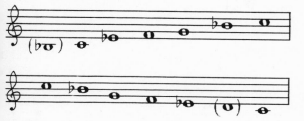

Raga Dhanashri

This raga belongs to the Kafi thata[148] and is to be performed in the early afternoon. N. A. Willard offers the following pictorial description of it:

> Dhunasree . . . We cannot but sympathise with solitary
> grief in a beautiful female . . . . The misfortunes . . .
> proceed from the absence of her lover, and that she has
> languished is evident from her emaciated frame. Her
> dress is red, and avoiding the society of her friends,
> she sits alone under a Moulsree tree, venting her griefs
> to the woods.[149]

This description stands in sharp contrast to the present concept of Dhanashri. Today this raga is considered to represent a light cheerful mood which is far removed from grief over an absent lover.

The vadis are PA (G) and SA (C). There is considerable similarity between Dhanashri and Bhimpalasi, but their difference can be easily recognized by their vadis and moods; Dhanashri is at the present time lighter and more cheerful than Bhimpalasi. The vadi is very strong and the notes RE (D) and DHA (A) are avoided in ascent. If NI komal (B♭) is followed in ascent by a SA (C or c), the former note will be intoned slightly sharp. In some notated songs the ascending NI is often notated shuddha (B), while in descent NI komal (B♭) is always used.

RAGA DHANASHRI   (Chautal)   BH, VI, 100

Tone material

Raga Bhim

This very rare raga can be ascribed to the Kafi thata. Its vadis
are probably PA (G) and SA (C). The note GA (E) always appears in
its shuddha form, and GA komal (E♭) is never used. The notes of the
upper tetrachord of the descending Bhim scale are treated in the same
way as are those of raga Bhimpalasi. The lower tetrachord contains
in descent several vakra steps which are shown below. The ascent of
the Bhim scale is remarkable. It consists either of an octave jump or
an octave gliding step from the low NI komal (B♭) to its octave above;
or it begins from the low NI komal (B♭), avoids the notes SA, RE, GA,
and DHA (C, D, E, and A) and moves via MA (F) and PA (G) to the
upper NI komal (B♭) and SA (c). If NI komal (B♭) is followed by SA
(C or c), the former note is intoned slightly sharp and is usually performed with a small fast vibrato.

The descent uses the following <u>vakra</u> steps:

Tone material

Raga Patadipaki (Patadip, Pradipaki)

This raga is to be performed in the early afternoon. Its <u>vadis</u>
are <u>SA</u> (C) and <u>MA</u> (F) or, according to some musicians, <u>MA</u> and <u>SA</u>.
The notes <u>RE</u> (D) and <u>DHA</u> (A) are avoided in ascent and are treated
weakly; they are often intoned slightly low in descent. A scrutiny of
several <u>Patadipaki</u> performances shows that there are three basic
types of this raga:

a) <u>Patadipaki</u> with <u>GA</u> <u>komal</u> (E♭) and <u>NI</u> <u>shuddha</u> (B), the most
   widely used type of this raga;

b) <u>Patadipaki</u> with <u>GA</u> (E) and <u>NI</u> (B) in ascent, and <u>GA</u> <u>komal</u> (E♭)
   and <u>NI</u> <u>komal</u> (B♭) in descent;

c) <u>Patadipaki</u> with <u>GA</u> (E) in ascent, <u>GA</u> <u>komal</u> (E♭) in descent, and
   <u>NI</u> (B) in both ascent and descent.

These three types rarely appear in their pure forms; generally preferred are combinations of one and another, and variants in which <u>NI</u>
<u>komal</u> (B♭) is used in ascent, usually intoned slightly sharp. Similarly,
the note <u>GA</u> <u>komal</u> (E♭) may show a microtonally high alteration if, in

ascent, it is followed by MA (F). These two high-altered notes are
mostly performed with a small fast vibrato. The note MA (F) is strong
in all three types of this raga. This feature constitutes the main difference between Patadipaki and Haunskankani.[150] In the latter raga the
note MA (F) is of little importance, but GA (E) is stressed.

Some North Indian musicians hold the view that the names
Patadipaki and Pradipaki represent two different ragas. According to
them, Pradipaki is the older form, with NI komal (B♭) in both ascent
and descent, but with GA (E) in ascent and GA komal (E♭) in descent.
In Pradipaki specimens the notes RE (D) and DHA (A) in descent are
often microtonally low-altered.

The same musicians consider raga Patadipaki to be the younger
raga. NI (B) or a slightly high intoned NI komal (B♭) appears in ascent, and a normally intoned NI komal (B♭) is used in descent.

Melodies in this raga, particularly those which employ the so-called "Pradipaki" material, move mainly in the low and middle octave regions.

The question of whether or not Pradipaki and Patadipaki are two different ragas cannot be answered with any certainty. The following example may illustrate the problem by showing the various possibilities of intonations in the Patadipaki scale and by showing how closely the three types of Patadipaki are linked to Pradipaki:

The phrase 1. is said to be characteristic (of Patadipaki), but experience shows that this phrase is not one of the strictly required features. The note NI komal (B♭), 2., can appear slightly raised—it can be notated as B natural, or it can be B♭; the note DHA (A), 3., may show similar inconsistencies in its intonation; the same applies to the notes GA komal (E♭), 4., and RE (D), 5.

Some musicians will say that the following song specimen represents raga Pradipaki; others will describe it as a variant of Patadipaki.

RAGA PRADIPAKI (PATADIPAKI)   (Jhumra)   BH, VI, 106

Asthayi

Antara

Tone material

Raga Barva

This raga belongs to the Kafi thata and is to be performed in the afternoon. There are some musicians who believe that Barva is a serious raga; others, however, think that it is light and flirtatious. There are also differing views on the vadis and general performance rules of raga Barva. One group of musicians believes that the vadi is RE (D); others state that it is SA (C). The samvadi, of little importance in Barva, is usually described as PA (G).

Whenever Barva is regarded as a light raga, the shuddha and komal forms of the notes RE (D and Db), DHA (A and Ab), and NI (B and Bb) may be used. In instances when the raga is considered to be a serious one, the notes RE komal (Db) and DHA komal (Ab) are strictly avoided, and only the shuddha forms RE and DHA (D and A) are used.

Generally speaking and implying no rule, it can be stated that the DHA notes exclude the subsequent NI notes, and vice versa. Characteristic and important is the fact that the note GA komal (Eb) is avoided in ascent. The note MA (F) is strong. The steps PA GA komal (G Eb) in descent and the vakra phrase GA RE GA komal RE (E D Eb D) appears frequently. If NI komal (Bb) precedes SA (C or c), the former note is often intoned slightly high. In some rare instances NI komal (Bb) can be raised even to NI shuddha (B) and can be notated as such.

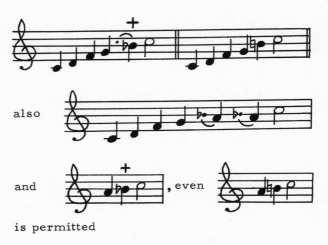

also

and   , even

is permitted

Occasionally musicians speak of a raga called Punjabi-barva. This
raga differs from Barva in that it uses the note GA shuddha (E) instead
of GA komal (E♭) in both ascent and descent.

RAGA BARVA   (Jhaptal)   BH, VI, 87

In the preceding song specimen, NI (B) predominates in ascent and NI komal (B♭) in descent, with the exception of the second bar of the sixth line, where NI komal (B♭) appears in ascent, a liberty which is particularly permissible in the light form of Barva.

Tone material

Raga Sindhura (Sindura, Sendhora, Sindhoda, Saindhvi, Sindhvi, Sindhuvi

The performance time of this ancient raga is uncertain, and its rasa can be either serious or joyful. In a raga-mala text in Bengali written in 1881[151] the following pictorial description is offered:

Sindhuvi (Saindhavi): She was expecting her lord Sindhuvi, and has now given up that hope. The appointed hour has gone by. Still the beloved has not come. This has led to deep resentment; she has assumed the robes of an ascetic. Having cast aside her scarlet robes, she has assumed russet ones (proper to ascetics). Casting aside jewelry, she has be-decked herself with strings of rosaries . . . and crystals. She abjured the fragrance of aguru . . . and besmeared all her body with ashes. Making pendants from Vandukha flowers, she wore them on her ears. Taking a trident, and the counting-beads in her hands, Sindhuvi is worshipping Śankara (Śiva). A heptatonic

melody having its abode in the note "sa", the succession
of notes being sa-ri-ga-ma-pa-dha-ni. Proper for the
six seasons, beginning with autumn, you should sing it at
the end of the day.[152]

Some old musicians state that in the past a distinction was made between Sindhura and Saindhvi and that the two names represented two
different ragas. At present this is not the case, although musicians
still speak of two types of the same raga which may be called by either
of the two names. The vadis of both types are SA (C) and PA (G). A
distinction can be made between pure Sindhura and a combination of
Sindhura and Kafi elements.

In pure Sindhura the notes GA komal (Eb) and NI (B) are avoided
in ascent. In the second type of this raga the note NI (B) is used in
ascent, particularly when it is followed by SA (C or c). All Sindhura
melodies usually ascend quickly to the region of the upper SA (c).
The following example shows the ascending succession of the notes MA
PA DHA SA (F G A c) which is characteristic of the first type of this
raga, the pure Sindhura.

The characteristic ascent of the pure Sindhura changes to MA PA NI
SA (F G B c) in the second type:

The note <u>GA komal</u> (E♭) is performed in both types with a small vibrato.

The song specimen immediately following represents the first type of raga <u>Sindhura</u>, the next song specimen, the second type.

RAGA SINDHURA   (Trital) First type   BH, VI, 73

Asthayi

Antara

RAGA SINDHURA   (Dhamar Tal)   Second type   BH, VI, 82

Asthayi

The second song specimen is a <u>Hori</u>, a Hindu religious song sung at the time of the <u>Holi</u> festival, when all participants are joyful and be-smear themselves and each other with paint. Despite the serious <u>Dhamar</u> <u>tal</u>, this song is performed in lively tempo.

Tone material

First
type

Second
type

Comparison of the Auffuehrungspraxis of the Ragas
Sindhura and Kafi, and Sindhura and Barva

The difference between Sindhura and Kafi lies mainly in the use or
avoidance of the notes GA komal (E♭), NI komal (B♭) or NI (B) in
ascent. If these notes, particularly GA komal (E♭), are used, the
Sindhura scale becomes very similar to that of Kafi.

The difference between Sindhura and Barva can be shown in the
following:

Sindhura	Barva
Melodies move in the middle and upper octave regions; The note PA (G) is strong.	Melodies move in the middle and low octave regions; The note PA (G) is weak; MA (F) is strong.

Raga Sindh

This rare and little known raga is usually played, hardly ever
sung. Its performance time and performance rules are vague. The
vadis of this raga are SA (C) and probably MA (F). The notes GA (E)
and NI (B) are used in ascent, GA komal (E♭) and NI komal (B♭) in
descent. The note GA komal (E♭) is usually performed with a small
vibrato. Melodies in this raga generally move in the middle and low
octave regions. At one of the very rare performances of this raga, I
noticed that the scale was transposed a pure fourth upward, whereby

SA would have to be transcribed not as C but F. It is impossible to state whether this use of the modern "MA-grama" is a rule or not. In the present discussion of this raga the note SA is represented, as usual, by the note C.

RAGA SINDH   (Trital)   BH, VI, 85

Asthayi

Antara

Tone material

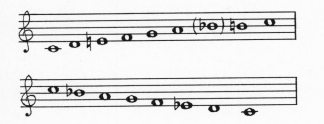

Raga Haunskankani (Hanskankani)

This rare raga is ascribed to the Kafi thata and is to be performed in the early morning. Its vadis are PA (G) and SA (C). The notes GA (E) and NI (B) are used in ascent, GA komal (E♭) and NI komal (B♭) in descent. The performing artist must emphasize in descent the similarity with raga Bhimpalasi,[153] otherwise Haunskankani can be mistaken for raga Tilang.[154] There also exists a strong similarity between Haunskankani and raga Dhanashri.[155] The difference between these two ragas lies in the fact that Haunskankani uses the note GA (E) in its shuddha form in ascent while Dhanashri uses GA komal (E♭). There is one exception to the above-stated rule concerning Haunskankani, the occasional appearance of a descending gliding step GA-SA (E-C). The progression GA RE SA (E D C), however, is forbidden. Leaving aside this remarkable gliding step, Haunskankani can be described as a combination of elements taken from raga Tilang[156] in ascent and raga Bhimpalasi in descent.

In practice it can be noted that the notes <u>GA</u> (E) and <u>NI</u> (B) in ascent are not really <u>shuddha</u> but are mostly slightly high-altered forms of <u>GA komal</u> (E♭) and <u>NI komal</u> (B♭). It may happen quite frequently that one or both of these notes are notated in their <u>komal</u> forms, but the performing artists will invariably apply the required high microtonal intonation in each instance. This can be observed in the following song specimen in the first bar of the second and last lines.

RAGA HAUNSKANKANI   (Jhaptal)   BH, VI, 109

Tone material

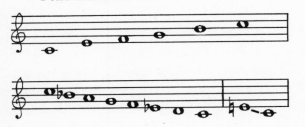

Raga Bageshri (Vagishvari)

This serious and "great" raga is to be performed at night. A pictorial description of this raga can be found in the Saṅgīta-Rāga-Kalpadrumā (p. 19):

> Bageshvari, the consort of Kaushik raga (Malkouns) is fair-complexioned, lovely and graceful. She has eyes like the lotus and loves playing the vina. She speaks charmingly when she is in the company of her lover.

The vadis of this raga are MA (F) and SA (C). The note RE (D) is avoided in ascent. PA (G) must be used only rarely and with caution. A total omission of this note, however, would destroy the character of Bageshri and would create too strong a similarity with raga Shriranjani.[157] The notes GA komal (E♭) and NI komal (B♭) appear in both ascent and descent. In practice, slightly high alterations of both notes can be observed in ascent if they lead to MA (F) and SA (c) respectively. In notated examples, shuddha forms of these two notes can be found which do not represent intonations of E and B naturals but only slightly high alterations of the komal forms.

These two altered notes are often performed with small vibratos.

The note PA (G), which is to be handled "with caution," usually appears in the following phrases:

The succession PA DHA NI komal (G A B♭) is permitted, but PA DHA NI komal SA (G A B♭ c) is forbidden. In the second instance the note PA (G) has to be avoided:

In descent, particularly in fast passages, the sequence NI komal DHA PA MA (B♭ A G F) may be observed because it is easier to sing than NI komal DHA MA (B♭ A F). In ascent, however, even in fast passages, the sequence MA DHA NI komal SA (F A B♭ c) must be maintained.

A similar method may be observed in the treatment of the note RE (D). This note is to be avoided in ascent. An exception to this rule may be made if RE (D) becomes the first (or last) note of a phrase:

If this note is not the lowest and first note of an ascending phrase, it has to be avoided. The succession SA RE GA komal MA is strictly forbidden.

RAGA BAGESHRI   (Jhaptal)   BH, III, 439

Asthayi

Tone material

Raga Bahar

This raga is to be performed at night. Its vadis are MA (F) and SA (C). Some musicians state that the note PA (G) is to be emphasized, an opinion which is not substantiated in practice. Raga Bahar represents a combination of elements taken from the raga Bageshri and the Kanada ragas.[158] The note NI (B) is generally used in ascent and NI komal (Bb) in descent. RE (D) is avoided in ascent. Bahar melodies often begin with the high SA (c), or NI komal (Bb), or move quickly up into this high region.

The Kanada phrase GA komal MA RE SA (Eb F D C) with a

characteristic vibrato on GA komal (E♭) is important in this raga.
The vibrato is performed in the following manner:

The ascent distinctly shows the relationship of Bahar to Bageshri:

or

In order to avoid too strong a similarity with Bageshri, musicians
often use the step SA MA (C F) in ascent:

The note GA komal (E♭) in ascent must not be followed by PA (G),
but by MA (F). The following steps are permitted in ascent: MA
PA (F G), MA DHA (F A) and MA NI komal (F B♭). PA (G) in
ascent may be followed by NI komal (B♭), but never by DHA (A).
In descent the note MA (F) is followed by RE SA (D C). The note
PA (G), however, may be followed by GA komal (E♭) or by the
Kanada phrase GA komal MA RE SA (E♭ F D C).

RAGA BAHAR   (Tivra Tal)   BH, IV, 597

Asthayi

Antara

Tone material

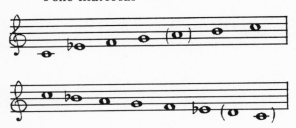

The creation of new ragas by combining elements of two or more
other ragas, a method much favored during the Mogul period, is to
some extent still in use.   These new compound ragas are always
greatly admired as great achievements.   It is important to state here
that the numerous new ragas which have been put together by such a
method are frequently far removed from the old complex forms, and
much of the ancient beauty and charm is missing.

     Bahar is a raga which is often combined with other ragas, into
Hindol-bahar, Vasant-bahar, Bhairav-bahar, Bageshri-bahar, Adana-
bahar, and many others. Hindol-bahar, for instance, is usually performed in such a manner that the musician confines himself to a
rendering of Bahar and then, without transition, suddenly changes
one or two passages to Hindol. This method is anything but satisfactory, because no artistic combination of the ragas is achieved —
only a poorly connected succession of materials of the two ragas.
There are, however, a few musicians who do not aim at surprising
their audiences with such sudden changes but create artful links

between the two ragas. In such instances the musician has to find a
note common to the two ragas, a note of sufficient musical weight,
across which a transition from one raga to the other can be effected.
A note which will cause no jarring effect is DHA (A) which, if carefully handled, will permit a plausible transition from Bahar to Hindol.

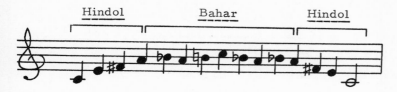

Another example of compound ragas is Vasant-bahar, in which the
common note SA (c) can serve as a transitional medium:

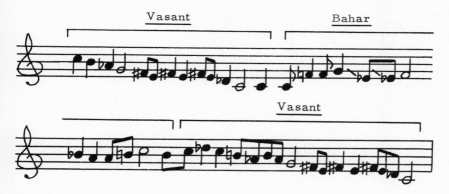

Raga Pilu

Pilu is a light, popular raga which is often described as being
of Persian origin. This raga is generally performed in the evening,
although the majority of musicians state that Pilu may be performed
at any time. As in other popular ragas, musicians usually tune their
instruments a pure fourth higher, whereby SA can be read as the note
F. In the present discussion of Pilu features, no such transposition
is made, and SA will be transcribed as C.

As Pilu is a light raga, its performance rules are so loose that
nearly all notes of the chromatic scale may be used. The vadis, which
are described as GA komal (E♭) and NI shuddha (B) are much less
important than in other ragas. The notes RE (D) and RE komal (D♭),

GA (E) and GA komal (E♭), DHA (A) and DHA komal (A♭), and NI (B)
and NI komal (B♭) can be employed ad libitum. Shuddha notes may
appear in ascent and their komal forms in descent, but it is equally
possible that komal notes may be used in ascent and their shuddha
forms in descent.

One frequently used phrase in Pilu is:

Further Pilu features are:

Even the note MA tivra (F#), a note foreign to the Kafi family, may
be used as a very lightly touched ornament in ascent before PA (G):

RAGA PILU   (Punjabi Tal)   BH, III, 621

Asthayi

Antara

The tone material of this raga changes from one performance to the
other; hence it is impossible to present a clearly defined scale.

Raga Palasi

This rare and little known raga is ascribed to the Kafi thata.
There are some musicians who deny the separate existence of the
ragas Palasi and Bhim[159] and insist that they are only variants of
raga Bhimpalasi.[160] Despite these arguments, raga Palasi can be
heard occasionally, and thus a claim is made for its separate existence.

Very little is known of raga Palasi. It has very few performance rules and no certain performance time. Its similarity to
raga Dhani is remarkable.[161] The vadis of Palasi are PA (G) and
SA (C). Here is the difference between Palasi and Dhani: in the
former raga the note PA (G) is strong, in the latter this note is
weak. The note DHA (A) is totally avoided in raga Palasi, and
RE (D) is usually omitted in ascent. The note RE (D) is used in
descent, a fact which contributes toward the similarity to raga
Dhani.

If the note NI komal (B♭) leads in ascent to SA (C or c), it is intoned slightly high. In the following song specimen, of which only sections are shown, both forms of NI, shuddha (B) and komal (B♭), are found notated in ascent. Both forms represent and require the microtonally high alteration of NI komal (B♭).

RAGA PALASI   (Jhaptal)   BH, VI, 113

Sanchari

Abhog

Tone material

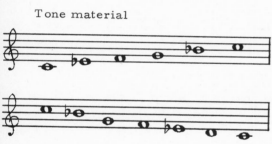

The Mallar Ragas

The Mallar (occasionally written Malhar) ragas are ascribed
to the Kafi thata. These are ragas which are performed primarily
during the monsoon, the rainy season which lasts from the middle of
June to the end of September. During the monsoon the Mallar ragas
can be performed at any time of the day or night. Outside of the
rainy season, however, the ragas are performed only in the late
afternoon or evening. Some of the Mallar ragas consist more or
less of the material of other ragas, to which are added characteristic Mallar phrases. The most important of these phrases are:

Another Mallar feature is the particular treatment of the note GA
komal (E♭). Whenever this note appears in Mallar ragas (with the
exception of fast passages) it is performed with a heavy gamak
(ornament) which here represents a heavy type of vibrato. The
note GA komal (E♭) is not distinctly intoned; it is approached, from
approximately MA (F), by means of several small successive descending gliding steps which do not exactly stop at GA komal (E♭)
but move slightly lower toward the note RE (D). There are instances

where the terminal point of these descending gliding steps indeed is the note RE (D). In general, however, this Mallar feature consists of several descending gliding steps moving vaguely between MA (F) and RE (D) which in all instances touch the note GA komal (Eb) in passing. This Mallar gamak, if notated, could be shown in the following manner:

It may be of some interest to compare here the Mallar gamak on GA komal (Eb) with the gamak performed on the same note in the Kanada ragas.[162] In the Kanada ragas the note GA komal (Eb) is the lowest point, the basis of a waving, slow vibrato in which the fundamental note remains comparatively unaltered. In the Mallar gamak, however, the note GA komal (Eb) is only vaguely touched upon, because the gliding steps move across it. The two gamakas can be presented graphically as follows:

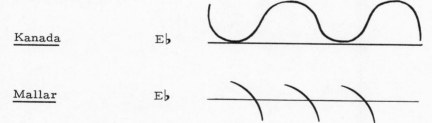

Kanada   Eb

Mallar   Eb

Raga Megh-mallar (Megha-mallar, Megh)

In the Sāngīta-Darpana (2, 76) the following pictorial description of Megh-mallar can be found:

> The Megha raga has the complexion of a blue lotus flower, and his face is beautiful and radiant like the moon. Dressed in yellow, he resides in the clouds. Sweetly smiling, the

तागमचमलार ...राःहाहुगाैडुः ककुः न्राैरयुूजर॑ःिन॑गालाबिसासःतिनहा
मिेचमलार नृपःिचतलकारतिबलासःचौपइः मेघमलारचतुरनपुनकिःनि
लतलकरतःश्रानहसहकिःप्रितबसनकाछएमग छालाःबरनसावनैेनविश्
लाःउमएणबिविधिनातीभ्रगबीयैःबनितासबेसाजकरलमेःउघतसबद
नालततकारःःबाजतउपगगहैरःभुएणनरीःश्रत्यअनबरएणपटामकाीश्रा
ःूमकतचमकतबरषाला याःडोहाःसंमोमुहावनसरसरितिःदेपतकरतकल
लःगावतानःतरगा राःगा हरारसबि न ॥३॥

Plate XIX. Raga Megh-mallar

DOHA: The king Megh-mallar is to be found with Gaud, Kukubha, Gurjari, Bangali, and Bibhas and spends his time dancing and in joyous sport.

CHAUPAYI: Megh-mallar is a good, wise king. He dances well and enjoys the pleasures of life with gay abandon. Of a slightly dusky complexion with bright shining eyes, king Megh-mallar is dressed handsomely, wearing a tiger skin, and adorned with various kinds of bright ornaments. He is in the company of beautiful maidens bedecked with jewels. The king dances with them to the resounding beat of drums and of clapping. The dancing and music bring forth clouds of various colors in the sky. The moving clouds thicken to the accompaniment of thunder and lightning, which brings the rain.

young Megha is the bravest of the brave. The thirsty
chataka bird which drinks only rain drops, craves when
he beholds him.

Popley offers the following description of this raga:

> The Megh-mallar raga is supposed to be able to produce
> rain. It is said that a dancing girl in Bengal, in a time
> of drought, once drew from the clouds with this raga a
> timely refreshing shower which saved the rice crop.
> Sir W. Ousley, who related many of these anecdotes,
> says that he was told by Bengal people that this power
> of reproducing the actual conditions of the raga is now
> only possessed by some musicians in western India,
> and by people in western India that such musicians can
> only be found in Bengal.[163]

The vadis of this raga are SA (C) and MA (F). Although the tone
material comes close to that of the Khamaj family, Megh-mallar has
been ascribed (e. g., by Pandit Bhatkhande) to the Kafi thata. The
gamakas require a slow, heavy performance.

There are three types of this raga. The first type totally avoids
the notes GA (E) and DHA (A). The note NI (B) appears in ascent
and NI komal (B♭) in descent. Of great interest are the gamakas in
the first type which do not occur on GA komal (E♭) but on the notes
RE (D), MA (F), PA (G), and on NI komal (B♭). Similar to the previously described gamak on GA komal (E♭), the gamak on RE (D)
consists of several, usually three, successive descending gliding
steps which begin with MA (F) and distinctly end RE (D):

The following specimen shows how the other gamakas on MA (F), PA
(G), and NI komal (B♭) are performed.

A second type of this raga employs the note <u>GA</u> <u>komal</u> (E♭) with the characteristic <u>Mallar</u> <u>gamak</u>:

In this type the note <u>GA</u> <u>komal</u> (E♭) must not be succeeded immediately by the note <u>RE</u> (D). However, the <u>gamak</u> on <u>RE</u> (D) may follow because it begins with the note <u>MA</u> (F).

A third type of <u>Megh-mallar</u> employs the note <u>DHA</u> (A) but avoids the <u>GA</u> <u>komal</u> (E♭) of the second type:

The following song specimen represents the first type, the one most frequently used. This type often employs the following phrases: <u>MA</u> <u>RE</u> <u>PA</u> (F D G), <u>MA</u> <u>RE</u> <u>SA</u> (F D C), <u>NI</u> <u>komal</u> <u>PA</u> <u>NI</u> <u>SA</u> (B♭ G B C [or c]), <u>NI</u> <u>komal</u> <u>PA</u> <u>SA</u> (B♭ G c), and <u>NI</u> <u>komal</u> <u>PA</u> <u>MA</u> (B♭ G F).[164]

RAGA MEGH-MALLAR   (Jhaptal)   First type   BH, VI, 227

Asthayi

Antara

The next song specimen represents the third type of this raga.

RAGA MEGH-MALLAR   (Trital)   Third type   BH, VI, 231

Asthayi

Antara

Tone material

First type

Second type

Third type

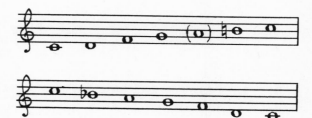

Raga Miyan-ki-mallar (Miyan-mallar)

    This raga is said to have been created by Miyan Tansen, the
famous court musician of Akbar the Great. He added the note GA
komal (E♭) with the gamak already described to the descending Mallar
scale. Miyan-ki-mallar is often called a "great raga" and only artists
with "great voices" should attempt to perform it. N. A. Willard presents the following pictorial description of this raga:

> . . . this raginee is delineated of a complexion wan and
> pale; she is decorated with the white jessamine, and sits
> sad and solitary, endeavouring to sooth and dissipate her
> melancholy, with the tones of the Veen, in happier days
> her delight. . . .[165]

The vadis of this raga are SA (C) and MA (F) or, according to some
musicians, MA (F) and SA (C). The note GA komal (E♭) is always
avoided in ascent. Once, in a song, I heard the sequence GA komal
MA PA (E♭ F G); but this was a very rare exception. In descent GA
komal (E♭) appears with the famous gamak and is followed by the
vakra phrase MA RE SA (F D C). This sequence (E♭ F D C) appears
also in the Kanada ragas, but there the note GA komal (E♭) is clearly
intoned, while in Miyan-ki-mallar it is partly hidden in the gliding
steps of the gamak. The note PA (G) must be succeeded in ascent
not by DHA (A) but by NI komal (B♭). The ascending NI komal (B♭)
is vakra and cannot be succeeded by the upper SA (c), but the (ascending) line has to perform a detour via DHA (A) which is followed
by NI shuddha (B). Only then may the upper SA (C) be used. The
correct ascent in Miyan-ki-mallar is therefore:

The preceding example shows that the direct ascent SA RE MA PA
(C D F G) is strictly forbidden.

    The descent in Miyan-ki-mallar also contains a number of
vakra steps which are characteristic. The note DHA (A) has to
be avoided and is generally hidden by the gliding step NI komal-PA

(Bb-G). If <u>DHA</u> (A) is used, the descending line has to turn upward
to <u>NI komal</u> (Bb), from where it may begin the gliding step toward
<u>PA</u> (G). The step <u>PA</u> <u>MA</u> (G F) is permitted, but after <u>MA</u> (F) the
melody has to return to <u>PA</u> (G), whereupon <u>GA komal</u> (Eb) follows
with the <u>Mallar gamak</u>, or the descending line may, in rare instances, avoid the note <u>GA komal</u> (Eb) and move straight to <u>RE</u> (D). <u>GA</u>
<u>komal</u> (Eb) is always followed by the sequence <u>MA</u> <u>RE</u> <u>SA</u> (F D C).

The treatment of the notes <u>NI komal</u> (Bb) and <u>NI</u> (B) in ascent requires
attention. Both notes, with <u>NI komal</u> (Bb) always <u>vakra</u>, appear in
wide ascending phrases. In order to reach <u>NI</u> (B), <u>NI komal</u> (Bb)
first has to move to a very short interpolated <u>DHA</u> (A), often called
a <u>kan</u>, as shown in the following example:

The gliding steps between <u>NI komal</u> (Bb) and <u>DHA</u> (A) have to be
performed slowly.

RAGA MIYAN-KI-MALLAR   (Ektal)   BH, IV, 557

Asthayi

Antara

Tone material

Raga Gaud-mallar

This raga can be ascribed to the Kafi or to the Khamaj thatas.
Gaud-mallar is usually a very serious raga which has to be performed

with much dignity in slow tempo.   There are five types of this raga:

1) Gaud-mallar with MA (F) as vadi; its scale employs GA (E),
    never GA komal (E♭);

2) Gaud-mallar with PA (G) as vadi; its scale employs GA (E);

3) Gaud-mallar with PA (G) as vadi; its scale employs GA komal
    (E♭), never GA (E);

4) Gaud-mallar with PA (G) as vadi; its scale employs both degrees
    of GA: GA shuddha (E) and GA komal (E♭);

5) Gaud-mallar with either MA (F) or PA (G) as vadi; its scale
    avoids both GA (E) and GA komal. This latter form is occa-
    sionally called Shuddh-mallar;[166] it resembles Megh-mallar.
    The difference between the fifth type of Gaud-mallar and Megh-
    mallar lies in the type of gamakas used. Megh, as we know,
    uses heavy gamakas, while the fifth type of Gaud-mallar has
    only light ornamentations. As a matter of fact, the character
    of this type of Gaud-mallar is much lighter than that of the
    former.

All five types of Gaud-mallar employ NI (B) in ascent and NI komal
(B♭) in descent and have the note SA (C) as samvadi.

First type

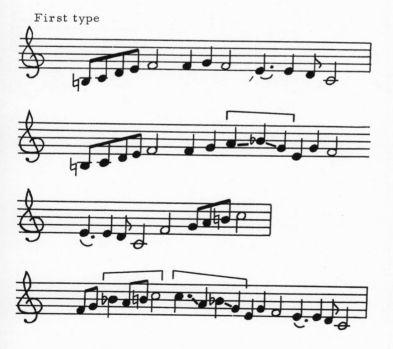

The note RE (D) is weak in both ascent and descent. The phrases
DHA NI komal PA (A B♭ G) or SA DHA NI komal PA (c A B♭ G), and
NI komal DHA NI SA (B♭ A B c) are characteristic of all Mallar ragas.

RAGA GAUD-MALLAR   (Trital)   First type   BH, IV, 542

Second type

This type differs from the first one only in the treatment of the notes
MA (F) and PA (G). As already mentioned, PA (G) is here the vadi.
The note RE (D) is treated in the Mallar manner: it is approached
twice or thrice by means of short descending gliding steps from MA (F

As there are no further differences between the first two types, the
second type requires no illustrative song specimen.

Third type

The use of the note <u>GA</u> <u>komal</u> (E♭) brings this type very close to
<u>Miyan-ki-mallar</u>. The difference between this type of <u>Gaud-mallar</u>
and <u>Miyan-ki-mallar</u> lies mainly in the tempo: this type of <u>Gaud-</u>
<u>mallar</u>, although stately, has a somewhat lighter character and gen-
erally requires a faster tempo for performance than does the heavy,
severe, slow <u>Miyan-ki-mallar</u>. The small gliding steps characteristic of all <u>Mallar</u> ragas are treated much lighter in this type of <u>Gaud-</u>
<u>mallar</u> than in the other <u>Mallar</u> ragas. Furthermore the wide gliding
step <u>NI</u>-<u>NI</u> <u>komal</u>-<u>NI</u> (B-B♭-B) of raga <u>Miyan-ki-mallar</u> does not
occur in the third type of <u>Gaud-mallar</u>. Another distinguishing sign
is that in this type of <u>Gaud-mallar</u> the step <u>PA DHA</u> (G A) is permitted; in <u>Miyan-ki-mallar</u>, however, it is forbidden.

Gaud-mallar   Miyan-ki-mallar

In fast passages

RAGA GAUD-MALLAR   (Trital)   Third type   BH, IV, 541

Asthayi

Antara

Fourth type

The uttaranga, the upper tetrachord of the scale, of this type of
Gaud-mallar is the same as those of the previously shown types.
In purvanga (lower tetrachord), however, GA (E) appears in
ascent, and GA komal (E♭) in the vakra phrase GA komal MA RE
SA (E♭ F D C).

RAGA GAUD-MALLAR   (Chautal)   Fourth type   BH, IV, 547

Asthayi

Antara

Fifth type

This type is occasionally called Shuddh-mallar and avoids both GA (E)
and GA komal (Eb). It is, however, possible to observe in some rare
instances the ornamental and subtle use of GA (E) immediately before
the note MA (F), as in the following song specimen in bars one and four
of the sixth line.

RAGA GAUD-MALLAR   (Trital)   Fifth type   BH, IV, 527

Asthayi

Antara

A comparison of the preceding song specimen with that representing
the third type of this raga may be of interest.

Tone material

First and
Second types

Third type

Fourth type

Fifth type

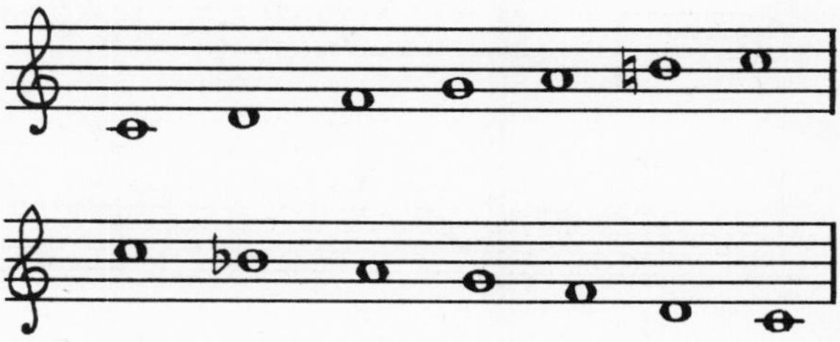

Raga Shuddh-mallar

Besides the fifth type of Gaud-mallar, there exists another Shuddh-mallar, which allegedly represents the original form of Mallar before it was altered by Tansen.   There are numerous arguments concerning the correctness of this raga, and many important North Indian musicians state that the fifth type of Gaud-mallar is the only correct form of Shuddh-mallar.   Other musicians, however, insist that Shuddh-mallar is a raga of its own and is not derived from Gaud-mallar.   The pictorial representation of Shuddh-mallar is described in several works.   In the Sangita-Darpana (2, 77) we find:

> The fair-bodied Mallarika has become pale and weak and sings sadly like the cuckoo. Her singing reminds her of her master, her beloved. In pain and sorrow with the pangs of separation she starts playing a sorrowful tune on her vina.

In the Rāga-Sāgara (3, 7) we read:

> I think of Mallari who is pure and chaste and worships Lord Shiva devoutly. Dwelling under the divine tree, she is like a lotus flower blossoming in the cold months, and her body has the complexion of winter clouds.

This raga is very rare and differs from the fifth type of Gaud-mallar in that it avoids not only both forms of GA, GA komal (E♭) and GA shuddha (E), but also both forms of NI, NI komal (B♭) and NI shuddha (B). Despite this rule, the note GA (E) is occasionally employed as a subtle ornamentation before MA (F). The vadis of this raga are PA (G) and SA (C).

The following example shows the characteristic Mallar phrases MA RE PA (F D G) and MA RE SA (F D C).

No song specimen of this raga could be found.

Before considering the next Mallar raga, it may be of interest to compare similar forms such as Shuddh-mallar, Durga (Bilaval thata),[167] and Jaladhara-kedar.[168]

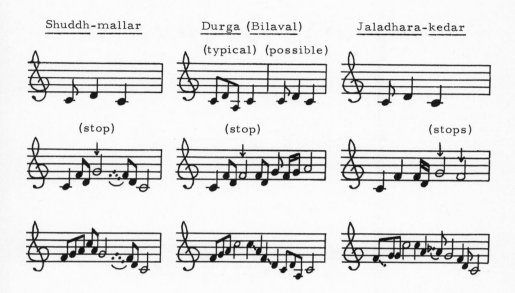

Shuddh-mallar   Durga (Bilaval)   Jaladhara-kedar
                 (typical) (possible)

(stop)   (stop)   (stops)

Raga Nath-mallar

This raga consists of material taken from raga Nath[169] and Mallar phrases. The vadis are MA (F) and SA (C). Two types of this raga can be distinguished: 1) Nath-mallar which employs only GA shuddha (E). This type is greatly favored by the musicians of Rampur and has come into use by an increasing number of musicians in North India; 2) Nath-mallar which uses GA (E) in ascent and GA komal (E♭) in descent, a rare type. There is no distinguishing feature between the two types other than the use of one or both forms of the note GA. The purvanga (lower tetrachord) of this raga shows more or less Nath affinity, particularly to raga Chhayanath.[170]

Nath

<u>Mallar</u> phrases appear also in other parts of ascent and descent:

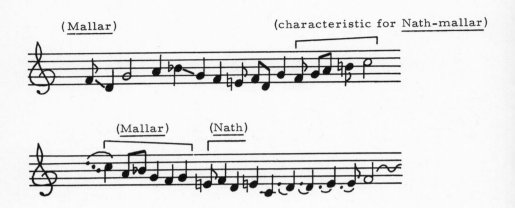

First type

A characteristic <u>Nath</u> phrase often used in this raga is:

There exists a certain similarity between this type of <u>Nath-mallar</u>
and the first type of <u>Gaud-mallar</u>. The difference lies in the treatment of the note <u>RE</u> (D). In <u>Gaud-mallar</u> this note is weak, in

<u>Nath-mallar</u> it is strong.

Gaud-mallar   Nath-mallar (very slow)

It may be anticipated here that the second type of <u>Gaud-mallar</u> cannot
be easily mistaken for <u>Nath-mallar</u> because the <u>vadis</u> in the two ragas
are different.   The main distinction, as has already been stated, is
that the singer has to treat the note <u>RE</u> (D) weakly in <u>Gaud-mallar</u>
and strongly in <u>Nath-mallar</u>.   Deviation from this rule would cause
considerable confusion.

RAGA NATH-MALLAR   (Tilvada)   First type   BH, VI, 267

Asthayi

Antara

Second type

Of interest is the succession <u>GA</u> <u>komal</u> <u>GA</u> <u>shuddha</u> (E♭ E), in which both notes are performed with the characteristic <u>Mallar</u> <u>gamak.</u>

RAGA NATH-MALLAR   (Trital)   Second type   BH, VI. 266

Asthayi

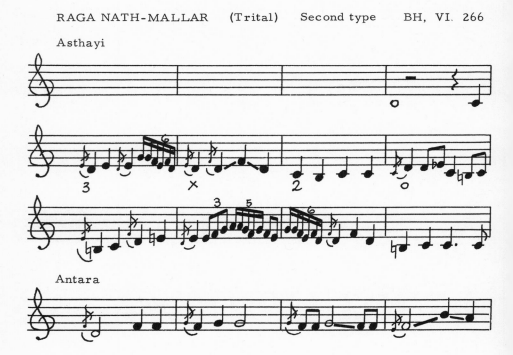

Antara

Tone material

First type

Second type

Raga Sur-mallar

The vadis of this raga are MA (F) and SA (C). Sur-mallar represents a combination of elements taken from the raga Sarang[171] to
which are added Mallar phrases. The note GA (E) is totally avoided.

DHA (A) has to be treated extremely weakly but must not be fully
avoided, because its use prevents too strong a similarity with
Sarang.   There are some songs in which DHA (A) is avoided entirely; in such instances a good performer will introduce the note
DHA (A) in his alap.   This note appears usually as an appoggiatura before NI komal (B♭), or it may be interpolated in descent as
a very weak note between NI komal (B♭) and PA (G).   As in
numerous other ragas, NI (B) is used in ascent and NI komal (B♭)
in descent.

There are a few instances in which the note GA komal (E♭) is
used in descent as a very weak ornament. Any stronger treatment of this note would create confusion, and raga Sur-mallar
could then be mistaken for the ragas Adana[172] or Suha.[173]   The
similarity of raga Sur-mallar with raga Sorath[174] has already
been mentioned.

     The following song specimen is a thumri, a popular love song.

RAGA SUR-MALLAR   (Trital)   BH, VI, 251

Asthayi

Antara

Tone material

Raga Ramdasi-mallar

The performance rules of this raga are indistinct, and even the
revered dhrupad melodies, which usually offer information on the
correct performance of a raga, show many discrepancies. The vadis
of Ramdasi-mallar are MA (F) and SA (C). In ascent usually GA (E)
and NI (B) appear, although the low SA (C) is reached (in ascent)
from the low NI komal (B♭). In descent GA komal (E♭) and NI komal
(B♭) appear. The note GA komal (E♭) in descent occurs in the vakra
phrase GA komal MA RE SA (E♭ F D C).

Indian musicians occasionally speak of a type of Ramdasi-mallar
which uses GA komal (E♭) both in ascent and descent. It was impossible to gain any further information about this unusual type.

The characteristic phrases of Ramdasi-mallar are:

The phrases MA NI komal PA (F B♭ G) and MA RE PA (F D G), the

Mallar gamak on GA komal (E♭), the scarce use of the note DHA (A)
which appears only in ascent, and the sequence SA RE GA MA PA (C
D E F G), which is strictly forbidden in Miyan-ki-mallar, all play
an important role in this raga. As the note DHA (A) is avoided in
descent, the descending gliding step NI komal-PA (B♭-G) can be
observed frequently.

RAGA RAMDASI-MALLAR   (Dhamar Tal)   BH, VI, 263

Asthayi

Tone material

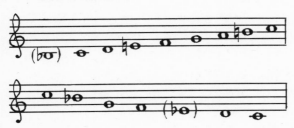

Raga Rupamanjari-mallar

Little is known about this rare raga. A few musicians of the
old school know some songs in these obscure ragas, songs which are
never presented to audiences and are only very rarely handed down
from teacher to pupil. The vadis of this raga are probably MA (F)
and SA (C), or PA (G) and SA (C). The very rare performances of
Rupamanjari-mallar create the impression that it consists of materials taken from three ragas: Mallar, Bilaval,[175] and Des.[176] In the
majority of instances the note GA (E) appears. However, in one
phrase GA komal (E♭) is used, which shows the affinity with raga
Kafi. The note DHA (A) appears generally between two NI komal
(B♭). NI komal (B♭) is used both in ascent and descent, but, as in
other Mallar ragas, NI shuddha (B) may occasionally appear in ascent.

RAGA RUPAMANJARI-MALLAR   (Rupak)   BH, VI, 278

Asthayi

Antara

Tone material

Raga Mirabai-ki-mallar

The "Mallar of the Mirabai" consists of a combination of phrases taken from Adana-kanada[177] and Mallar. The vadis are SA (C) and PA (G), or MA (F). The notes GA (E), DHA (A), and NI (B) are used in ascent; and GA komal (Eb), DHA komal (Ab), and NI komal (Bb) in descent.

Mallar

Adana-kanada

characteristic from
Mirabai-ki-mallar

Kanada (or Mallar)

The last phrase in the preceding example can be ascribed either to
the Kanada or Mallar forms, depending on the manner in which the
note GA komal (Eb) is rendered. If it is performed with successive
descending gliding steps which move toward RE (D) and only touch GA
komal (Eb), it assumes an affinity with Mallar. If, however, the
note GA komal (Eb) becomes the lowest point in a waving, light vibrato and is intoned slightly low, it points toward the Kanada group of
ragas. The preceding example shows, besides the treatment of GA
komal (Eb), two further microtonally low alterations, one on the
note GA shuddha (E) and the other on DHA (A), both appearing in a
phrase characteristic of Mirabai-ki-mallar.

RAGA MIRABAI-KI-MALLAR   (Chautal)   BH, VI, 272

Asthayi

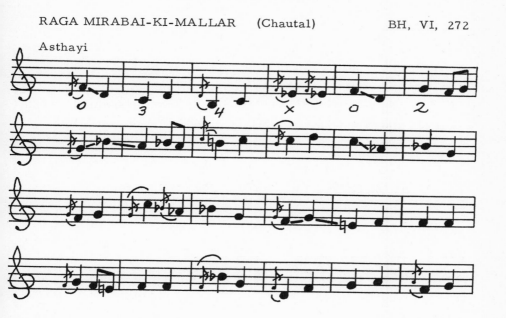

Antara

Tone material

Raga Naiki-mallar

This raga is very rare and its performance rules are obscure. The vadis are probably MA (F) and SA (C), or SA (C) and MA (F). Naiki-mallar, as indicated by its name, is a combination of phrases taken from Naiki-kanada[178] and Mallar. It was impossible to obtain an adequate song specimen. The constituent phrases are:

Naiki (or Mallar)

Naiki

Mallar

Each of these three phrases may be followed by the phrase shown below, a phrase which also contains elements from <u>Naiki</u> and <u>Mallar</u>.

Naiki   Mallar

The tone material can be derived from the scales of <u>Mallar</u> forms and <u>Naiki-kanada</u>.

Raga Jayant-mallar

<u>Jayant-mallar</u> is another of the obscure <u>Mallar</u> forms. The <u>vadis</u> are <u>PA</u> (G) and <u>SA</u> (C), or vice versa. This raga represents a combination of <u>Mallar</u> elements with one or more phrases taken from raga <u>Jayjayvanti</u>.[179]   Usually <u>Mallar</u> features appear in ascent, and <u>Jayjayvanti</u> material in descent, particularly in the <u>purvanga</u>, the lower tetrachord. No adequate song specimen could be obtained.

Jayjayvanti

The tone material can be derived from the scales of Mallar forms
and Jayjayvanti.

Raga Charajuki-mallar

As far as I know, there exists only a single song melody in this
raga. It is shown below, a melody which is hardly ever sung but can
be heard occasionally during the rainy season as an instrumental
piece. The vadis are PA (G) and SA (C). The notes GA komal (E♭)
and DHA (A) are used only in descent, and the lower SA (C), the
first note of the middle octave region, can be reached in descent only
from GA komal (E♭), not from RE (D). In the upper octave region,
however, the descent GA komal RE SA (e♭ d c) is permitted.

There is a strong similarity between Charajuki-mallar and raga
Sindhura.[180] The difference between the two ragas lies in the fact
that the sequence GA komal RE SA (E♭ D C) in the middle octave
region is forbidden in Charajuki-mallar, while it is allowed in
Sindhura.

The following is a typical Charajuki-mallar alap fragment:

As in the majority of Mallar ragas, NI (B) appears in ascent and NI komal (B♭) in descent.

RAGA CHARAJUKI-MALLAR   (Chautal)   BH, VI, 273

Asthayi

Antara

Tone material

Raga Des-mallar

Des-mallar is another obscure Mallar type ascribed to the Kafi
family. As the name indicates, we are dealing here with a combination of elements taken from Des[181] and Mallar. The combination depends on the ingenuity of the performing musician. Although there
are numerous possibilities of combining elements of the two ragas,
three possibilities seem to be the favorites of modern North Indian
musicians:

a) The use of Des material in ascent and Mallar material in descen

Des   Mallar

b) The use of Mallar material in ascent and Des material in the
    uttaranga (upper tetrachord) of the descent:

c) The use of Mallar material in ascent and in the uttaranga of the
    descent, and Des material in the purvanga (lower tetrachord)
    of the descent:

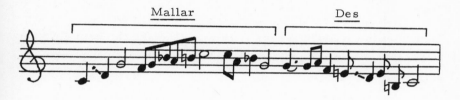

The performance rules of this raga are somewhat ambiguous; if the
Mallar features predominate, Des features (vadi, etc.) have to appear
on the sam in order to create a balance between the two ragas; and,
conversely, if the Des features predominate, Mallar material will
be observed on the sam. The features of the raga "opposing" the
predominant raga usually represent on the sam the beginning of the
melody.

No adequate song specimen was obtained.

Raga Chanchalasasa-mallar

Chanchalasasa-mallar can be heard only rarely. It consists of
several phrases taken from the ragas Sarang,[182] Kanada,[183] and Mallar
and possesses a few characteristic features of its own. Its vadis are
MA (F) and SA (C). The note DHA (A) is totally avoided.

Of interest is the use of the note GA komal (E♭). It appears only in
the Kanada phrase, which usually occurs only once or twice in a song.
The note NI komal (B♭) may be intoned slightly high in ascent. The
last phrase, which is annotated with Chanchalasasa and is characteristic of this raga, has a certain similarity with raga Devsakh;[184] the
difference between it and Devsakh is that in Devsakh the note GA komal
(E♭) is used, while in the related Chanchalasasa phrase this note is
avoided.

RAGA CHANCHALASASA-MALLAR   (Chautal)   BH, VI, 274

Asthayi

Antara

Tone material

Raga Dhulia-mallar

The groups of the Mallar ragas end with raga Dhulia-mallar. The vadis of this raga are PA (G) and SA (C). Occasionally the note MA (F) is treated so strongly that it can be considered as the vadi. In this raga the Mallar features are subordinate, and phrases taken from the ragas Des and Sarang predominate.

The descent from PA (G) to SA (C) is usually performed PA MA RE GA komal SA (G F D Eb C). The direct sequence PA MA GA komal RE SA (G F Eb D C) is never used.

There is a certain similarity between this raga and raga Lankadahan-sarang. The difference between the two ragas lies in the treatment of the note GA komal (Eb). This note has a much greater importance in <u>Lankadahan-sarang</u> than in <u>Dhulia-mallar</u>.

The note <u>DHA</u> (A) is employed either in ascent or between two <u>NI</u> <u>komal</u> (B♭). <u>NI</u> (B) appears in ascent and <u>NI</u> <u>komal</u> (B♭), in descent.

RAGA DHULIA-MALLAR   (Chautal)   BH, VI, 275

Tone material

Raga Chandrakauns

The performance time of this raga is uncertain. The vadis
are MA (F) and SA (C). In two of the three types of this raga the
notes RE (D) and PA (G) are totally avoided. The three types of
Chandrakauns are:

a) Chandrakauns with DHA (A) and NI komal (B♭)

    This resembles raga Bageshri.[185] The difference between the
    two ragas lies in the use of the note PA (G); in Bageshri this
    note can be used occasionally; in Chandrakauns, as has already
    been stated, it is strictly forbidden. The same is applicable to
    the use and avoidance of the note RE (D). Raga Chandrakauns
    also shows some similarity with raga Shriranjani,[186] which
    will be discussed below.

or:

The note GA komal (E♭) is often performed with the Mallar vibrato.

b) Chandrakauns with DHA komal (A♭) and NI (B)
This type, which is rather far removed from the Kafi family,
was created by Professor Deodhar of Bombay.

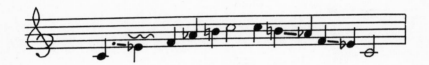

The Chandrakauns characteristic in this type is the total avoidance of the notes RE (D) and PA (G).

c) Chandrakauns with RE komal (D♭), PA (G), DHA komal (A♭),
and NI komal (B♭)
This type is still further removed from the Kafi group and show
hardly any relationship with the typical Chandrakauns features—
the avoidance of the notes RE (D) and PA (G).   In this type PA
(G) and the komal form of RE (D♭) appear in descent.   One
could describe this type as a combination of the raga Malkauns[1]
in ascent and raga Bhairavi[188] in descent.   It is a type favored
by the musicians of the Agra school.

The notes MA (F) and GA komal (E♭) are usually vakra in
descent, particularly when they appear for the first time. MA
(F), instead of leading in descent to GA komal (E♭), requires
the performer to turn back to PA (G), from where a partially
straight descent may be made, PA MA GA komal (G F E♭).
At GA komal (E♭) in descent another vakra turn has to occur by
by turning back to MA (F). Only after this MA (F) can the
low SA (C) be reached in descent by the progression MA GA
komal RE komal SA (F E♭ D♭ C).

The following song specimen represents the first type of
this raga.

RAGA CHANDRAKAUNS   (Sultal)   First type   BH, VI, 289

Asthayi

Antara

Tone material

First type

Second type

Third type

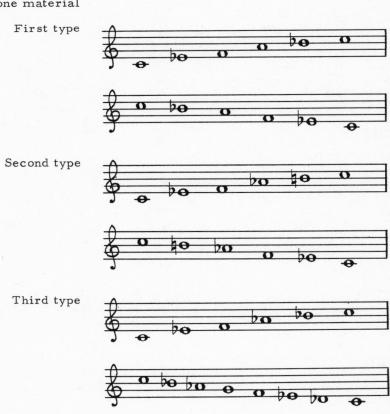

Raga Shriranjani

Shriranjani can be ascribed to the Kafi thata. Its vadis are MA (F) and SA (C). The note PA (G) is totally avoided. RE (D) has to be avoided in ascent but may be used in descent. This feature constitutes the difference between Shriranjani and the first type of raga Chandrakauns, where the note RE (D) is also avoided in descent. A strong similarity between Shriranjani and Abhogi-kanada[189] can cause occasional dissension among performers. The difference between these two ragas lies again in the use of the note RE (D). In Abhogi-kanada this note can be used in ascent while it is forbidden (in ascent) in Shriranjani. This latter rule is not always observed; there are some performers who employ RE (D) in the ascending line of Shriranjani, particularly in fast passages; a habit which does not find approval by serious musicians.

RAGA SHRIRANJANI   (Ektal)

BH, VI, 281

Asthayi

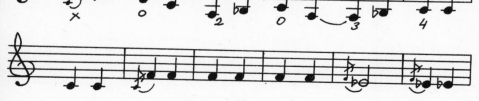

Antara

Tone material

Raga Patmanjari

There exists another raga with the same name, occasionally also called Bangal-bilaval,[190] which is ascribed to the Bilaval family. Raga

Patmanjari of the Kafi thata is to be performed in the afternoon in a
manner similar to the Sarang ragas.[191]   Its vadis are SA (C) and PA
(G). There are two types of this raga:

a) Patmanjari, Sarang-anga (Patmanjari similar to the Sarang
types), in which the Sarang phrase SA RE MA PA (C D F G)
plays a considerable role. The notes GA komal (E♭) and DHA
(A) are avoided in ascent. In fast passages, however, a performer may use the sequence RE GA komal MA GA komal RE
SA (D E♭ F E♭ D C) instead of RE RE MA GA komal RE SA (D
D F E♭ D C) because it is easier to sing and play. Of interest
is the fact that the note PA (G), the samvadi, is avoided in
descent in all those instances when the melody begins its descent from a note higher than PA (G). If, however, PA (G) is
the highest note of a descending phrase, no restrictions are
prescribed. Steps such as PA MA (G F) and PA SA (G C) are
permitted. The descending steps PA GA komal (G E♭) and PA
RE (G D), however, are either avoided or are used very rarely.
The note NI komal (B♭) in ascent is often altered microtonally
high. In notated songs one can observe occasionally the note
NI shuddha (B), although a well-informed musician will know
that this note is always a slightly high intoned NI komal (B♭).

RAGA PATMANJARI   (Adachautal)   First type   BH, VI, 153

Asthayi

Antara

b) Patmanjari with GA shuddha (E) and GA komal (E♭)

This type of Patmanjari resembles to some extent raga
Patadip,[192] particularly in its uttaranga (upper tetrachord).
Both GA (E) and GA komal (E♭) are used in the following
manner:

In this second type of Patmanjari the microtonally high intonation of

NI komal (B♭) is occasionally so intense that the result is a distinct
NI shuddha (B).   The Sarang phrase which plays an important role
in the first type of this raga does not occur here.

No adequate song specimen could be found.

Tone Material

First type

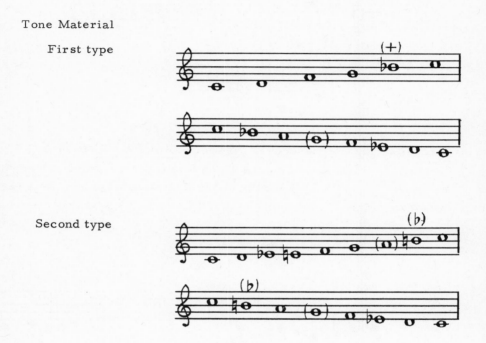

Second type

Raga Malgunj (Malgunji)

It can be assumed that the vadis of this little known raga are MA
(F) and SA (C).   The note GA (E) is used in ascent and GA komal (E♭)
in descent.   PA (G) is avoided in ascent.   RE (D), too, is either avoided in ascent or is treated so weakly that it has no other function than
that of a subtle appoggiatura.   The note GA komal (E♭) is often performed with a small, gentle vibrato.   Both NI shuddha (B) and NI komal
(B♭) may be used, and one may be substituted for the other.

In raga Malgunj the descent SA NI komal DHA PA MA (c B♭ A G F) is straight. This is the feature which distinguishes between Malgunj and raga Bageshri,[193] where the direct descent occurs only as a rare exception to the rule.

RAGA MALGUNJ   (Chautal)   BH, VI, 414

Asthayi

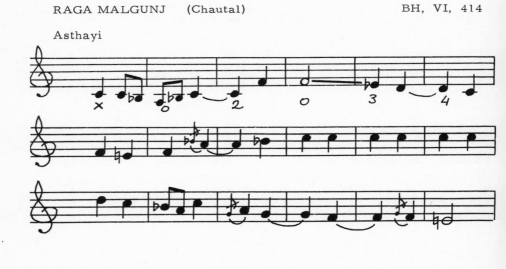

Antara

Tone material

Raga Gaud

This raga is to be performed in the afternoon. Its vadis are MA (F) and SA (C). Gaud consists to a great extent of Kanada and Mallar phrases. It is important to note that GA komal (E♭) is performed in this raga with the Kanada vibrato and not with the Mallar gamak. The note NI (B) is used in ascent and NI komal (B♭) appears in descent.

As there is very little known about the performance rules of this raga,
the following song specimen is shown in its entirety.

RAGA GAUD   (Jhaptal)   BH, VI, 292

Sanchari

Antara (Abhog)

Tone material

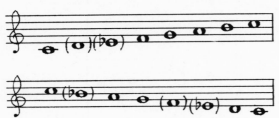

The Sarang Ragas

The majority of the group of Sarang ragas belongs to the Kafi thata. Most Sarang types are to be performed at noon or in the early afternoon. Some of the Sarang ragas show strong relationships with the Kalyan, Bilaval, and Khamaj thatas. For instance, raga Gaud-sarang,[194] which is ascribed to the Kalyan thata, has been described before. Similar examples are the ragas Badhauns-sarang[195] and Nur-sarang.[196]

Raga Bindrabani-sarang (Sarang)

This raga is the prototype of the Sarang group and is often called simply Sarang. Sarang is supposed to represent the quiet and tender mood of the noonday. In his Rāga Mālā, Puṇḍarika Viṭṭhala describes the pictorial aspect of this raga in the following manner:

> His body of a dark green hue, dressed in yellow, he holds the conch, the lotus, the mace and the chakra and a quiver filled with arrows tied to his waist [This is the description of Lord Vishnu, who is traditionally known to carry shankh, the conch horn, the chakra, a discus, the gada (mace), and the padma (lotus) in his four hands]. He rides on his mount, the Garuda bird. Sarang is to be sung in the [early] afternoon.

In the Cattvārimsacchata-Rāga-Nirūpanam (p. 16) this raga is des-cribed as follows:

> Sarang, the leader among the ragas, is fond of flowers and bouquets and he delights in liquor. He is the pride of the god of love.

The vadis of this raga are RE (D) and PA (G). The note GA (E) is totally avoided, and DHA (A) is avoided in ascent and appears only as a weak ornament in descent. The note NI shuddha (B) is employed in ascent and NI komal (B♭) in descent. Bindrabani-sarang has no vakra steps, and melodies in this raga can move rather freely. In descent there are two gliding steps which are frequently used, NI

komal-PA (B♭-G) and MA-RE (F-D). Both are performed lightly
and quickly, in contrast to the much heavier steps of the Mallar ragas.
The Sarang formula can be shown as follows:

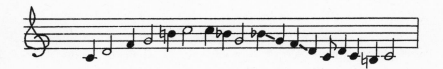

RAGA BINDRABANI-SARANG   (Dhamar Tal)   BH, III, 552

Asthayi

Antara

Tone Material

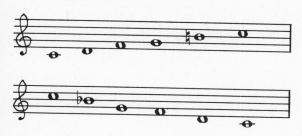

Raga Madhyamadi-sarang (Madhmadi)

For centuries this raga was considered to be obscure, and its performance rules were vague and confusing. During a conference of Indian musicians held twenty or twenty-five years ago, the characteristic features and performance rules were finally clarified, and today Madhyamadi-sarang is comparatively distinct. The vadis are RE (D) and PA (G). The notes GA (E) and DHA (A) are totally avoided. The note NI komal (Bb) appears both in ascent and descent, in contrast to Bindrabani-sarang, where NI shuddha (B) is used in the ascending line. The descending step PA RE (G D) represents a characteristic feature of this raga, while MA RE (F D) is characteristic in Bindrabani-sarang.

Despite the recently postulated rule that NI komal (Bb) also has to be used in ascent, some musicians employ NI shuddha (B) instead. This confuses the distinction between Bindrabani and Madhyamadi-sarang. But even in such ambiguous instances, we are able to keep the two ragas apart if the characteristic step PA RE (G D) occurs. The similarities between Madhyamadi-sarang and Badhauns-sarang[197] will be considered below.

Madhyamadi melodies usually begin with the upper NI komal (Bb) and continue with a descending motion. The essential phrases of this raga are:

RAGA MADHYAMADI-SARANG   (Jhaptal)   BH, VI, 119

Tone material

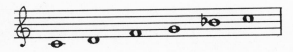

Raga Badhauns-sarang

Pandit Bhatkhande ascribes this raga to the Kafi thata. Some
musicians place it in the Khamaj, others even in the Bilaval thata.
Badhauns-sarang is rare and its performance rules are indistinct.
There is a gramophone recording made in the 1930's on which Amanath
Khan performs a song with the title Rangadi Jiva. The record label
states it is in raga Madhyamadi, but careful listening shows that the
raga is Badhauns. The differences between the two ragas are small
but can be noticed, as will be shown below.

The vadis of Badhauns are RE (D) and PA (G). The note MA
(F) is very strong. As in Bindrabani-sarang, the notes GA (E) and
DHA (A) are, in theory at least, avoided. In practice, however, both
notes are occasionally used. NI (B) appears in ascent, NI komal (B♭)
in descent, a rule which is also not always strictly obeyed. Badhauns
melodies, similar to those of Madhyamadi, usually begin with a descending movement from the upper NI komal (B♭) or, in instances
where musicians feel free to disregard rules, even from NI shuddha
(B).

In order to describe this raga, a comparison between Badhauns
and Madhyamadi may be of use. Badhauns melodies may be interrupted or stopped not only on the vadis, but also on the notes MA (F)
and NI komal (B♭). The descending step MA RE (F D) in Badhauns
is important. Madhyamadi melodies, however, can be interrupted
or stopped on PA (G) and their characteristic step is the descending
PA RE (G D).

Badhauns-sarang

Madhyamadi-sarang

It is more difficult to define the differences between Badhauns and Bindrabani-sarang. One could say that Badhauns is a type of Bindrabani in which the performance rules, particularly those forbidding the use of the notes GA (E) and DHA (A), have been relaxed. There are some musicians who purposely employ these two notes in Badhauns in order to create a distinct difference from Bindrabani. This practice is not acceptable to serious musicians.

RAGA BADHAUNS-SARANG   (Jhumra)   BH, VI, 135

Tone material

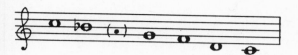

Raga Miyan-ki-sarang

This serious raga was created by the court singer Tansen. The vadis are RE (D) and SA (C) or PA (G). Miyan-ki-sarang represents a combination of elements of Sarang and Mallar. Mallar features are observed mainly in the uttaranga (upper tetrachord), particularly in the phrase NI komal DHA NI SA (Bb A B c), in which DHA (A) appears immediately after NI komal (Bb). In songs, never in alaps, we can also find the progression NI DHA SA (B A c) or NI SA DHA PA DHA (B c A G A). NI shuddha (B) usually appears in ascent and NI komal (Bb) in descent. The note DHA (A) is often performed with a short, shallow, smooth vibrato and the note GA (E) is totally avoided.

Important phrases of this raga are:

typical

Mallar

The descending (gliding) step MA-RE (F-D) appears frequently.

RAGA MIYAN-KI-SARANG   (Tilvada)   BH, VI, 142

Asthayi

[sic]

Antara

Tone material

Raga Lankadahan-sarang

In the Saṅgīta-Sāra, a Hindi work written by the Maharajah Sawai Pratap Sinha Deo of Jaipur, we find the following description of this raga:

> Now the picture (image) of Lanka-dahan is written. His complexion is fair, he is dressed in a white robe, he is turning a lotus in his hand, his eyes are large, his tresses are long, he is an adept in the Art of Love, his body is soft, he wears jewels on all his limbs, he carries a staff in his other hand, he is contemplating in his heart on the God Siva, he is associated with his friends. A raga thus visualized should be recognized as Lanka-dahan.[198]

Its vadis are RE (D) and PA (G). This raga represents a combination of elements of Sarang in ascent and of Kanada in descent. The Kanada feature in this raga emphasizes the typical vibrato on GA komal (E♭). The note NI (B) appears in ascent and NI komal (B♭) in descent.

RAGA LANKADAHAN-SARANG   (Dhamar Tal)   BH, VI, 148

Asthayi

Antara

Tone material

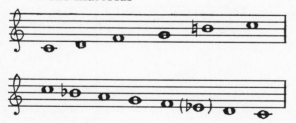

Raga Samant-sarang

The vadis of this raga are RE (D) and PA (G). Samant-sarang represents a combination of Bindrabani-sarang and one phrase, in which the note DHA (A) appears in descent, taken from raga Des.[199] As is to be expected, GA (E) is avoided, and NI (B) and NI komal (B♭) appear in the usual way, the former in ascent, the latter in descent.

The phrase borrowed from raga <u>Des</u>, <u>NI komal DHA PA</u> (B♭ A G),
usually begins in <u>Samant</u> with the note <u>MA</u> (F); <u>MA NI komal DHA PA</u>
(F B♭ A G).

RAGA SAMANT-SARANG   (Jhaptal)   BH, VI, 139

Asthayi

Antara

Tone material

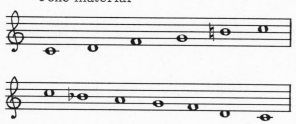

Raga Nur-sarang

This unusual raga concludes the Sarang group. It cannot be ascribed to the Kafi thata because it uses MA tivra (F#) instead of MA shuddha (F). This raga is better ascribed to the Kalyan thata than to any other family. The matter of classifying this raga becomes somewhat complex because there are three types of Nur-sarang which differ from each other and, with changes in their scales, claim affinity to various thatas. The vadis of Nur-sarang are RE (D) (or SA [C]) and PA (G).

The first type of Nur-sarang has nearly the same features as Bindrabani-sarang, except that this type of Nur-sarang employs only NI shuddha (B) in both ascent and descent.

A second type of this raga adds the notes MA (F) and NI komal
(B♭) to the scale of the first type. These changes create features
which are extremely rare in North Indian music; we observe the unusual descending gliding steps NI-NI komal (B-B♭) and MA tivra-
MA (F# -F).

A third type of Nur-sarang employs a slightly touched DHA (A)
in descent, where it appears between NI (B) and PA (G). If the descent proceeds from NI komal (B♭) to PA (G), the note DHA (A) is
avoided. In the mandra saptaka (low octave region) NI DHA SA (B A
C) occasionally appears, which creates some resemblance to the
raga Shuddh-sarang.[200]

No adequate song specimen could be found.

Tone material

First type

Second type

Third type

THE ĀSAVARI THĀTA

The scale of this thāta represents the material of the eighth family of North Indian ragas.

Raga Asavari (Asaveri)

The pictorial representations and descriptions of this important raga differ considerably. In the Cattvārimsacchata-Rāga-Nirūpanam (p. 22) we read:

> The sages hold that Asavari, deeply fond of music, looks majestic with her breasts decorated with crimson powder, sitting near her lover.

In the Rāga-Sāgara (3, 65) we find:

> I remember Asavari, clad in red, fair and beautiful with charming nails, in the posture of bending low and looking up while she supports her round breasts with her arms and tries to cover them with her garment which is loosely falling off.

In the Saṅgīta-Darpana (2, 75) and several other works the description is:

> Her complexion is of a shining blueish tint. Dressed with the feathers of a peacock and wearing a charming necklace of rare pearls, Asavari drags serpents from the sandal tree on the peak of a mountain, and wears them boldly as bracelets.

Despite the varying interpretations, Asavari is considered to be a quiet, even gentle, raga which is to be performed in the morning.

There are two types of Asavari:

a) Asavari (representing the scale of the Asavari thata) with RE shuddha (D);

b) Asavari with RE komal (Db), a type which stands close to raga Bhairav and occasionally is also ascribed to the Bhairav thata.

Raga <u>Asavari</u> with <u>RE</u> (D):

The <u>vadi</u> is <u>DHA</u> <u>komal</u> (A♭) and the <u>samvadi</u> is <u>GA</u> <u>komal</u> (E♭).
The ascending scale of this type of <u>Asavari</u> is <u>SA</u> <u>RE</u> <u>MA</u> <u>PA</u> <u>DHA</u>
<u>komal</u> <u>SA</u> (C D F G A♭ c) and the descending scale has the additional
notes <u>NI</u> <u>komal</u> (B♭) and <u>GA</u> <u>komal</u> (E♭). These two notes are performed (in descent) with a short, very light vibrato.

RAGA ASAVARI   (with RE)   (Chautal)   BH. II, 349

Asthayi

Antara

रागनिन्त्रासावरी:॥३५॥चांप रू न्यालसबर्धिन्त्रासावरारात्ती॥पार्थीबिंत्रोगंबिरह्त्व
कुलाएल्॥बिरह्अनिलशीहिहरेच्नारे॥ हेहराधस्यामकरीडारा॥कामछ्रप्बिबि
धसंगंघेलै॥सुघन्चटंगकरपलवमेलै॥मुक्तमालाआभरणसंगसाजै॥मोरद
चंद्रपटकिकीनीरांए॥त्रासनकरौसीबिरिगिरिजाहि॥चंद्नबिरिघश्वांह
गहराड॥डोह॥पीयमगु चाहतन्त्रासावरी॥चढीमलिया चलक्राय॥त्रांडि
सर्पछीघडतजी:रहेहेहलपिटाइ॥॥३५॥॥   ॥   ॥

Plate XX. Ragini Asavari

CHAUPAYI: The queen Asavari is lingering and idle. Having been left alone, she is melancholy and anguished. The fire of this anguish has burnt her heart, and her complexion has darkened. Kamdeva, the lord of Love, plays with other women while cobras sting her hands and her body. He [Kamdeva] wears a necklace of pearls, the feathers of the peacock adorn his body, and he wears tinkling bells on his feet. Searching for her lover, she comes to the top of the mountain and rests beneath the dark, shady [branches] of a sandal tree.

DOHA: Looking for her lover, Asavari climbs "Malayachal." Abandoning all comforts and fine food, she has come here to be surrounded by serpents. They encircle her limbs.

Plate XXI. Asavari Ragini

Asavari is longing for her husband and climbs the Malaya mountains. All the snakes
desert their sandal trees and writhe and coil their bodies. (Rajasthan, Jodhpur, 18th c.
George P. Bickford Collection)

Tone material

Raga <u>Asavari</u> with <u>RE komal</u> (D♭):

This second type of <u>Asavari</u> is often ascribed to the <u>Bhairav</u> <u>thata</u>. There are some musicians who believe that this type repre-sents the original form of <u>Asavari</u>. One cannot state with certainty which type is the older. However, the first type of this raga is much more in use than the second.

The <u>vadis</u> are the same as those of the first type. Melodies may be interrupted on the notes <u>MA</u> (F), <u>PA</u> (G) and on the <u>vadi</u>, <u>DHA komal</u> (A♭). Instead of <u>RE</u> shuddha (D), the note <u>RE komal</u> (D♭) is employed. The notes <u>DHA komal</u> (A♭) and <u>GA komal</u> (E♭) are performed with the same typical vibrato forms as the first type uses.

It is unusual for <u>Asavari</u> melodies to descend into the low octave range,
as can be observed in the first bar of the third line of the following
song specimen. <u>Asavari</u> melodies usually have a tendency to rise
quickly into the upper half of the middle octave region and do not dwell
for any length of time on notes below <u>PA</u> (G). This is not a strict
rule but a habit which can be noted in numerous <u>Asavari</u> performances.
The descent into the regions of the low middle or lower ranges may
show the relationship of this second type of <u>Asavari</u> with raga <u>Bhairav.</u>

RAGA ASAVARI (with RE Komal)   (Dhamar Tal)   BH, II, 382

Asthayi

Antara

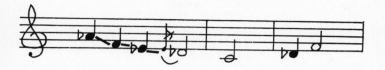

Tone material

There are a few instances where musicians combine both types of Asavari by using RE (D) in ascent and RE komal (D♭) in descent.

Raga Jaunpuri (Jivanpuri, Yavanapuri)

The name Jaunpuri is derived from the Indian city Jaunpur, where, we are told, Sultan Hussein and his court musicians created this raga.

Jaunpuri belongs to the Asavari thata. It is often mistaken for the first type of raga Asavari, and there are only a few musicians who are able to create in their performances a distinct difference between the two ragas. Indian musicians still occasionally engage in more or less severe arguments concerning the correct performance rules of this raga. As has already been stated, one group of musicians states that Jaunpuri is nothing but the first type of Asavari. Another group, however, insists that Jaunpuri is a distortion of the ancient raga Gandhari, [201] which appears here without the note RE komal (D♭). Despite such arguments, Jaunpuri is an independent raga, is performed comparatively often, and must be discussed separately. Although Jaunpuri has indeed the same tone material as the first type of Asavari, a careful listener will notice that some of the Jaunpuri notes receive a treatment different from those of Asavari (I).

Jaunpuri is to be performed in the late morning. Its vadis and

their use are the same as those in Asavari — DHA komal (A♭) and GA
komal (E♭). The note NI komal (B♭) is used both in ascent and descent. In descent this note may assume some importance. In order
to show the characteristics of Jaunpuri, a comparison of its important
phrases with those of Asavari (I) may be of use.

   Jaunpuri employs the note NI komal (B♭) in descent, a feature
which does not occur in Asavari (I):

In Jaunpuri the note NI komal (B♭) is strong; in Asavari (I) this note
is merely the starting point from which the vibrato on DHA komal (A♭)
is approached.

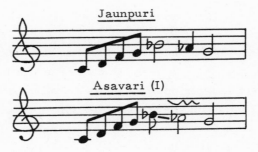

The vibratos on GA komal (E♭) and DHA komal (A♭) in Jaunpuri are
still lighter and more shallow than those in Asavari (I). Jaunpuri
melodies often begin with MA (F), PA (G), or RE (D).

RAGA JAUNPURI   (Trital)   BH, III, 640

Asthayi

Antara

Tone material

Raga Shobhavari

Even the name of this obscure raga is uncertain. It was impossible to obtain a song specimen of this raga. The little information
derived from hearsay is that Shobhavari could be ascribed to the
Asavari thata and that its scale is believed to be that of Jaunpuri without the notes GA komal (E♭) and NI komal (B♭). The Shobhavari
scale is therefore:

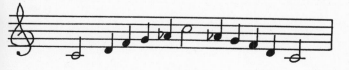

Raga Gandhari

This raga, supposedly an ancient one, belongs to the Asavari
family. Some musicians perform it in the morning, others in the
evening. The vadis are DHA komal (A♭) and GA komal (E♭). The
note RE (D) is used in ascent, and RE komal (D♭) in descent. The
note GA komal (E♭) appears in descent, as in most Asavari types.
The two vadis are performed with a shallow vibrato similar to that
of raga Jaunpuri.

There are some Gandhari melodies in which RE komal (D♭) is used
in ascent and RE shuddha (D) in descent. The confusion caused by
this practice becomes especially manifest in songs of recent origin.
Musicians permit themselves other liberties, such as the use of NI
shuddha (B) in ascent. Although this note is notated in its shuddha
form, experienced musicians will always treat it as a microtonally
high intoned NI komal (B♭).

RAGA GANDHARI   (Dhamar Tal)   BH, VI, 331

Asthayi

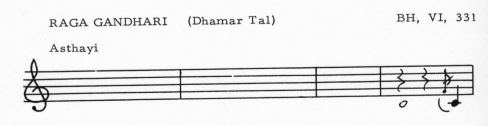

Asavari Thata

Antara

Tone material

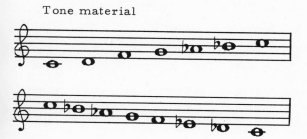

राग नी देव गंधारी ॥ ॥ ७ ॥ बेष ई तपसी उपजंधारी जोरी बिरहल हरिजन मैश्व
ती जारी ॥ बिरचित थें दुबेल दे ही ॥ पल पल में चित चढे सनेही ॥ मुकलत केसने
सबै रागी पीस ॥ के नाम जप ला गी ॥ जोग जटा आसन दृढ कीये ॥ नव न छाडी
बैगली मैं ॥ मनसा महे ध्यान ज में भरई ॥ साई मोही ममा नेक करई ॥
दोहा ॥ करतट हल संगस हचरी ॥ सोउ न पेट बैराग मानु
सुरती ॥ चीत्र की रहे पे मल वला गी ॥ ॥ ७ ॥ ॥

Plate XXII. Ragini Devagandhari

CHAUPAYI: The lady Gandhari appears as an ascetic. There is much anguish in her heart
at having been parted from her lover. Her body is frail, and her love for him is pitiful.
She is dressed as a recluse, with long, flowing hair. She sits in a rigid posture and has
deserted her home. She prays incessantly and hopes that God will have pity on her and
unite her with her beloved.

DOHA: The companions of Devagandhari are also ascetic in temperament. Worshipping
the idol, she pictures her lover in her mind. Her love is very deep.

[See "Note on Plates," p. xii]

Raga Devgandhar (Devagandhari)

This rare and obscure raga is to be performed in the morning. Its vadis are DHA komal (A♭) and GA komal (E♭). Despite its obscurity, musicians speak of three types of Devgandhar:

a) A type in which the name Devgandhar, actually Dvigandhar, "two Gandhar, " indicates the use of both forms of GA, shuddha (E) and komal (E♭). With the exception of the use of these two notes, the scale and other features of this type of Devgandhar are the same as those of raga Jaunpuri.

b) An indistinct type in which only the komal form of GA (E♭) is used, and thus the "two-Gandhar" feature is ignored. This second type of the raga represents a combination of elements of ragas Dhanashri[202] and Jaunpuri. Material of Dhanashri appears in the lower, and material of Jaunpuri in the upper, tetrachord.

c) A very rarely used type which is nothing but Gandhari combined with the characteristic Devgandhar phrase containing GA shuddha (E) to produce SA RE GA MA (C D E F).

In all three types of this raga the vadis are performed with a shallow vibrato which is started from above, from approximately NI komal (B♭) and MA (F) respectively.

The most frequently used type is the first one:

The preceding example shows that GA (E) appears in ascent and GA komal (E♭) in descent.

The second type, as has already been stated, employs GA komal in ascent and descent. This excludes the characteristic Devgandhar phrase (with E in ascent). The notes RE (D) and DHA komal (A♭) are avoided in ascent:

The third type shows Gandhari features with the characteristic Devgandhar phrase:

The following song specimen represents the first type of this raga.

RAGA DEVGANDHAR   (Ektal)   (First type)   BH, VI, 335

Asthayi

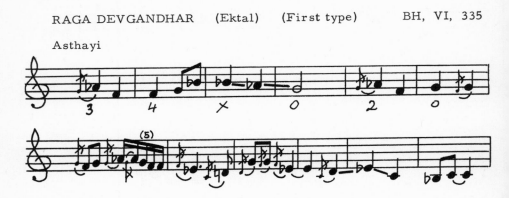

Antara

Tone material

First type

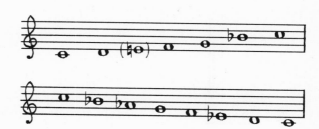

Second type

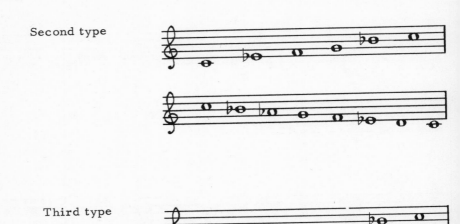

Third type

A comparison of the notes <u>RE</u> and <u>GA</u> (D and E) in the ragas <u>Jaunpuri</u>, <u>Gandhari</u>, and <u>Devgandhar</u> (I and III) shows the following:

Jaunpuri	Gandhari	Devgandhar (I and III)
<u>RE</u> (D) is <u>shuddha</u> in both ascent and descent.	<u>RE</u> (D) appears in ascent and <u>RE</u> <u>komal</u> (D♭) in descent.	<u>RE</u> (D) appears in ascent and <u>RE</u> <u>komal</u> (D♭) in descent. The important feature is the characteristic <u>Devgandhar</u> phrase with <u>GA</u> (E).
Only <u>GA</u> <u>komal</u> (E♭) is used.	Only <u>GA</u> <u>komal</u> (E♭) is used.	

<u>Raga Desi (Deshi)</u>

"Ragini Desi" is a serious, yet somewhat popular raga which belongs to the <u>Asavari</u> family. It is to be performed in the morning.

A "Contemplation of _Desi_" may be found in the Rāga-Sāgara:

> Living in a hut of Usira grass, holding a wreath of
> flowers in her hand, of a very fair complexion, clad
> in attractive robes, I contemplate on the youthful Desi.

> The visual picture of the melody is thus given in the
> Ratna-Mālā: With the slow movement of a king of ele-
> phant [sic], with eyes like that of a fawn, with a com-
> plexion like the lotus, with heavy hips, with her plaits
> dangling like a serpent [sic], with a frame quivering
> like a delicate creeper, this comes into view, the
> ragini Desi, sweetly smiling. This is Desi. [203]

In an anonymous Hindi text dealing with a number of raga-mala pictures, [204] _Desi_ is described as follows:

> Dressed in blue, and of shining complexion, she is
> standing near her lord, carrying a fan, full of desire
> for dalliance. She is burned by passion and has a
> voice like the cuckoo which captivates the heart of
> her beloved. Proud of her youth, and full of joy,
> she is called Desi ragini. [205]

One must be cautious not to mistake this raga for raga _Des._ [206] The
vadis of _Desi_ are PA (G) and RE (D). There are three types of this
raga:

a) _Desi_ with DHA komal (A♭);

b) _Desi_ with DHA shuddha (A),

c) _Desi_ with both forms, DHA komal (A♭) and DHA shuddha (A).

The notes GA komal (E♭) and DHA (A) or DHA komal (A♭) are avoided
in ascent. NI (B) usually appears in ascent and NI komal (B♭) in
descent, but occasionally performers deviate from this rule.

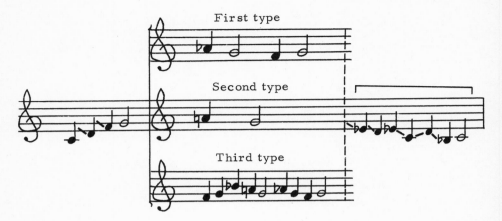

The phrase <u>GA</u> komal <u>RE GA</u> komal <u>SA RE NI</u> komal <u>SA</u> (E♭ D E♭ C
D B♭ C) is characteristic of all types of <u>Desi</u>.   Another typical feature is a descending gliding step from the upper <u>SA</u> (c) to <u>PA</u> (G).
The note <u>DHA</u> <u>komal</u> (A♭) in the first and third types usually appears
between two <u>PA</u> (G) and is approached by a small descending glide
from above, roughly from <u>NI</u> <u>komal</u> (B♭).

The note <u>GA</u> <u>komal</u> (E♭) of the middle octave region is approached in
all three types from above, roughly from <u>MA</u> (F) and is performed
with a shallow vibrato.

In a few exceptions the note <u>DHA</u> (A), although forbidden according
to the performance rules, may be observed in descent:

The notes above MA (F) determine the use of either NI komal (B♭) or
NI (B) in ascent. Usually the succession MA PA NI SA (F G B c) or,
in some exceptional and irregular cases, MA PA DHA NI komal SA
(F G A B♭ c) is used. This shows that if the note DHA (A) is used
in ascent, it has to be followed by NI komal (B♭). If DHA (A) is
avoided in ascent, according to the performance rule, the preceding
PA (G) has to be followed by NI shuddha (B).

     None of these rules are strictly observed. Desi is a popular
raga which allows musicians to take various liberties, such as the
progressions MA PA NI komal SA (F G B♭ c), RE NI SA (d B c), RE
NI komal SA (d B♭ c), and so forth.

     The following song specimen represents the third, most frequent-
ly used, type of this raga.

RAGA DESI   (Trital)   (Third type)   BH, VI, 299

Asthayi

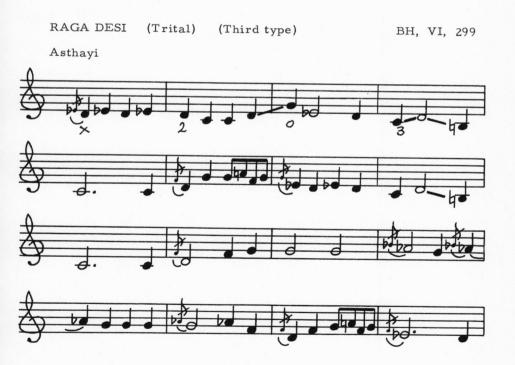

Antara

Tone material

First type

Second type

Third type

Raga Komal-desi

It happens not infrequently that certain popular ragas are altered in various ways and that these altered forms are given new names.
The names Komal-desi, Komal-ramkali, and similar ones indicate
by the word komal that one or more essential notes have been low-
altered by a semitone and that the komal-raga is to be distinguished
from the basic form.

Komal-desi, a raga which belongs to the Asavari thata, has the
same vadis as raga Desi, but differs from Desi in that in ascent RE
(D) appears, but RE komal (D♭) has to be used in descent; Komal-
desi employs only DHA komal (A♭) and NI komal (B♭) in ascent and
descent and avoids the note MA (F) in descent whenever the melody
moves from PA (G) to the lower SA (C); only when the descending line
ends with RE (D) and moves again upward—whereby the note RE (D)
becomes the first note in the ascending line—may MA (F) precede RE
(D). With the exception of these features, there is no difference between the two ragas.

In the following song specimen are shown the asthayi and only two lines
of the antara, sufficient material for illustrating Komal-desi.

RAGA KOMAL-DESI   (Dhamar Tal)   BH, VI, 319

Asthayi

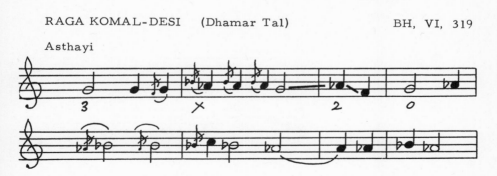

Antara

Tone material

Raga Khat

This rare raga is to be performed in the morning. Khat possesses a considerable number of variable phrases, and for that reason
some Indian musicians erroneously equate the name Khat with the
Sanskrit shat ("six"), implying that Khat represents a combination
of elements taken from six ragas. The great variability of some Khat
phrases can indeed lead a listener to believe that there are six, eight,
ten, or any other number of ragas involved in its composition. The
most obvious constituent phrases and ornaments can be derived from
the ragas Asavari, Bhairav, [207] and the Mallar types. [208]

The vadi of this raga is DHA komal (A♭), and the samvadi is
probably GA komal (E♭). There are some musicians who insist that
the vadi is PA (G). This difference of opinion is understandable, for
the variable material allows several points of view, or, better, points
of hearing. The predominance of the elements of one raga over those
of others becomes in compound ragas such as Khat a determining
factor in the choice of the vadi. Ornaments (gamakas) occur mostly
on GA komal (E♭), also on DHA komal (A♭), and less frequently on
NI komal (B).

The Khat scale contains RE (D), or, when the relationship with
raga Bhairav is emphasized, RE komal (D♭); similarly, it employs
GA (E) and GA komal (E♭), DHA (A) and DHA komal (A♭), and NI
(B) and NI komal (B♭). In short, with the exception of MA tivra (F#),
eleven degrees of the chromatic scale are in use. The following examples illustrate some of the possible ascents and descents.

Ascent from SA (C) to PA (G):

(Mallar gamak)

The use of NI (B) in ascent:

Ascent from PA (G) to SA (c):

NI komal (B♭) is used mostly in descent, but there are phrases which use this note also in ascent:

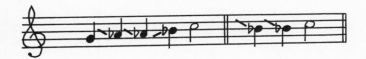

Besides the ascending progression DHA komal NI komal SA (A♭ B♭ c), we observe DHA shuddha NI komal SA (A B♭ c):

In ascent the vakra phrase leading from DHA komal (A♭) via NI DHA PA (B A G) to the upper SA (c) is permissible:

Descent from SA (c) to PA (G):

Descent from PA (G) to SA (C):

If the performer wishes to stress the relationship of Khat with raga Bhairav, he uses:

The preceding examples show the commonly used ascents and descents, but it is important to note that more varieties are possible. These varieties obstruct the postulation of fixed performance rules. The only rule which appears to have some general validity in this raga is the use of the indicated gamakas on GA komal (E♭) and DHA komal (A♭).

A Bhairav relationship can be observed in the following song specimen (fourth line, bars three and four):

RAGA KHAT   (Jhaptal)   BH, VI, 348

Asthayi

Antara

Tone material

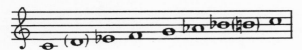

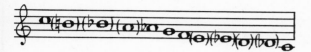

Raga Zhilaf

   This raga belongs to the Asavari thata and is to be performed
in the morning.   Another raga with the same name is ascribed to the
Bhairav thata. [209]
   The vadis of Zhilaf are DHA komal (A♭) and GA komal (E♭).
The raga consists of elements taken from the ragas Jaunpuri and Khat
or Jaunpuri and Bhairav, whereby the Bhairav feature of raga Khat
is employed.   Jaunpuri material appears in the lower, and Khat material in the upper, tetrachord of the Zhilaf scale.   The following example shows the Jaunpuri and Khat combination without the Bhairav
feature:

The Jaunpuri and Bhairav combination shows the former material in
the upper, the latter material in the lower, tetrachord of the scale:

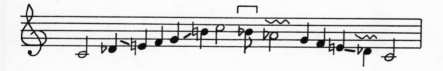

The preceding example shows a predominance of Bhairav material.
Khat is actually represented only by the single note NI komal (B♭).
The reason is that Khat and Bhairav materials overlap in the notes
PA (G) and DHA komal (A♭).

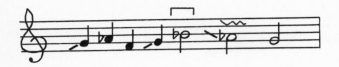

The following song specimen emphasizes the relationship with raga
Bhairav.

RAGA ZHILAF   (Dhamar Tal)   BH, VI, 367

Asthayi

The following is a fragment of a second song in Zhilaf in which the combination of Jaunpuri and Khat without the Bhairav phrase is utilized:

RAGA ZHILAF   (Jhaptal)   BH, VI, 366

Asthayi

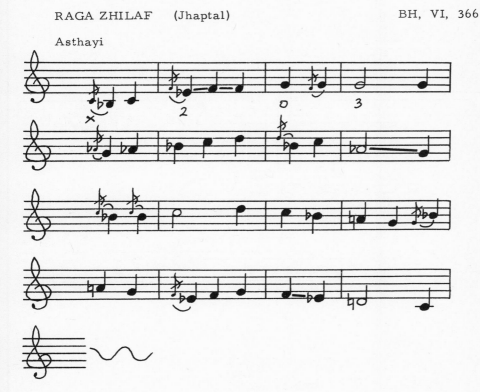

The tone material cannot be stated with certainty, because the scale may change from Jaunpuri to Khat, or vice versa, and may or may not add the Bhairav notes.

Raga Jangla (Jangala)

Jangla is a light, rare raga which belongs to the Asavari family and is quite distinct from raga Jangula of the Bhairav thata.[210] As

in all light ragas, the samvadi is never taken into consideration.
Jangla uses GA (E) and GA komal (E♭), DHA (A) and DHA komal
(A♭), and occasionally RE (D) and RE komal (D♭).

The note GA komal (E♭) is avoided in ascent, and GA shuddha
(E) usually appears between two MA (F) or between MA (F) and PA
(G). DHA (A) is used either before NI komal (B♭) or between two
NI komal (B♭). Whenever there is a straight step by step ascent from
PA (G) to the upper SA (c), the note DHA komal (A♭) is used. If the
ascent avoids PA (G), the note DHA shuddha (A) is employed. The
note RE komal (d♭) appears mainly in the upper octave region between
two SA (c). In lower regions RE shuddha (D) is used.

The following song specimen is a fragment. It represents the asthayi
and the first part of the antara.

RAGA JANGLA   (Dipchandi Tal)   BH, VI, 361

Asthayi

Antara

Tone material

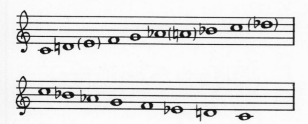

Raga Gopikavasant (Gopibasant)

This obscure raga can be ascribed to the Asavari thata. Its vadi is SA (C); the samvadi is probably PA (G). The note RE (D) is totally avoided. GA komal (E♭) and DHA komal (A♭) are often performed with a shallow, short vibrato. The descending gliding steps SA-MA (c-F) and PA-GA komal (G-E♭) seem to be characteristic features, although musicians never mention them as such. The vakra phrases in descent shown below occur often but can be avoided, hence they cannot be considered as characteristics of Gopikavasant. The following shows the common ascent and the three forms of descent of this raga:

RAGA GOPIKAVASANT   (Trital)   BH, VI, 374

Asthayi

The tone material, is the <u>Asavari</u> scale without the note <u>RE</u> (D).

Raga Sindh-bhairavi

This raga, allegedly of recent origin, is to be performed in the late morning. Its <u>vadi</u> is <u>DHA</u> <u>komal</u> (A♭), although some musicians believe it to be <u>MA</u> (F). The <u>samvadi</u> is never mentioned, but it can be assumed to be a note which is a fourth or a fifth distant from the <u>vadi</u>. The song specimen below shows the notes <u>GA</u> <u>komal</u> (E♭), <u>PA</u> (G), <u>MA</u> (F), and <u>DHA</u> <u>komal</u> (A♭) coinciding with the <u>sam</u>, which indicates that the <u>vadi</u>, as could be expected, has little or no significance in this raga. Although <u>Sindh-bhairavi</u> belongs to the <u>Asavari</u> family, North Indian musicians derive its tone material from the scale of raga <u>Bhairavi</u>.[211] The <u>Bhairavi</u> scale is:

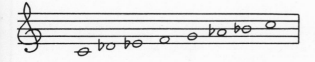

If this scale is transposed a fifth higher (beginning with G) and if a scale is made of these transposed notes, beginning with C, the <u>Sindh-bhairavi</u> material is achieved:

The difference between <u>Sindh-bhairavi</u> and <u>Bhairavi</u> lies in the use of <u>RE</u> <u>shuddha</u> (D) in the former and <u>RE</u> <u>komal</u> (D♭) in the latter. However, there are some songs in <u>Sindh-bhairavi</u> which employ both <u>RE</u> (D) and <u>RE</u> <u>komal</u> (D♭), for example in passages such as:

<u>Sindh-bhairavi</u> melodies frequently move in the middle and low octave ranges.   It is in the low octave range where the note <u>DHA</u> <u>shuddha</u> (A) may appear:

Other more or less characteristic phrases of this raga are:

RAGA SINDH-BHAIRAVI   (Trital)   BH, VI, 378

Asthayi

Antara

Tone material

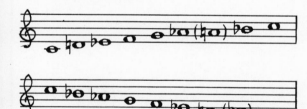

Plate XXIII. Ragini Kanhadi [Kanada]

CHAUPAYI: Kanhadi is dressed in male attire and is seated on her mount, holding a sword in her hand. Kanhadi is being dressed by her companions, and she raises her hand holding the sword. One of her companions is fanning a whisk over her head. She was victorious in battle, and all passion has left her. Her fair complexion has darkened with the deep anguish caused by her separation from her lover. But she returned only after she had been victorious in every field. She holds a sword in one hand, and her voice is deep.
DOHA: Confident in her lover's deep affection and donning the headgear of victory, she enjoys the boundless love of her paramour. She is matchless among women.

The Kanada Ragas

Ragas which belong to this group are ascribed to various thatas, particularly to the Asavari and Kafi thatas. In order to present the Kanada ragas in one group, several are listed below which belong to the Kafi thata.

The word Kanada refers to Carnatic, the name of a former province in the South between the Eastern ghats and the Coromandel coast, today included in the Madras Presidency.

All Kanada ragas possess·two characteristics:

a) The notes GA komal (Eb) and DHA komal (Ab) are vakra in descent and are used in phrases such as GA komal MA RE (Eb F D) and DHA komal NI komal PA (Ab Bb G).

b) The basis of all Kanada scales is the material of raga Sarang: [212] SA RE MA PA NI komal or NI shuddha (C D F G Bb or B). Even if the notes of a Kanada raga differ from Sarang in one or two degrees, the Sarang feature usually manifests itself in fast passages, where the performers are inclined to avoid the notes GA komal (Eb) and DHA komal (Ab) and thus bring out the underlying Sarang character.

Raga Darbari-kanada

Darbari (Durbar) means the audience hall, the room in which the ruling sovereign receives visitors. Darbari-kanada is a majestic raga which belongs to the Asavari thata. It is to be performed at midnight in a dignified, slow manner, and musicians are advised to apply as many gliding steps as the performance rules permit. The tone material of this raga is the same as that of raga Asavari with RE shuddha (D), but the manner of ornamenting the notes (gaiki) is quite different from that of raga Asavari. A pictorial representation of this raga may be found in the Saṅgīta Darpana (2, 66):

Kanada is an impressive regal figure holding a sword in one hand and the tusk of an elephant in the other. The gods and a host of bards are always singing his praises.

In the R̄aga-S̄agara (3, 34) we read:

I think of Kanada as a dark woman gorgeously dressed, with her long beautiful hair tied near the waist. Ever restless, she is exceedingly playful by the side of the banyan tree. She is domineering and an expert in the gentle fights of love.

The vadis of this raga are RE (D) and PA (G). The great majority of North Indian singers intone the notes GA komal (E♭) and DHA komal (A♭) slightly flat and with vibrato. This vibrato, the notes of which are not clearly definable because they are linked by tiny gliding movements, requires an unusual, forceful voice production which is unknown in the West. A rough idea of this vibrato can be obtained if a singer produces a note and simultaneously presses briefly four or six times against his abdomen. It is a vague up and down of the voice, together with the gliding from one vibrato note to the next. This characteristic vibrato is always started from the next higher note; thus the vibrato on GA komal (E♭) will be started approximately from MA (F) and that on DHA komal (A♭) from NI komal (B♭).

A more simple and shallow vibrato appears on the note SA (C). It starts on the note and requires no approaches from above or below.

The preceding example shows that the phrase NI komal DHA komal NI komal SA (B♭ A♭ B♭ C) is often used twice in succession.

In the preceding example the above mentioned <u>vakra</u> positions of <u>DHA</u> <u>komal</u> (A♭) and <u>GA</u> <u>komal</u> (E♭) can be observed.

The following song specimen shows that <u>Darbari</u> song melodies often move in the low octave range when the singer presents the <u>as-thayi</u>.

RAGA DARBARI-KANADA   (Jhaptal)   BH, IV, 650

Asthayi

Antara

Tone material

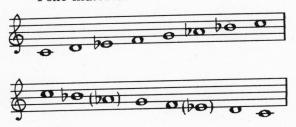

Comparison of the Auffuehrungspraxis of the Ragas

Asavari and Darbari-kanada

Asavari	Darbari-kanada
Melodies in this raga move quickly up toward DHA komal (A♭);	Melodies in this raga tend toward the low octave region in a slow, dignified tempo;
Straight descents, such as GA komal RE SA (E♭ D C) and NI komal DHA komal PA (B♭ A♭ G) are the rule;	Vakra phrases such as GA komal MA RE (E♭ F D) and DHA komal NI komal PA (A♭ B♭ G) are the rule;
The ornaments on GA komal (E♭) and DHA komal (A♭) are light; In descent melodies can be interrupted on SA (C);	The ornaments on GA komal (E♭) and DHA komal (A♭) are heavy; In descent the melody rarely stops on SA (C) but moves further down

The note NI komal (Bb) is
avoided in ascent.

into the low octave range;
The note NI komal (Bb) is used
in ascent.

Raga Adana-kanada

Adana-kanada, often simply called Adana, belongs to the Asavari
family. It is the light counterpart of Darbari-kanada. Adana is rich
with fast passages, while Darbari-kanada is too dignified for virtuoso
features. Nevertheless, it must be added that at the present time
numerous singers include fast passages in their Darbari-kanada performances, a habit which does not enhance the character of Darbari.

Adana is to be performed after midnight. Its vadi is SA (C),
usually the high SA (c); and the samvadi is PA (G). The notes GA
komal (Eb) and DHA komal (Ab) have the same vakra functions as in
Darbari-kanada, but they are intoned normally and are performed
with light, shallow vibratos. Occasionally the note NI komal (Bb) is
taken slightly sharp. This is the reason why this note is often notated as NI shuddha (B), although it is never clearly intoned as such.
In descent NI komal (Bb) shows no microtonal alteration. Numerous
Adana melodies begin with the high SA (c), a feature which cannot be
observed in Darbari-kanada. The general movements of melodies in
the two ragas can be shown graphically in the following manner:

Now and then an Indian singer may avoid the note DHA komal (Ab) in
ascent, as is the practice of, for instance, the famous Roshanara
Begum. The reason for this practice can be found in the fact that
these singers were pupils of tantakars (string players). String players have adopted the habit of omitting a note now and then, particularly in fast passages, when it lies uncomfortably on the fingerboard.

The habit was eventually taken over by the singer-pupils, who occasionally consider these deviations as performance rules.

The essential Adana-kanada (with DHA komal [A♭]) phrases are:

RAGA ADANA-KANADA   (Jhaptal)   BH, VI, 693

Asthayi

Antara

In the preceding song specimen can be seen the notation of NI shuddha (B) in ascent. This note will always be a microtonally high altered NI komal (B♭).

Tone material

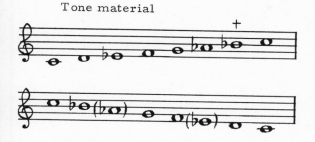

Raga Shahana-kanada

Shahana-kanada allegedly originated during the Mogul era. It is ascribed to the Kafi thata. Its vadis are PA (G) and SA (C). The lower tetrachord of the Shahana-kanada scale is the same as that of Adana-kanada. The note GA komal (E♭) is vakra in descent and appears in the characteristic Kanada phrase GA komal MA RE SA (E♭ F D C). GA komal (E♭) is performed with the same vibrato as in Adana-kanada. The upper tetrachord of the Shahana-kanada scale shows its relationship to Kafi. DHA shuddha (A) appears frequently, mainly in the vakra phrase DHA NI komal PA (A B♭ G), or between two NI komal (B♭). In all instances DHA (A) is to be followed by NI komal (B♭). If the note NI komal (B♭) in ascent is followed by SA (c), it is intoned slightly sharp. This is the reason why in some notated songs NI shuddha (B) can be found; it is always interpreted, however, as NI komal (B♭) with a microtonally high alteration. The direct step-by-step sequence PA DHA NI komal SA (G A B♭ c) is

rare in this raga. Usually one or the other note of this sequence is
omitted, and thus ascents such as <u>PA</u> <u>NI</u> <u>komal</u> <u>SA</u> (G B♭ c) or <u>MA</u>
<u>DHA</u> <u>NI</u> <u>komal</u> (F A B♭) become frequent features.

A few musicians speak of a second type of this raga, in which both
<u>GA</u> <u>shuddha</u> (E) and <u>GA</u> <u>komal</u> (E♭) are employed;

RAGA SHAHANA-KANADA   (Dhamar Tal)   BH, VI, 194

Asthayi

Antara

Tone material

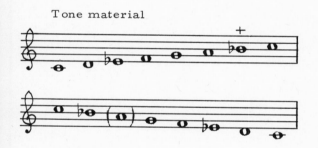

Raga Naiki-kanada

Naiki-kanada belongs to the Kafi thata and is to be performed at night. Its vadi is MA (F); the samvadi is SA (C). It is important to note that in present-day practice the note MA (F) is hardly ever emphasized. Emphasis can be observed on PA (G), which seems to have taken over the function of the vadi. Melodies are never interrupted on MA (F) but very frequently on PA (G). The note DHA (A) is avoided except as a subtle ornament, and is usually used before NI komal (B♭).

The <u>Sarang</u> background, which is not always clearly noticeable in the <u>Kanada</u> ragas, is particularly distinct in <u>Naiki-kanada</u>, which could cause a listener to describe this raga as <u>Sarang</u> to which has been added the note <u>GA komal</u> (E♭).

The note <u>GA komal</u> (E♭) is performed in this raga in two characteristic ways. Either it is provided with a <u>murki</u>, a chain of subtle grace notes:

or it is rendered in the form of a sequence of short descending gliding steps between <u>MA</u> (F) and <u>GA komal</u> (E♭), a feature which resembles the heavy <u>gamak</u> of <u>Darbari-kanada</u>:

In this second form of rendering <u>GA komal</u> (E♭), the note is taken slightly low.

The note <u>NI komal</u> (B♭) is treated and notated in the same manner as in raga <u>Shahana-kanada</u>. In descent it is normally intoned without any alteration. The characteristic <u>Kanada</u> phrase <u>GA komal MA RE SA</u> (E♭ F D C) also appears in this raga and is even hinted at in the <u>murki</u> shown above.

RAGA NAIKI-KANADA   (Trital)   BH, VI, 198

Asthayi

Antara

Tone material

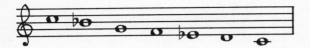

Raga Suha-kanada (Soha-kanada)

This raga belongs to the <u>Kafi</u> <u>thata</u> and is to be performed in the late morning. The night counterpart of this raga is <u>Naiki-kanada</u>. The <u>vadis</u> of <u>Suha-kanada</u> are <u>MA</u> (F) and <u>SA</u> (C). Both forms of the note <u>DHA</u> (A) are totally avoided. The <u>vadi</u> of this raga, although not particularly stressed in the song melody shown below, is emphasized in <u>alaps</u>. This strong <u>MA</u> (F) contributes toward a distinction between <u>Suha-kanada</u> and other <u>Kanada</u> types. The note <u>GA komal</u> (Eb) is <u>vakra</u> in its characteristic <u>Kanada</u> phrase and is often performed with a vibrato which is less heavy than that in raga <u>Naiki-kanada</u>.

Suha-kanada is often described as a combination of features taken from <u>Megh-mallar</u>[213] and <u>Darbari-kanada</u>.[214] Even if only the vibratos are compared, this does not appear to be a fully adequate description. The similarity between <u>Suha-</u> and <u>Naiki-kanada</u> is remarkable and will receive our attention below. The note <u>NI komal</u> (Bb) in ascent before <u>SA</u> (C or c) is microtonally altered, if at all, only very slightly high.

Essential phrases of this raga are:

RAGA SUHA-KANADA   (Jhaptal)   BH, VI, 156

Asthayi

Antara

Tone material

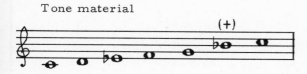

Some musicians speak of a second type of this raga in which the note
DHA komal (Ab) is employed in the following manner:

Comparison of the Auffuehrungspraxis of the Ragas

Naiki-kanada and Suha-kanada

Naiki-kanada	Suha-kanada
Although MA (F) is vadi, it has little importance; melodies may stop on PA (G).	MA (F) has to be strong, if not in song melodies, at least in alaps. Melodies may stop on MA (F).
The gamak on GA komal (Eb) is heavy.	The gamak on GA komal (Eb) is light.
Naiki uses the characteristic murki:	Suha has no murki.

Raga Sugharai-kanada

Sugharai-kanada belongs to the Kafi thata and is to be performed
in the late morning. Its night counterpart is Shahana-kanada. The
vadis of this raga are PA (G) and SA (C).

There are two types of Sugharai-kanada:

a) Sugharai-kanada with DHA shuddha (A)

This type is sometimes erroneously called Suha. The similarity

of this type with Shahana-kanada is remarkable. The note DHA
(A) appears in the characteristic phrase DHA NI komal PA (A
Bb G). DHA (A) is often performed in the same manner as in
raga Deshkar.[215] This note can also appear rarely in the phrase
DHA MA PA (A F G). There exist some songs which completely
avoid the note DHA (A) or touch upon it in such a manner that it
cannot be considered as a scale note. These features, however,
concern a second type of this raga, which will be discussed below.
As in other Kanada ragas, the note NI komal (Bb) is slightly
high in ascent. Occasionally it is even notated as NI shuddha
(B), but experienced musicians will always interpret this note
as a microtonally high altered NI komal (Bb).

The essential phrases of the first type of this raga are:

RAGA SUGHARAI-KANADA (Jhaptal) First type   BH, VI, 170

Asthayi

Antara

The slight high alteration of the note <u>NI</u> <u>komal</u> (B♭) may be indicated
by a notational <u>NI</u> <u>shuddha</u> (B): In the first bar of the third line of
the preceding song specimen, the notation indicates <u>NI</u> <u>komal</u> (B♭).
It means the same high alteration as described before. The note <u>DHA</u>
(A) appears only once in the preceding song specimen (last measure,
penultimate line). This single appearance is sufficient to describe
the song as the first type of <u>Sugharai-kanada</u>.

Before considering the second type of this raga, a brief comparison of the first type of <u>Sugharai-kanada</u> with <u>Shahana-kanada</u> may
be useful:

Shahana-kanada

The note DHA (A) appears
in ascent in:

Sugharai-kanada

The note DHA (A) appears
in ascent in:

The note GA komal (E♭)
is strong in descent:

The note GA komal (E♭)
is of minor importance:

Tone material

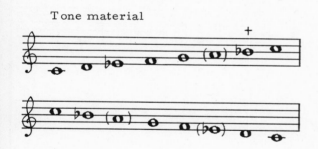

b) Sugharai-kanada without DHA (A)

This second type differs from Suha-kanada only in the fact that
Sugharai-kanada melodies must not be interrupted on MA (F),
while Suha-kanada performance rules not only permit such interruptions but require them. In this second type melodies may

be interrupted on the <u>vadi</u> (which is the same note as in the first type).

The intonation of <u>NI</u> <u>komal</u> (B♭) is the same as in the previously described <u>Kanada</u> ragas.

RAGA SUGHARAI-KANADA (Trital) Second type   BH, VI, 174

Asthayi

Antara

Tone material

Raga Devsakh (Deshakya, Desakh)

    Devsakh, related to the Kanada and Mallar groups, belongs to the
Kafi thata and is to be performed in the late morning, before noon.
N. A. Willard presents the following pictorial description of this raga:

    Desakh, the wife (ragini) of Hindol:

    In treatises on the ragas, this raginee is described as
    an enraged Amazonian [sic], wielding a naked sword in
    her hand, with which she has overcome a number of foes
    and defended her lover who stands by her side; but the
    general representation in the Ragmala is quite ambig-
    uous; there she is drawn in the figure of several ath-
    letic young men engaged in various gymnastic exercises,
    such as wrestling, casting hugh masses of stone, & [sic].
    It is quite uncertain what gave rise to this preposterous
    representation.[216]

The vadis of this raga are PA (G) and SA (C); some musicians state
that the vadis are MA (F) and SA (C).

    There are two types of Devsakh:

a) Devsakh without DHA (A);

b) a very rare type of Devsakh in which the note DHA (A) can be
    used occasionally.

Melodies and phrases in both types may be interrupted on PA (G) or
MA (F). The step GA komal PA (E♭ G) is characteristic. In some
songs (never in alaps) both forms of GA, GA komal (E♭) and GA shuddha (E), may occur. Similarly, both NI komal (B♭) and NI shuddha
(B) may be employed.

    The treatment of GA komal (E♭) shows a gamak which consists
of several short descending gliding steps which are clearly detached
from each other. Each step begins roughly at MA (F) and ends at
GA komal (E♭). The note GA komal (E♭) is intoned slightly low.
This gamak resembles to some degree the gamak used in raga Megh-
mallar, but it is not the same in rendition.

    The characteristic Kanada phrase GA komal MA RE SA (E♭ F D C)

plays an important role in this raga. The following example shows
the gamak on GA komal (E♭), the step GA komal PA (E♭ G), and the
Kanada phrase:

If the note NI komal (B♭) is followed by SA (C or c), it is altered microtonally high. In descent, however, NI komal (B♭) shows no alteration:

    The performance rules in most Kanada ragas are often indistinct,
and musicians have differing opinions about performance practices.
Devsakh, for instance, is closely related to the Kanada ragas Suha
and Sugharai, and at some performances the similarities between these
ragas become so strong that the fine, characteristic distinctions of the
ragas are completely ignored. Musicians love to argue about these
ragas and try to point out the distinguishing features of each type.
Even if a raga has been described verbally with some care, the performance usually shows that the fine distinctions were only words.
    One feature seems to be the avoidance of the note GA komal (E♭)
in ascent in the first type of Devsakh. In descent it appears in the
typical Kanada phrase where the note is vakra, that is, it leads first
upward to MA (F), whereupon the descent follows. This vakra position
of GA komal (E♭) can be misunderstood occasionally, and a less-
informed musician may employ this note in ascent. At the present
time the situation is such that it is difficult to ascertain which of the

two methods is correct. Such matters often lead to lengthy, fruitless discussion. Whenever GA komal (Eb) appears, usually in the pseudo ascent in the Kanada phrase, it is performed with the characteristic gamak. The avoidance of GA komal (Eb) in straight ascent causes the appearance of the Mallar phrase SA MA RE PA (C F D G).

The second type of Devsakh has a striking similarity with raga Sugharai. The difference between the ragas may lie in the vadis and in the somewhat uncertain avoidance of the note GA komal (Eb) in ascent in Devsakh.

The note DHA (A), which represents the characteristic feature of the second type of this raga, is always vakra in descent. It appears in DHA NI komal PA (A Bb G). DHA (A) is ornamented as in raga Sugharai. The difference between the second type of Devsakh and Sugharai in the DHA (A) region is that this note is not always vakra in Sugharai; it is possible to find in Sugharai the straight descending progression NI komal DHA PA (Bb A G), which does not occur in the second type of Devsakh. In ascent the second type of Devsakh may employ rarely the straight progression PA DHA NI komal SA (G A B̄b c).

The following song specimen represents the first type of Devsakh. The step NI komal SA (Bb c), containing the microtonally high altered NI komal (Bb), is notated as NI shuddha (B).

RAGA DEVSAKH   (Trital)   First type   BH, VI, 212

Asthayi

Antara

The next song specimen represents the second type of Devsakh.

RAGA DEVSAKH   (Jhaptal)   Second type   BH, VI, 214

Asthayi

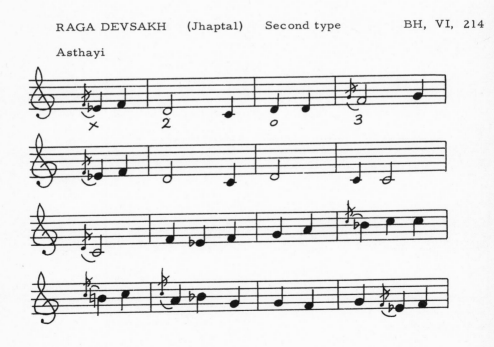

Antara

Tone material

First type

Second type

Raga Kaushik-kanada (Kaunsi)

There are two types of this raga. One belongs to the Asavari
thata, the other to the Kafi thata. Both are to be performed at night.

a) Kaushik-kanada (Asavari thata) represents a combination of
material taken from raga Malkouns [217] and the notes RE (D) and PA (G).
The performer has to watch that the Malkouns features do not become
too preponderant in his melody. If this threatens, he has to create a
counterbalance by using the notes RE (D) and PA (G).

The vadis are MA (F) and SA (C) in both types. The note GA
komal (Eb) is performed in both with a shallow, fast-moving vibrato
which oscillates roughly within the range of a semitone. DHA komal
(Ab), a note which appears only in the first type of this raga, is performed with a similar vibrato which has, however, a slightly wider
range. If the notes GA komal (Eb) and NI komal (Bb) are followed in
ascent by MA (F) and SA (c), respectively, both are intoned slightly
sharp.

RAGA KAUSHIK-KANADA (Ektal) (Asavari thata) BH, VI, 223

Asthayi

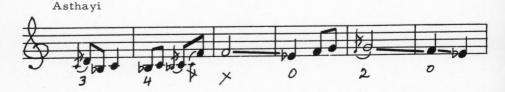

Even a superficial examination of the preceding song specimen shows how weak the relationship is between the first type of this raga and the Kanada family.

   b) Kaushik-kanada (Kafi thata) stands much closer to the Kanada group.   Its vadis are the same as those of the first type.   This type of Kaushik-kanada can be described as a combination of phrases taken from the raga Bageshri [218] and from the Kanada group.

In raga Bageshri the note PA (G) is weak and rarely used. In Kaushik-
kanada this note has considerable importance. The relationship to
the Kafi family in general becomes manifest by the use of DHA shuddha
(A), an essential note of Bageshri. The note GA komal is performed
with a shallow vibrato, but the note shows no microtonal alteration
in ascent or descent. The note NI komal (B♭) is treated in the same
manner as in the first type.

RAGA KAUSHIK-KANADA (Chautal) (Kafi thata)   BH, VI, 221

Tone material

First type

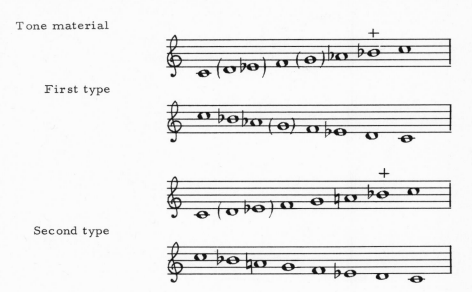

Second type

Raga Husseini-kanada

This rare raga belongs to the Kafi thata. Its name points toward a Mohammedan origin. Husseini-kanada is to be performed at night. The vadis are SA (C) and PA (G). Its scale resembles that of raga Darbari-kanada except that Husseini-kanada employs the note DHA shuddha (A) and not DHA komal (Ab). DHA (A) is performed without any vibrato, and NI komal (Eb) is altered microtonally high in ascent before SA (C or c). Melodies in this raga prefer the range of the low octave region. A characteristic feature of this raga consists of two heavy successive ascending gliding steps, both starting with PA (G) and ending with NI komal (Bb). The note GA komal (Eb) is performed in the characteristic Kanada manner, that is, with heavy descending gliding steps. The Kanada phrase GA komal MA RE SA (Eb F D C) can be replaced in Husseini-kanada by GA komal MA GA komal RE SA (Eb F Eb D C).

No adequate song specimen can be shown.

Tone material

Raga Abhogi (Abhogi-kanada)

Abhogi or Abhogi-kanada belongs to the Kafi family. Its vadi is SA (C); the samvadi is indistinct, probably MA (F). The notes PA (G) and NI komal (Bb) are totally avoided. NI komal (Bb) may appear occasionally as a subtle appoggiatura before DHA (A) but never as a melody note. Abhogi has few Kanada features. It uses rarely the Kanada phrase GA komal MA RE SA (Eb F D C) and the characteristic gamak on GA komal (Eb). The straight Bageshri descent MA GA komal RE SA (F Eb D C) occurs much more frequently than the Kanada phrase doe

In fast passages singers are inclined to approach most notes of this raga from above:

The use of the Kanada phrase GA komal MA RE SA (E♭ F D C) depends upon the choice of the performer. A total avoidance of this phrase would completely destroy the Kanada character of this raga. In a gramophone recording the great Abdul Karim Khan sings his Abhogi in a manner which immediately emphasizes the Kanada feature. The following song specimen does not show the Kanada phrase clearly. Instead the phrase used reminds one much more of Bageshri (seventh line, bar two and three).

RAGA ABHOGI   (Jhaptal)   BH, VI, 284

Asthayi

Antara

Tone material

Raga Bageshri-kanada

This rare raga belongs to the Kafi thata. It represents a combination of phrases taken from the ragas Bageshri and Darbari-kanada.
This combination of Kanada and Kafi (Bageshri) elements has been observed before, for instance in Kaushik-kanada, and it is doubtful
whether sufficiently distinct differences between Bageshri-kanada and
Kaushik-kanada can be found. The only difference which can be observed is the regular use of the Kanada phrase GA komal MA RE SA
(E♭ F D C) in Bageshri-kanada, while in Kaushik-kanada the straight
descent MA GA komal RE SA (F E♭ D C) is permitted. If a short
passage of Kaushik-kanada is shown in which the Kanada phrase is
used (which is permissible), there is no distinction between the two
ragas, because even the vadis, MA (F) and SA (C), are identical.
Darbari-kanada and Bageshri phrases are linked in the following
manner in this raga:

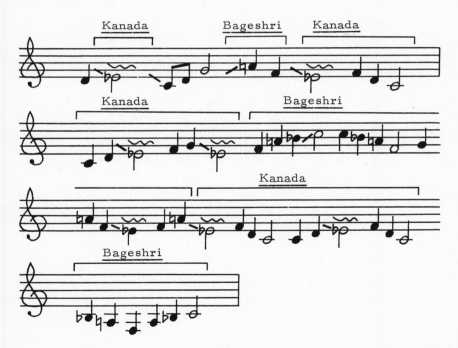

No adequate song specimen of this raga can be presented.

Raga Kafi-kanada

This very rare raga can be ascribed to the Kafi family. It was performed by Kesar Bai, a pupil of Aladiya Khan Saheb of Bombay. One can assume that this raga originated with Aladiya Khan and became the more or less exclusive property of his well-known pupil. The vadis are PA (G) and SA (C). As indicated by the name, this raga consists of phrases taken from Darbari-kanada and Kafi. According to the taste of the performer, it can be rendered either in "Kafi-style" or in "Bageshri-style." The note DHA (A) is weak in Kafi but is important in Bageshri. Thus the two "styles" will be characterized by the lesser or greater use of the note DHA (A).

a) Kafi-kanada in "Kafi-style" either avoids the note DHA (A) or uses it very weakly:

b) Kafi-kanada in "Bageshri-style," which occasionally is also called Kafi-bahar, employs the note DHA (A):

Of interest is the characteristic phrase shown at the beginning of the two preceding examples. It is believed to be a reliable indicator of Kafi-kanada. Apart from this phrase, the following few distinctions between Kafi-kanada, Bageshri-kanada, and Abhogi-kanada can be observed:

Kafi-kanada	Bageshri-kanada	Abhogi-kanada
The normally intoned NI komal (Bb) does not occur in ascent; the note is always altered microtonally high if followed by SA (C or c);	NI komal (Bb) is used in ascent;	NI komal (Bb) is not used;
The note PA (G) is used.	The note PA (G) is used.	The note PA (G) is not used.

No adequate song specimen of Kafi-kanada can be presented.

काननजेरखु रागमः बापदरराजकुबारतेरेबारावः देंघाछुननराजालेचांलहैन
शीसगनसबसुरतिबिसर्ति राधिमिनोरधसिवमरुहाशीः वोहेत्तजातिकैगुजाल
शीः लमिताल्करसुजसुसुनावामनयहीवनेरखुपावाःयहनिमनलचितगाहु
लारेः पासमनेहनहीनेकबिसारेः हैहाः मानसरोवुरबिमलजलःपंघाकरे
तकीलीलःतिहतरसानीसिमिनबएःरजितदुचित्तअमोल ॥ २ ॥ रामः ॥

Plate XXIV. Ragini Bhairavi

CHAUPAYI: This unmarried princess is Bhairavi. Bhairava was overwhelmed by her beauty and tempted by her charms. At this auspicious turn, she came to the temple of Lord Shiva. She devoutly prayed to the Lord for the fulfilment of her desires. Beating the drums with her hands, she sings praises of the Master and sincerely prays for the hand of Bhairava. She has set her heart on her chosen one, and she does not forget him even for a single moment.

DOHA: Near the sacred waters of the Manasarovar in Kailash [Mount Kailasa], where countless birds of all kinds chatter, there is the abode of Lord Shiva in enchanting surroundings.

THE BHAIRAVI THATA

The scale of this thata represents the material of the ninth family of North Indian ragas.

Raga (Ragini) Bhairavi

Bhairavi, always represented in female form, usually as the wife of Bhairav, is frequently described in its pictorial aspect. The following can be found in the Cattvārimsacchata-Rāga-Nirūpanam (p. 13), in the Rāga-Kalpadruma (p. 17), and in the Saṅgīta-Darpana (2, 48):

> The great poets sing of Bhairavi, the consort of Lord Bhairava, worshipping her Lord seated on a carved crystal on the peak of Mount Kailasa with soft leaves of full blossomed lotus flowers. She holds the cymbals in her hands, and her eyes sparkle with a yellowish glint.

Bhairavi is to be performed in the late morning in a peaceful, serious, occasionally also sad mood. Its vadis are MA (F) and SA (C). The performance rules of this raga are unusually relaxed, and there are neither weak and strong notes nor are there any vakra steps. Some musicians take the liberty of using RE shuddha (D) in ascent and even the sequence MA MA tivra (F F#) in their songs. These are deviations which cannot be considered as characteristic features. The ascent and descent of the first five notes of the Bhairavi scale are straight and show no remarkable features.

The note DHA komal (A♭) is often performed with a small, shallow

vibrato, and the progressions DHA komal NI komal SA (A♭ B♭ c) and
SA RE komal SA (c d♭ c) are frequently used.

Although one cannot speak of fixed performance rules, musicians are
inclined to avoid occasionally the note PA (G) in ascent, except in
"garlands" and fast passages:

RAGA BHAIRAVI   (Dhamar Tal)   BH, II, 419

Asthayi

Antara

The avoidance of the note RE komal (D♭) in ascent in the preceding song specimen is purely incidental. As has already been mentioned, various liberties may be taken in this raga.

Tone material

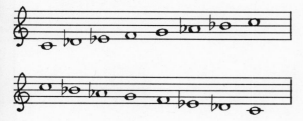

Raga Malkouns (Malkauns, Malkous, Malkos)

In a comparatively recent raga-mala text by Gangadhar[219] the following pictorial descriptions of Malkouns is given:

> Malkous wears a robe of blue; he holds a white staff in his hand. He wears on his shoulders a string of pearls; he is accompanied by a number of lady companions. Dressed in a blue robe, his shining complexion puts to shame the prince of Kausaka (?). With garlands on his shoulders and a white staff in his hand he is the very picture of the purity of the flavour of Love. He overpowers the heart of women, and by his beauty attracts the gaze of all. At early dawn he is up and seated. Hero and Lover, he is contemplating his colourful exploits of Love.[220]

Malkouns is to be performed at night in a very serious mood. Its vadis are MA (F) and the upper SA (c). The notes RE komal (D♭) and PA (G) are totally avoided, whereby an anhemitonic pentatonic scale is achieved: SA GA komal MA DHA komal NI komal SA (C E♭ F A♭ B♭ c). Some musicians intone the notes DHA komal (A♭) and NI komal (B♭) slightly flat, a habit which, however, is not a rule. The notes GA komal (E♭) and DHA komal (A♭) are often performed

रागमालकोसिक ॥गा दोहा गौरगौरारामकली चनावितश्रितिष्ठ ब इनसंगलागगुण
सरी मालकोसिकमहबूब ॥चौपय॥ मालकोसकनूप चतुर बिनानी कंचण देहसुबरा
छ्यानी देरेमहलतमतपरछाही बेरचौरुरावुरावतछांही जिनके रूपनरंझाही कांम
सरूपकामिणी सोछी सुझयएसुनगवनावबनावही तिहियेछम ल्सीनापा वहहै पानमात
बिरक रूलिये मनरसमगनमौनसुखकी चे ॥दोहा॥ सह बानिकनूपदिषिकरि
माल कोसिकसिरबेग अबबरनउछबिकांमिल

Plate XXV. Raga Malkaushika [Malkouns]

DOHA: Gauri, Gaura, Ramkali, Khambavati, Gunashri, all treat Malkaushika as the loved one.

CHAUPAYI: Malkaushika is very wise and ingenious. Golden-complexioned, he has a sweet tongue. He is seated on his throne in his palace attended by a number of women whose charm and beauty are matchless. They are exceedingly desirable and tempting. They are wearing bright and glistening ornaments that have added brilliance because they adorn such beautiful bodies. Chewing betel leaves and holding betels in their hands, the women are happy and full of joy.

DOHA: Beholding the majesty and dazzling brilliance of King Malkaushika, how would I now describe the charm and beauty of the maidens?

with a small, shallow vibrato, a practice which also is not required.
In short, all five notes of the <u>Malkouns</u> scale have practically equal
importance, and melodies may be started or interrupted on any of
these notes. This raga, having no characteristic phrases, offers
the performer a comparatively wide field for free improvisation.

RAGA MALKOUNS   (Ektal)   BH, III, 719

Asthayi

Antara

Tone material

Raga Bilaskhani-todi (Vilaskhani-todi)

Bilas Khan (Vilasa Khan) was the son of the famous Tansen.
After his father's death, Bilas Khan became court singer, and it is
reported that of his numerous creations Bilaskhani-todi is the most
beautiful.   There are, we have seen, a number of compound ragas
which date back to the time of the Mogul emperors, particularly to
the time of Akbar the Great. Mohammedan and Hindu musicians were
assembled at his court and when the Muslim musicians performed their
own melodies, the Hindu musicians in competition created new ragas
by combining two or more ragas into new forms.   Bilaskhani-todi,
for instance, represents a combination of materials taken from the
ragas Bhairavi and Todi.[221] It is to be performed in the morning.
The vadis are DHA komal (A♭) and GA komal (E♭).   The notes RE
komal (D♭) and GA komal (E♭) are treated in the same manner as in
Todi; that is, they are intoned slightly low and are linked in ascent
by a gliding step.   In descent both notes are taken normally without
any microtonal alterations.

The notes above MA (F) are taken from the Bhairavi scale. MA (F)
is used very little in ascent, and DHA komal (A♭) (in ascent) is performed with a slight vibrato:

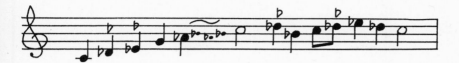

In descent the note RE komal (D♭), and rarely DHA komal (A♭), are performed with a vibrato. A straight descent from SA to SA (c to C) is generally avoided.   The vakra feature begins with PA (G) in the phrases DHA komal PA NI komal DHA komal MA (A♭ G B♭ A♭ F) or DHA komal PA DHA komal MA (A♭ G A♭ F).   Below PA (G), the descent usually progresses in the following manner: PA DHA komal MA GA komal RE komal GA komal RE komal SA (G A♭ F E♭ D♭ E♭ D♭ C). GA komal RE komal GA komal RE komal (E♭ D# E♭ D♭) is particularly characteristic. The upper SA (c) is often hidden by the descending gliding step RE komal-NI komal (d♭-B♭). A similar procedure may be observed in the occasional descending gliding step DHA komal-MA (A♭-F) by which the note PA (G) is avoided.

At times musicians avoid the note NI komal (B♭) and descend without gliding from the upper SA (c) to DHA komal (A♭).

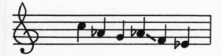

RAGA BILASKHANI-TODI   (Jhumra)   BH, VI, 384

Asthayi

Antara

Tone material

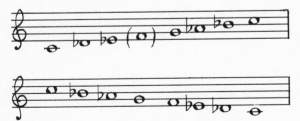

There are some musicians who state that Bilaskhani-todi is very similar to raga Todi and that, ignoring a few minor deviations, the Todi
scale may be used in both instances. This is an erroneous. There
exists a similarity between the ragas Todi and Bahaduri-todi,[222] and
some confusion arises from the fact that Bahaduri-todi occasionally
and incorrectly is called Bilaskhani-todi.

Raga Bhupal-todi

Bhupal-todi is a "little" and rare raga which may be ascribed
to the Bhairavi thata. Its scale represents a combination of notes
taken from the ragas Bhupali[223] and Bilaskhani-todi. The vadis are
DHA komal (Ab) and GA komal (Eb). The scale of this raga has a
pentatonic feature similar to that of Bhupali, but the notes RE, GA,
and DHA (D, E, and A) are here not only performed in their komal
forms, RE komal, GA komal, and DHA komal (Db, Eb, and Ab),
but the first two notes are microtonally low altered as in Bilaskhani-
todi, and the third note, DHA komal (Ab), is performed with a slight
vibrato. In contrast to Bilaskhani-todi, the note PA (G) assumes
greater importance in descent.

RAGA BHUPAL-TODI   (Chautal)   BH, VI, 392

Asthayi

Antara

The preceding song specimen shows the occasional use of the note NI
komal (B♭). This is not a scale note, but serves only as an indication
that the succeeding note DHA komal (A♭), performed with a vibrato,
has to be approached from above.

Tone material

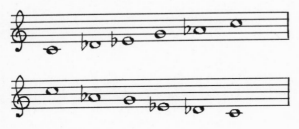

Raga Sunderkauns

This very obscure raga may be ascribed to the Bhairavi family.
Its alleged origin is the Punjab. Sunderkauns has the same scale as
raga Malkouns,[224] to which is added the note PA (G) in the phrase MA
PA DHA komal NI komal MA (F G A♭ B♭ F). Even the vadis of this
raga are uncertain. At the only hearing of Sunderkauns I experienced
in fourteen years, it was noticeable that the note MA (F) was treated

strongly. Although the performing musicians were unable or unwilling to offer any information, one can assume that MA (F) is the vadi
of this raga.

No adequate song specimen can be presented.

Raga Dhanashri

There are two ragas with the name Dhanashri. One is ascribed
to the Kafi thata,[225] while the raga here under consideration belongs to
the Bhairavi family. It is to be performed in the morning. This raga
Dhanashri is not much more than a modification of Dhanashri of the
Kafi thata. In Dhanashri of the Bhairavi thata the microtonally high
alteration of the note NI komal (B♭) of Dhanashri (of the Kafi thata)
does not occur, and in the Bhairavi form RE komal (D♭) instead of
RE shuddha (D) (or the Kafi form) is used.

With the exception of the above-mentioned two differences, there are
no other distinctions between the two Dhanashri ragas, and the performance rules of the Kafi form can also be applied to the Bhairavi.

The Bhairavi form of Dhanashri is very rare, and no song specimen can be shown.

Raga Motki (Motaki)

This rare and obscure raga can be ascribed to the Bhairavi thata.
Its vadis are probably PA (G) and SA (C). Motki represents a combination of materials taken from Bhairavi, the Mallar,[226] Kanada,[227]
and Sarang[228] groups, to which are added one or two individual and
characteristic phrases. The Motki scale uses both forms of RE, RE
komal (D♭) and RE shuddha (D), both forms of DHA (A), and both
forms of NI (B). In descent the note MA (F) is avoided.

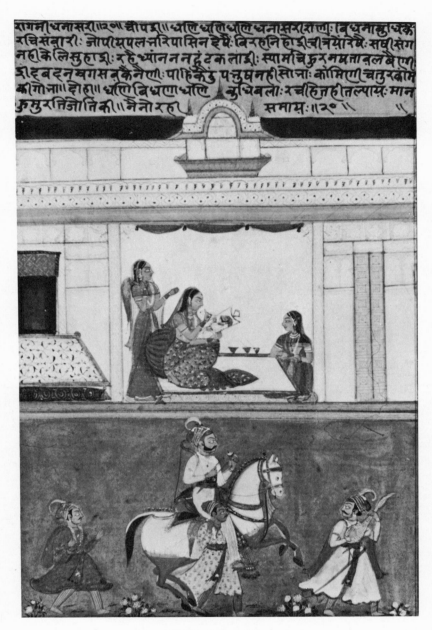

Plate XXVI. Ragini Dhanashri

CHAUPAYI: Twice blessed is ragini Dhanashri, who has been created by the Lord with such great skill. If her lover is not by her side, even for a little while, she feels exceedingly dejected in her heart, and in her sadness she begins to draw lines on the ground. She does not relish any company and stares about vacantly. She is very well proportioned. She has long hair that reaches to her feet. Her face is like the moon, and her eyes are those of a young deer. The beauty of the ornaments she is wearing is enhanced by being worn on such a lovely body.

DOHA: Praise be to the Lord who created this body with such great care and skill in order to torment men and make them restless. Her graceful body is like a well-cut bright jewel and [our] eyes do not tire of looking at this heavenly sight.

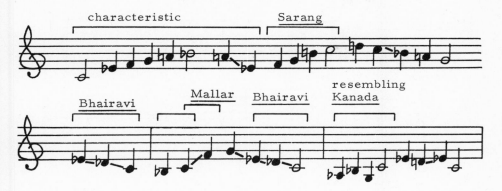

The low DHA komal (A♭) appears in a phrase which resembles Kanada.
In the middle octave region the note DHA shuddha (A) is used in both
ascent and descent. NI shuddha (B) is used in ascent only; NI komal
(B♭), however, may be employed both in ascent and descent. The
note RE shuddha (D) is mainly employed in ascent but may also occur
in descent. RE komal (D♭), however, appears only in descent. These
rules are subject to the performer's taste and the manner in which he
combines phrases of the Sarang, Kanada, etc., ragas. The resulting
tone material will then determine whether, for instance, the note RE
shuddha (D) and NI shuddha (B) can be used in ascent and descent,
and whether restrictions in their use are required.

        RAGA MOTKI   (Jhaptal)   BH, VI, 389

        Asthayi

Antara

Tone material

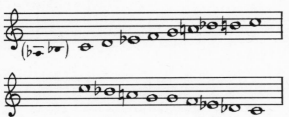

Raga Utari-gunkali

Neither performance time, performance rules, nor <u>vadis</u> of this very rare and obscure raga are known. It is said that this raga consists of <u>Bhairav</u> material into which are interpolated three short Asavari[229] progressions.

The ragas <u>Utari-gunkali</u> and <u>Asavari</u> (with <u>RE</u> komal) are very similar. The distinction between the two ragas lies in the fact that <u>Utari-gunkali</u> employs the notes <u>GA</u> komal (E♭) and <u>NI</u> komal (B♭) in ascent while <u>Asavari</u> (with <u>RE</u> komal) avoids them.

RAGA UTARI-GUNKALI   (Trital)   BH, VI, 394

Asthayi

Antara

Tone material

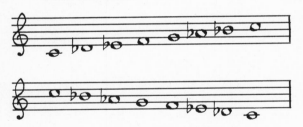

Raga Vasant-mukhari

The name and the scale of this rare raga have their counterparts in the South. Vasant-mukhari is to be performed in the morning. Its vadis are DHA komal (Ab) and RE komal (Db). The lower tetrachord of the scale takes its material from raga Bhairav,[230] the upper tetrachord from raga Bhairavi. In contrast to Bhairav, in Vasant-mukhari the note RE komal (Db) is often avoided in ascent.

RAGA VASANT-MUKHARI   (Jhaptal)   BH, VI, 396

राग न टोडा ॥१॥ चौपाइ ॥ परम बिचित्र रची बि घटो डा ॥ तिहुं लोक रबिक
न छोडी करद्रभत बाग म होगढी पेम सुरति उपजावत गढी सुनैनाद
म्रगाजूथ चुलानै देप्रतनैन छबि निपट लजानै उ नजिनिक व सरोवर तीर न
मल जल मानौ गंगा नीर सारंग सुरं र गहाप्रन्यौ हौ रामौ अपने कर आपन
कर बुलामो ॥ दोहा ॥ नैन उमाहि पीय ब से जीय में पेम बैराग मन बोरा
ब त म्रगन सुं स्तुटोडी ग ढी बाग ॥१७॥ ॥

Plate XXVII. Ragini Todi

CHAUPAYI: The Almighty has made a wondrous creature in Todi. He appears to have spared no charm and grace in this act. Holding the nectar [vessel] in her hands, she stands in a garden, and the world around her is filled with deep love. Hearing the enchanting sounds of Todi, herds of deer lose their way. The beauty of Todi is so enchanting that eyes drop after a glance at her. Nearby is a pond of clear, sweet water, sacred as "Gangajal." Taking her to be his own, Sarang extends his hands and beckons her to his side.

DOHA: The lover always dwells inside her eyelids, but the lover has become an ascetic in his heart. Her mind is as confused as the deer, and she stands still in one spot in the garden.

THE TODI THATA

The scale of this thata represents the material of the tenth family
of North Indian ragas.

Raga (ragini) Todi

Todi is one of the most important ragas of North India. If one
looks in museums or art institutes for pictorial representations of
ragas, the picture of Todi, with its gentle, lovely atmosphere, will
always stand out. The following description can be found in the
Cattvārimsacchata-Rāga-Nirūpanam (p. 15) and in the Saṅgīta-Darpana
(2, 53):

> With a fair erect body like the white lotus, and delicate
> like the gleaming dew drop, Todi holds the vina and pro-
> vides fun and frolic to the deer deep in the forest. Her
> body is anointed with saffron and camphor.

Todi pictures nearly always show a gentle, beautiful woman, holding
a vina and standing in a lovely green forest. She is surrounded by
deer. Numerous pictures of this raga show in the background buildings
of a distant town or palace. Only rarely do we find a different pictorial
representation such as in the Rāga-Sāgara (3, 45);

> I always shall remember Todi, with her charming face
> rested in the palm of her hand, and the right hand hold-
> ing a crystal cup filled with delicious wine. She is car-
> rying the robe of her lover on her left shoulder.[231]

Todi is to be performed in the late morning. H. A. Popley in his
Music of India (p. 68)[232] states that the performance time is noon.
but his time is very late for this raga. Todi represents the mood of
delighted adoration in a gentle, loving sentiment.

The vadis are DHA komal (A♭) and GA komal (E♭). The note
RE komal is a vishrantisthan. The scale of the Todi thata is SA,
RE komal, GA komal MA tivra, PA, DHA komal, NI shuddha, and
SA (C, D♭, E♭, F#, G, A♭, B, c). In the raga, however, some

important microtonal alterations are made in ascent: the notes RE
komal (D♭), GA komal (E♭), and DHA komal (A♭) are intoned slightly
low, and MA tivra (F #), very sharp.   In descent the intonation of all
these notes is normal.

The note PA (G) is of very little importance in this raga and it is
avoided in ascent.   North Indian musicians hold differing opinions
about the use of this note, some believe that if PA (G) is used, the
raga becomes Miyan-ki-todi, a creation of the famous Tansen; others
state that there is no difference between the ragas Todi and Miyan-ki-
todi and that PA (G) can be used only in descent.

        The three low-altered notes in ascent are approached from
below and are often performed with a small, shallow vibrato.

MA tivra (F#), too, can occasionally be performed with a small vibrato which is less articulated than the vibratos on the low-altered
notes.   NI shuddha (B) is usually intoned normally in ascent, although
there are some musicians who perform it slightly sharp.

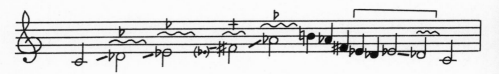

The phrase GA komal RE komal GA komal-RE komal (E♭ D♭ E♭-D♭),
although not strictly required, appears in numerous Todi songs and
could be considered as a characteristic feature.

In some instances the ascent is performed without the note SA
(C):

The descent is usually rendered in the following manner:

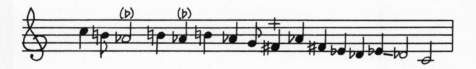

or in this manner:

The succeeding song specimen uses the note PA (G) rather frequently,
perhaps too much for the conventional Auffuehrungspraxis of Todi.

RAGA (RAGINI) TODI   (Trital)   BH, II, 432

Asthayi

Antara

Tone material

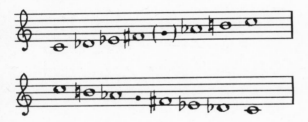

Raga Multani

This raga, named after the city of Multan, is to be performed in the late afternoon.[233] Multani is supposed to represent quiet, loving contemplation. Its scale is the same as that of Todi, but the treatment of the individual notes differs considerably in the two ragas. The vadis are PA (G) and SA (C). The notes RE komal (Db) and DHA komal (Ab) appear only in descent and are treated very weakly.

The note SA (C) is often performed with a small ornament. If we "enlarge" it, it can be notated as follows:

GA komal (E♭) in ascent is approached from above, roughly from MA
tivra (F#), and is usually intoned slightly sharp. MA tivra (F#), too,
is taken sharp, as in Todi, but it is performed without any vibrato.
The note PA (G) is strong in Multani, in severe contrast to Todi.
Melodies may be interrupted at this point. NI shuddha (B) in ascent
is taken sharp.

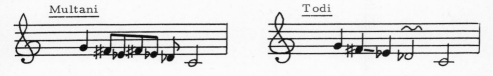

In descent no microtonal alterations are used, and the notes are in-
toned normally. Of importance is the quick moving phrase MA tivra
GA komal MA tivra GA komal (F# E♭ F# E♭) or MA tivra GA komal
MA tivra PA MA tivra GA komal (F# E♭ F# G F# E♭), which repre-
sents a noticeable distinction from the slow moving Todi step MA tivra-
GA komal (F# -E♭).

Multani   Todi

The vibrato on the descending RE komal (D♭) is short in contrast to
the one in Todi.

In order to perform the preceding phrase in <u>Todi</u> it would have to be:

The <u>Multani</u> descent is performed in the following manner:

RAGA MULTANI   (Trital)   BH, IV, 736

Asthayi

Antara

Tone material

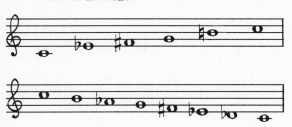

Occasionally musicians speak of a second type of raga <u>Multani</u> in which the notes <u>RE komal</u> (D♭) and <u>DHA komal</u> (A♭) are replaced in descent by their <u>shuddha</u> forms. This type at times is called raga <u>Ambika.</u> Its scale is:

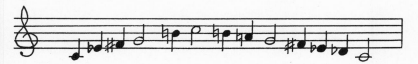

Raga Bahaduri-todi

<u>Bahaduri-todi</u> (or, simply <u>Bahaduri</u>) is a rare raga. Its performance rules are uncertain, and musicians occasionally speak of different types of this raga without describing their details. As far as I can ascertain, there are two basic types of <u>Bahaduri-todi</u>:

a) <u>Bahaduri-todi</u> which strongly resembles <u>Bilaskhani-todi,</u> in which the note <u>NI komal</u> (B♭) of the latter raga is raised to <u>NI shuddha</u> (B);

b) <u>Bahaduri-todi</u> which utilizes the scale of <u>Todi</u> without ever using the note <u>PA</u> (G).

There are some other variants of this raga, for instance, one in which the second type employs the notes <u>MA</u> (F), <u>MA tivra</u> (F♯), and <u>PA</u> (G) in descent. Another type uses both forms of <u>RE</u>, <u>RE komal</u> (D♭) and <u>RE shuddha</u> (D), and so forth.

In all types <u>DHA komal</u> (A♭), of the low octave region, is the vadi and <u>GA komal</u> (E♭), the <u>samvadi.</u>

The following example illustrates a type of <u>Bahaduri-todi</u> in which the notes <u>MA</u> (F), <u>MA</u> <u>tivra</u> (F#), and <u>PA</u> (G) are employed in descent:

While in <u>Todi</u> the note <u>MA</u> <u>tivra</u> (F#) is altered microtonally high, it is intoned normally in <u>Bahaduri-todi</u>. A similar difference in intonation can be observed in the performance of the note <u>DHA</u> <u>komal</u> (Ab): it is low-altered in <u>Todi</u> and is normal in <u>Bahaduri-todi</u>.

The following song specimen represents neither the first nor the second type of this raga. It uses the note <u>PA</u> (G) both in ascent and descent. Its melodic line resembles so much that of <u>Miyan-ki-todi</u> [234] that there is hardly any essential distinction noticeable between the two ragas. Only one slight difference may be pointed out. In contrast to <u>Miyan-ki-todi</u>, melodies in <u>Bahaduri-todi</u> begin usually in the low octave region and move gradually upward.

RAGA BAHADURI-TODI   (Jhaptal)   BH, VI, 408

Antara

It is impossible to state a fixed tone material of this raga because the various types require different notes.

Raga Gujri-todi (Gurjari-, Ghurjari-, Gojri-todi)

In the earliest known Sanskrit text which deals with the iconography of ragas, the Rāga-Sāgara (Chapter Rāga-dhyāna-vidhānam), the following description of this raga is given:

> Contemplation of Ghurjari: Covered with a white mantle (armor), playing with her companions with balls in her hands, swaying in a dance (?), I worship,

in the region of my heart, Ghurjari.[235]

N. A. Willard offers the following description of Gujri, ragini (wife)
of Megh:

> The tenor of this picture is not evident. It presents a
> young female minstrel of a delicate voice and engaging
> mien, dressed in yellow short stays and red saree, and
> adorned with jewels.[236]

The possibilities of transforming a raga, for instance, Todi, are
numerous. A good musician can change any raga by altering its notes,
by interpolating various passages, or by combining or adding two or
more features from different ragas. Gujri-todi is one of these forms.
Its scale is the same as that of Todi, but it avoids the note PA (G) in
both ascent and descent. This similarity can be observed not only between the Todi thata and the Todi ragas but also between some of the
minor ragas subordinated to Todi. For instance, Gujri-todi and the
second type of Bahaduri-todi are strikingly similar. The difference
between these two ragas lies in two minor features. First, the vadi of
Bahaduri-todi is the note DHA komal (Ab) of the low octave region,
while the vadi of Gujri-todi is the same note but an octave higher. The
second point is the use or avoidance of the note PA (G); in Bahaduri-
todi the note PA (G) may be used in ascent; while in Gujri-todi it is
totally avoided. One can add that Bahaduri-todi melodies often begin
in the low octave region, and Gujri-todi melodies usually start and
move in the middle octave region.

The vadi of Gujri-todi is DHA komal (Ab); the samvadi is GA
komal. None of the microtonal alterations which occur in Todi appear
in Gujri-todi. Particularly the note MA tivra (F#) is not high-altered,
perhaps because the note PA (G) is omitted and no "leading note" effect
is required.

RAGA GUJRI-TODI   (Brahmtal; 28 matras)   BH, VI, 402

Asthayi

Antara

Tone material

Raga Khat-todi

This raga can be ascribed to the Todi thata or, if Khat [237] material predominates, to the Asavari thata. As the name indicates, the
raga represents a combination of Todi and Khat materials. It is left
to the performing musician either to create a good balance between
the two or to purposely stress for a little while one or the other elements, a method which creates unusual interest for an educated listener.

The vadis of this raga are DHA komal (A♭) and GA komal (E♭).
In order to illustrate the liberties a performer can take with Khat-
todi, an alap fragment is shown below which contains only a single
Khat phrase. If there is only limited Khat material and the melody
moves mainly within the realm of Todi, Khat features are usually presented at the end of the alap and at the end of the asthayi and antara.
If there is more Khat material, the combination with Todi can be made
in any manner the performer finds suitable.

Khat

In the following song specimen the combination of Khat and Todi elements is made in a manner different from that shown in the preceding
alap fragment. The asthayi represents only Khat, while the antara
more or less shows Todi features. The only trace of Khat in the antara
can be found in the second line, bar four, where the note RE shuddha
(D) defies the surrounding Todi array.

RAGA KHAT-TODI   (Ektal)   BH, VI, 358

Asthayi

Antara

No fixed tone material can be postulated because the combination of Khat and Todi depends upon the choice of the performer.

Raga Ahiri-todi

The performance rules of this extremely rare and obscure raga are unknown. All that is known is that the Ahiri scale employs both forms of MA, MA shuddha (F) and MA tivra (F#), and that Todi material prevails.

As in raga Todi the notes RE komal (Db), GA komal (Eb), and occasionally also the low NI shuddha (B) are performed with a short, shallow vibrato. The microtonal alterations in this raga are the same as those in Todi.

No adequate song specimen can be shown.

Raga Lachari-todi

The name of this rare raga indicates its affinity to the Todi family. Hence, the raga has been ascribed to this thata. However, it has little in common with Todi. It would be more adequate to relate Lachari-todi to raga Desi,[238] for Desi phrases, although occasionally somewhat modified, occur frequently in this raga. The vadi is MA (F); the samvadi is probably SA (C). The Lachari-todi scale employs, in addition to the notes SA (C), MA (F), and PA (G), the notes RE shuddha (D), GA komal (Eb) and GA shuddha (E), DHA shuddha (A) and DHA komal (Ab), and NI shuddha (B) and NI komal (Bb).

DHA komal (Ab) is performed with a very shallow, fast vibrato. Occasionally this vibrato may also be used in the performance of GA komal (Eb).

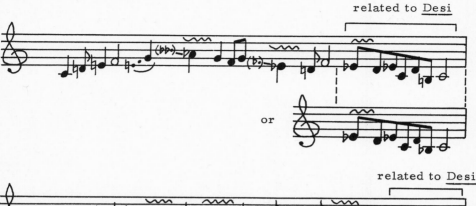

The ascent from MA (F) to the upper SA (c) can be made in two ways.

Either   or

but never

If the ascending line extends only up to NI komal (B♭), then the use of DHA (A) is permissible:

Opinion about the performance rules of this raga is divided. A very well-known singer of Bombay used to sing songs in raga Desi, but invariably called the raga Lachari. Whichever way Lachari-todi is evaluated, an educated listener will always regard it as a form of Desi in which the notes GA komal (E♭), GA shuddha (E), DHA komal (A♭), DHA shuddha (A), NI shuddha (B) and NI komal (B♭) are used, and in which the note <u>MA</u> (F) is occasionally treated strongly.

RAGA LACHARI-TODI   (Trital)   BH, VI, 405

Tone material

Raga Lakshmi-todi (Laxmi-todi)

This obscure raga is ascribed to the Todi thata, although little relationship with Todi can be observed. Its vadi is probably PA (G). Pandit Bhatkhande presents two songs in this raga. If they are compared with each other, the reader has the impression of two utterly different ragas. The performance rules are as good as unknown. I shall try, however, to derive some rules from the scanty material available. A heavy gamak consisting of two or three successive heavy descending gliding steps between NI komal (B♭) and DHA komal (A♭) seems to be characteristic. In descent appear both forms of RE, RE shuddha (D) and RE komal (D♭), and both forms of DHA (A and A♭). The notes GA shuddha (E) and GA komal (E♭) appear in ascent, but in descent only the komal form of this note is used. Another gliding step, descending from MA (F) to GA komal (E♭) and in a vakra movement in ascent, seems to be of some importance.

In ascent can be noted the frequent omission of NI komal (B♭) before the upper SA (c).

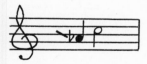

Between two upper SA (c) the note NI komal (B♭) may be used:

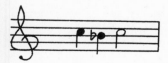

In descent the avoidance of <u>NI</u> <u>komal</u> (B♭) between the upper <u>SA</u> (c)
and <u>DHA</u> <u>komal</u> (A♭) may represent a rule:

If the descent does not begin with the upper <u>SA</u> (c) but with <u>NI</u> <u>komal</u>
(B♭), the progression uses not <u>DHA</u> <u>komal</u> (A♭) but <u>DHA</u> <u>shuddha</u> (A):

RAGA LAKSHMI-TODI   (Sultal)   BH, VI, 406

Asthayi

Antara

Tone material

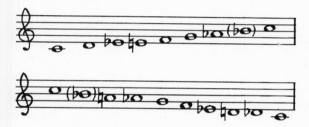

Raga Anjani-todi

The performance rules of this very obscure raga are indistinct, and there is hardly a singer at the present time who performs Anjani-todi. The vadi is probably PA (G). The note DHA komal (A♭) is performed with a fast vibrato which is approached from above, approximately from NI komal (B♭). Both forms of DHA (A and A♭) and of NI (B and B♭) are in use. The purvanga (lower tetrachord) of the Anjani-todi scale uses Desi material, the uttaranga (upper tetrachord) shows Kafi and Asavari features. This arrangement represents no strict rule; other combinations are equally permissible. Some characteristic features are shown in the following examples:

or

The preceding examples show that <u>Anjani-todi</u> does not use <u>RE komal</u> (Db); it uses only <u>RE shuddha</u> (D). The note <u>GA komal</u> (Eb) is avoided in ascent.

RAGA ANJANI-TODI   (Chautal)   BH, VI, 411

Asthayi

Antara

Tone material

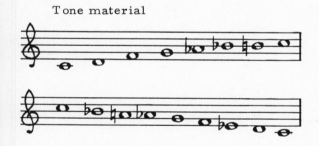

OBSCURE RAGAS

Although a number of obscure ragas have already been discussed, there are some others which do not fit into the system of the ten thatas. These indistinct ragas are mentioned here in order to complete the survey of northern ragas. Most of them are more or less the "private property" of certain singers who have either created them or inherited them from their teachers. These ragas are usually not accessible and can only be studied par distance and on rare occasions.

Raga Madhyamavati (Madhumadhavi)

The vadis of Madhyamavati are probably SA (C) and PA (G). The song specimen shown below consists of phrases of a number of ragas which seem to represent the constituent material of this raga:

Khamaj

Sindhura

Jhinjhoti (in the antara)

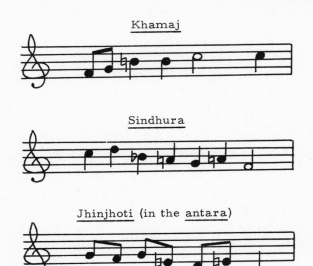

RAGA MADHYAMAVATI   (Jhaptal)   Vaze, 46

Asthayi

Antara

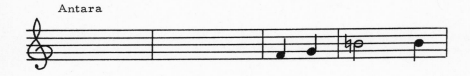

Plate XXVIII. Ragini Madhumadhavi [Madhyamavadi]

CHAUPAYI: Madhumadhavi is a beautiful woman dressed in green and adorned with numerous shining ornaments. Sages turn pale when they behold her. When she steps out from the palace dark clouds gather in the sky and thunder softly. Lightning appears, and the "kural" birds sing pleasantly in great delight.

DOHA: Expecting to meet her lover, she is exultant and stands on the doorstep in a state of great happiness. She awaits the arrival of her master and is, therefore, very happy, her heart filled with pleasure.

No tone material can be postulated in these compound ragas.

Raga Lankeshri

This raga supposedly represents a combination of materials
taken from the ragas Khamaj (particularly Rageshri[239]) and Jhinjhoti.
Its vadis are MA (F) and SA (C). In contrast to raga Rageshri, the
note GA (E) in Lankeshri receives a vakra treatment. While in Rageshri
the progression MA GA RE SA (F E D C) is permitted, it seems to be
modified to the vakra phrase GA MA RE SA (E F D C) in Lankeshri.
The song specimen shown below shows both progressions, the vakra
in the third line and the straight one in the sixth line. Whether or not
the vakra feature is required in ascent cannot be stated with any certainty. The phrase SA MA GA PA MA DHA PA (C F E G F A G) seems
to indicate such a practice. NI shuddha (B) appears only in ascent;
NI komal (Bb), however is used in both ascent and descent.

RAGA LANKESHRI   (Adachautal)   Vaze, 52

Asthayi

Antara

Raga Manzh

This raga consists of a combination of elements taken from the
ragas Bilaval,[240] Khamaj, and Mand.[241] Its vadis are GA (E) and
DHA (A). The note RE (D) is treated in the same manner as in raga
Bhatiyar of the Bilaval thata.[242]

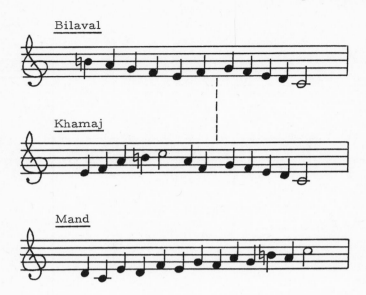

Bilaval

Khamaj

Mand

RAGA MANZH   (Trital)   Vaze, 53

Asthayi

Antara

Raga Raysakanada

This raga is said to consist of a combination of phrases taken
from the ragas Naiki-kanada[243] and Bahar.[244] Its vadis are SA (C)
and PA (G). The very limited available sources show that Bahar
material is used in the lower, and Naiki-kanada material in the upper,
tetrachord of the scale.

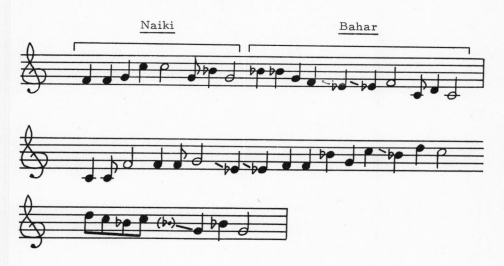

RAGA RAYSAKANADA   (Jhaptal)   Vaze, 55

Asthayi

Antara

Raga Banskanada

This raga is said to use various phrases of raga Kafi.[245] As far as is known, not a single musician at the present time performs this raga. Its performance rules are totally unknown. The following song specimen is the only available material of Banskanada.

RAGA BANSKANADA   (Ektal)   Vaze, 61

Asthayi

Antara

The preceding song melody yields the following information. The ascending <u>NI</u> <u>shuddha</u> (B) appears only in the low octave region before <u>SA</u> (C). <u>DHA</u> (A) or <u>DHA</u> <u>komal</u> (A♭) is avoided in ascent. The descent

employs all seven notes but shows two vakra features in SA DHA komal
NI komal DHA komal NI komal PA (c A♭ B♭ A♭ B♭ G).

Raga Adana-bahar

This raga consists of a combination of phrases taken from the
ragas Adana-kanada [246] and Bahar. [247] Its vadis are either MA (F) and
SA (C) or SA (C) and MA (F). The note NI shuddha (B) appears in
ascent and NI komal (B♭) in descent, a feature which can be observed
in a large number of ragas. Here it may emphasize the relationship
with raga Bahar. The ascent is performed either as indicated in the
following song specimen or it has to use the progression GA komal
MA DHA NI shuddha SA (E♭ F A B c). The note DHA komal (A♭) may
be touched upon in descent very lightly.

RAGA ADANA-BAHAR   (Trital)   Vaze, 65

Raga Gara-bageshri

This raga is occasionally used in light popular music. Its vadis
are MA (F) and SA (C). As indicated by its name, this raga uses
phrases from the ragas Gara[248] and Bageshri.[249] Gara-bageshri melodies move mainly in the low and middle octave regions in fast tempo.
In ascent appears GA shuddha (E), in descent GA komal (Eb). The
note NI komal (Bb) is used in both ascent and descent.

RAGA GARA-BAGESHRI

Asthayi

Antara

Raga Jaitshankara

This raga represents a combination of materials taken from either the ragas Shankara [250] and Jait (Jayat), [251] or Shankara and Jayat-kalyan. [252] If Jait elements are used, the note RE komal (D♭) has to be employed; if Jayat-kalyan elements are used, RE shuddha (D) has to be applied. In this latter instance, which is represented in the following song specimen, some care is necessary to avoid any resemblance with Shuddh-kalyan, [253] where the note RE (D) often appears in conjunction with GA (E).

Students of Aladiya Khan Saheb of Bombay employ in this raga both forms of RE (D and D♭) and DHA (A and A♭).

RAGA JAITSHANKARA   (Trital)   Vaze, 72

Asthayi

Antara

The preceding song melody points toward some performance rules which could only be ascertained if more material were available. The rules hinted at are: melodies in this raga begin in the high octave region; the note MA (F) is totally avoided; RE (D) is omitted in ascent and DHA (A) in descent.

Raga Khokar

Although Khokar is obscure and rare, musicians speak of two types of this raga. Both types have the vadis SA (C) and PA (G).

a) Khokar as performed by the pupils of Aladiya Khan Saheb. It is a combination of phrases taken from the ragas Khamaj [254] and Bihagda: [255]

Khamaj   Bihagada

b) Khokar as shown by R. N. Vaze in his Sangit Kala Prakash: [256]

The following song specimen represents the second type.

RAGA KHOKAR   (Ektal)   Second type   Vaze, 89

Raga Gara-kanada

This raga represents a combination of phrases taken from Gara[257] and the Kanada family.[258] As has previously been stated, raga Gara is itself a combination of elements taken from the ragas Jhinjhoti,[259] Pilu,[260] and Khamaj.[261] Its vadis are SA (C) and PA (G).

RAGA GARA-KANADA   (Trital)   Vaze, 125

The tone material cannot be stated with any certainty because the
scale of this raga is derived from four ragas. The preceding song
specimen indicates that the note NI komal (Bb) is avoided in ascent
and that a remarkable vakra feature, PA GA shuddha MA RE GA komal
RE (G E F D Eb D), can be observed in descent. The use of GA shuddha (E) and NI shuddha (B) in ascent can also be noted in other songs
in GA MA DHA NI shuddha SA (E F A B c).

Raga Jog

       This raga appears in two types. Both have the vadis GA (E)
and NI (B).
       a) Jog representing a combination of material taken from raga
Malkouns [262] and a few features from Naiki-kanada. [263]

Naiki-kanada

       b) Jog as shown by R. N. Vaze, representing a combination of
Nath [264] and Nand [265] elements.
The following song specimen represents the second type of this raga.

       RAGA JOG   (Ektal)   Second type   Vaze, 139

       Asthayi

Raga Salang

This raga is said to be a derivative of raga <u>Sarang</u>.[266] Its <u>vadis</u> are probably <u>SA</u> (C) and <u>MA</u> (F). The following song specimen shows that the notes <u>GA</u> (E) and <u>DHA</u> (A) are totally avoided and that <u>MA</u> (F) is omitted in ascent.

RAGA SALANG   (Jhaptal)   Vaze, 92

Asthayi

Antara

Raga Khamaji

This raga is supposed to consist of Jhinjhoti [267] and Khamaj [268] elements. Its vadis are probably GA (E) and NI (B). In ascent appears the note NI (B), in descent NI komal (B♭). Two progressions

are said to be characteristic of this raga <u>GA MA PA NI SA</u> (E F G B
c) and, in the low octave region, <u>MA PA DHA SA</u> (F G A C).

    During my long stay in India I only once heard a musician refer-
ring to this raga, which he called <u>Khamaji-kanada</u>. Despite my efforts
I did not find a single musician who knew anything about this totally
obscure raga. One could assume that this song specimen represents
<u>Khamaji</u> with <u>GA komal</u> (E♭), at least in descent, in order to indicate
some relationship with the <u>Kanada</u> group.[266]

RAGA KHAMAJI   (Jhaptal)   Vaze, 141

The following ragas are still more obscure than the ones mentioned above. They can hardly ever be heard and are listed here only for the sake of completeness.

Raga Arabhi (Arabi)

A counterpart of this raga may be found in the music of the South. In the Cattvārimsacchata-Rāga-Nirūpanam this raga is described as follows:

> Always attended by her lover, covered with nava-malika flowers and engaged in drinking, sweet-speaking Arabhi is thus described.[270]

It differs from raga Durga (Bilaval thata)[271] only in the additional use of the note GA (E) in descent:

Raga Kamodnath

A combination of Kamod and Nath (?). The vadis of this raga are possibly SA (C) and PA (G).

Raga Shankara-aran

The name of this raga may point to the South, the scale does not. The vadis are possibly SA (C) and PA (G).

Raga Shankarabharan

Dhirashankarabharanam is the name of a famous South Indian raga. The northern raga may have the vadis PA (G) and SA (C); its scale only partially resembles the southern raga.

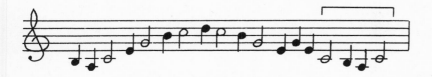

Raga Bhavsak

The vadis are possible MA (F) and SA (C).

Raga Takka (Dhakka)

This raga has an ancient name. Allegedly it is sung in honor of the god Rudra. A pictorial description of this raga can be found in Bhava Bhatta's Anūpa-Saṅgīta-Vilāsa (345, p. 139):

A youth of bluish complexion, with his body besmeared with saffron, awaiting at the trysting-place, at the bidding of his beloved, smitten with desire, such is Takka-kaisika.[272]

Its performance rules are totally unknown. Its vadis are probably PA (G) and SA (C). I once heard a singer perform Takka; the note MA (F) was used both in ascent and descent. This created the impression that the ascent was related to Bhimpalasi[273] and the descent to Bhairavi.[274]

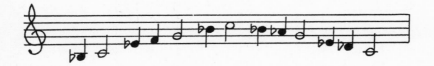

Raga Khem-kalyan

This raga represents a form of Kalyan[275] in which the note RE (D) is treated strongly in descent with the gamak indicated below. The vadis are probably the same as those of Kalyan.

Raga Abhir

The name of this raga points to the southern name Abheri. The vadis are PA (G) and SA (C).

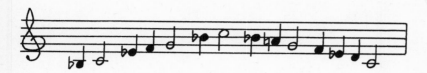

Raga Godhani

This raga is possibly identical with the raga Gorakh-kalyan.[276]
Its vadis are MA (F) and SA (C).

Raga Godhani-todi

Despite its name, which indicates some relationship with Todi,
this raga appears to be in a combination of materials of Barva[277] in
the lower half and Bageshri[278] in the upper half of the scale.

BRIEF NOTE ON THE DIFFERENCES
IN INTERPRETATION OF THE
RAGAS OF NORTH INDIA

This study of North Indian ragas is based on an investigation which I made during my fourteen years in India. Ragas with the same names were compared as they were performed in Bombay, Delhi, Lahore, Lucknow, Calcutta, etc., and great care was exercised in order to obtain correct information about widely applied performance practices. Despite this care, it is necessary to state that the music of northern India is represented by a number of more or less stylistically different schools which show their influences in the performances of various musicians. Students may move from one master to another and thus acquire different, often contradictory, practices in their performances, which may diffuse the original forms of ragas or, at times, enhance them. At the present time the study of Auffuehrungs-praxis has become enormously complex, and there are only a few features left which still show the characteristics of the different schools and thus enable us to distinguish between the various interpretations of ragas. One of the distinguishing points still observable is the per-formance of the tans, the fast passages. The important North Indian schools and their characteristic ways of performing tans are:

Indore

The main representative of this school is Rajah Ali Khan. The tans of the Indore musicians aim at a noble simplicity. One rarely finds complicated passages; only tans in clear-cut scale forms are in use.

Rampur

Famous artists of this school are Mushtaq Hussein and Nisar Hussein. The tans of the Rampur school (called satta tans) very often extend across three octaves, which is a much larger gamut than in the other schools. The satta tans are noticeable for their bold curves and are,

597

of course, much more complex than the tans of the Indore musicians.

Patiala

The most important representatives of this school are Ashiq Ali Khan
and Abdul Aziz Khan, a Vichitra-vina player.[279] The tans of this school,
despite their complexity, are performed in very fast tempo. With all
due respect to the great artistry of the Patiala singers, the tans are
usually sung in a somewhat bleating voice.

Agra

The main representatives of this school are Fayyaz Khan, Vilayat
Khan, and especially Vilayat Khan's father, Nathan Khan. The Agra
musicians strive in every performance for the utmost rhythmic perfection. The tans are sung in a special nasal manner and are not
performed to the syllable "ah," as is usually done, but to parts of the
text of the song.

Kirana (Rajputana)

The greatest singer of northern India, who reached an unsurpassed
artistic peak during the first third of the twentieth century, Abdul
Karim Khan, is the main representative of this school. His brother,
Abdul Vahid Khan, is also held in high esteem by Indian audiences.
In this school, greatest importance is given to the clear intonation of
notes and to beautifully rounded melodies. When the curve of the
melody rises, the voice of the singer changes into a remarkable fal-
setto which has created much admiration among Indian listeners.
Abdul Karim Khan sings only a few ragas, but these are performed
in greatest perfection. Each note is rendered in crystal clear intonation, and the beauty of the raga, be it shown in slow and expressive
or in brilliant and fast tans, becomes overwhelmingly manifest. Even
inexperienced and foreign listeners have been deeply moved by the
performances of this great artist. Abdul Karim Khan's pupils still
imitate the style of their master, but they make the mistake of ignoring the relationship between weak (short) and strong (long) notes by
their constant aiming at the creating of "beautiful sounds." Disregard-
ing the weak and strong note relationship—a relationship which is still

scrupulously maintained in Abdul Karim Khan's performances—alters
and possibly spoils the character of the raga.

Aladiya Khan Saheb

This school is named after the great master of Bombay, who lived in
the late nineteenth and early twentieth centuries. Aladiya Khan Saheb
is one of the truly great artists of North India. His art, which incor-
porates Abdul Karim Khan's beautiful sounds, becomes manifest in
his stupendous technique and in his manner of performing incredibly
complex tans. In addition to his "fire works," Aladiya Khan has created a number of very beautiful ragas which remind us of the performances of Abdul Karim Khan. It is said that Aladiya Khan never handed
his own ragas over to his pupils; he believed that his creations were
his own private property; he performed them only at very rare occasions and guarded them like a precious treasure. His two sons,
both excellent musicians, have gained fame, but the importance of
Aladiya Khan's school dwindled with his death.

Gwalior

This school is represented by such celebrated musicians as Balkrishna
Boa, Ichalkarranjikar, and the famous Vishnu Digamber Paluskar.
The Gwalior school has an eclectic character. Its tans often assume
characteristic simple shapes such as C D C, C D E D C, C D E F E
D C, and so forth.

In addition to easily accessible contemporary recordings of
Indian music, the following list presents interesting recordings made
about twenty years ago by masters of the schools mentioned above.

HABIB KHAN ALADIYA KHAN (Patiala)

Ragas Darbari-todi, Manaranjani (a modified form of Lalit). Odeon 2308

MALLIKARJUN MANSUR (pupil of Aladiya Khan)

Ragas Todi, Kafi.   His Master's Voice N 15841

KESARBAI KERKAR (pupil of Aladiya Khan)

Ragas Jaunpuri, Lalit.   His Master's Voice HQ 1
Ragas Bihag, Malkouns.   His Master's Voice HQ 2

NISAR HUSSEIN (Rampur)

Ragas Jaunpuri, Todi.   His Master's Voice N 15721

VILAYAT HUSSEIN (Agra)

Ragas Deshkar, Bindrabani.   Odeon A 245115 A
Ragas Barva, Bahar.   Odeon SB 2434
Ragas Malkouns, Vasant.   Odeon A 245071 B
Ragas Bhimpalas, Gaud-sarang.   Odeon A 245038 B

FAYYAZ KHAN (Agra-Rangile School)

Ragas Todi, Paraj.   Hindusthan H 249 h
Ragas Nath-bihag, Bhairavi.   Hindusthan H 355
Ragas Jaunpuri, Kafi.   Hindusthan H 793

GULAM ALI KHAN (Lahore)

Ragas Adana-bahar, Bhairavi.   Hindusthan H 886
Ragas Dhun, a light song; Megh.   Hindusthan H 910
Ragas Marva, Sur-sarang.   Xenophone JP 751

ASHIQ ALI KHAN (Lahore)

Ragas Gunkali Bhairav, Bhairav.   Xenophone RB 5002

AMANATH KHAN (Indore)

Ragas Kedar, Madhmad-sarang.   Young India DA 11155

A larger list of recorded North Indian music may be found in Danielou, Northern Indian Music, Vol. II, pp. 264 ff.

RAGA-MALAS (NEPAL)

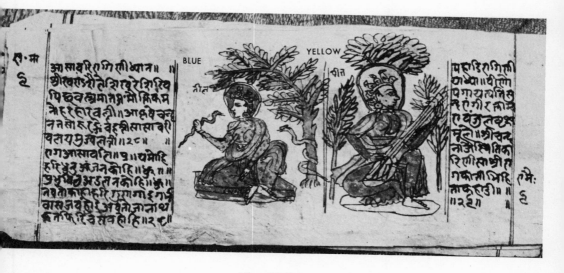

Plate XXIX

Raga Asavari   Raga Pahadi

Surpassing the sweet sound of the vina,
Shri Chandana is singing the raga under the
onjul tree.

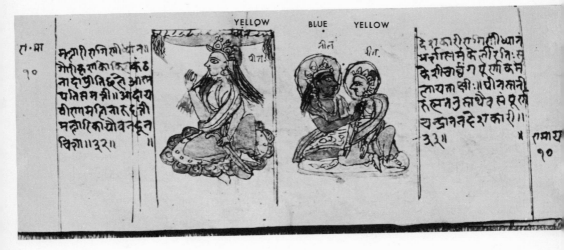

YELLOW   BLUE   YELLOW

Plate XXX

Raga Mallari

Gauri and Krishna are singing with beautiful
voices like those of the cuckoos. They have the
vina in their Mallari love-spot.

Raga Deshkar

This is Deshkari, soft as a lotus, with the most
beautiful hair, lovely breasts and the prime of youth

Plate XXXI

Raga Kakubha [Kukubh]

Raga Hindola

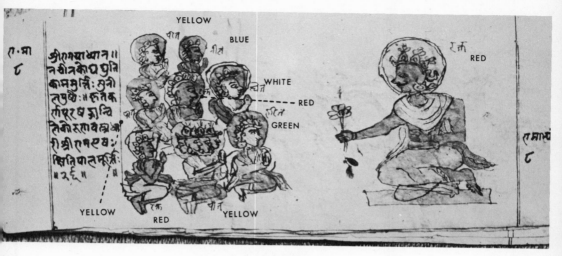

Plate XXXII Shri-raga

Here is the great image of Shri Ram-esh Kshiti, pala of Karnapur, who has an amazing capacity for work. He is wearing his *kuruna* dress.

Plate XXXIII

Raga Sarang

Raga Megh (Mallar)

With the vina in her hand she is singing the beautiful raga of Saranga while he is untying her hair.

Plate XXXIV

Raga Vasant   Raga Malavi

Plate XXXV

Raga Sarang   Raga Sauri

With the vina in his hand Krishna with a   In the luxuriant forest of Sauri, Shyama [Krishna]
sweet voice sings the famous raga Saranga.   is roaming about in this enchanting spot of beauty.
                                                He is wearing his beautiful gown made of
                                                sikhandi.

BIBLIOGRAPHY

Ahobala. Saṅgīta-Pārijāta. Calcutta: Sarasvati Press, 1884.

Barve, Manohar G. Manohar Sangitavali. Bombay, 1944.

Bharata. Nātyaśāstra; Kāvya Māla Series, No. 42, Bombay. Also Kashi Sanskrit Series, No. 60, Benares, 1926. Translated by Manmohar Ghose. Calcutta: The Royal Asiatic Society of Bengal, 1950.

Bhatkhande, V. N. Hindusthani Sangit Paddhati (6 Vols.), Bombay, 1934-37.

_____. Srīmal-Laksya-Saṅgītam. Bombay, 1921.

_____. Abhinava-Rāga-Mañjari. Bombay, 1921.

_____. "A Comparative Study of Some Leading Music Systems of the 15th, 16th, 17th and 18th Centuries," Sangita I, Lucknow, 1930-31, 1-4, pp. 3-6.

_____. A Short Historical Survey of the Music of Upper India, Bombay, 1939.

Bhāvabhaṭṭa. Anūpa-Saṅgīta-Vilāsa. Bombay, 1916, 1921.

_____. Anūpa-Saṅgīta-Ratnākara. Bombay, 1916, 1921.

_____. Anūpa-Saṅgītaṅkuśa. Bombay, 1916, 1921.

Clements, E. Introduction to the Study of Indian Music. London, 1913.

Daniélou, A. Northern Indian Music (2 Vols.), London, 1954 (Reference is made only to Vol. II).

Deodhar, B. R. Rāg-Bodh. Bombay, 1939.

Fox-Strangways, A. H. The Music of Hindostan. Oxford, 1914.

Gangoly, O. C. Rāgas and Rāgiṇīs. Bombay, 1935.

Gosvami, O. The Story of Indian Music. Bombay, 1957, 1961.

Kallinātha. Saṅgīta-Ratnākaratīka. Madras: Adyar Library, 1945.

Kaufmann, W. Musical Notations of the Orient. Bloomington: Indiana University Press, 1967.

_____. "The Forms of the Dhrupad and Khyal in Indian Art Music." The Canadian Music Journal. 1959, III, No. 2, pp. 25 ff.

Locanakavi. Rāga-Tarangini. Poona, 1918.

Matanga (Matangamuni). Bṛhaddeśi. Trivandrum Sanskrit Series XCIV, 1928, pp. 82-133.

Misra, Dāmodara. Saṅgīta-Darpaṇa. Calcutta: Stanhope Press, 1881.

Nārada. Cattvārimsacchata-Rāga-Nirūpanam. Bombay: Arya Bhusan Press, 1914.

Nārada. Saṅgīta-Makaranda. Baroda: Gaekwad's Oriental Series XVI, 1920.

Nāradīyā-Śiksā. Calcutta, 1890. Also, Benares Sanskrit Series, 1893; Mysore 1946.

Pārśvadeva. Saṅgīta-Samayasāra. Trivandrum Sanskrit Series LXXXVII, 1925.

Popley, H. A. The Music of India. Calcutta and London, 1921.

Prajnanananda (Swami). A History of Indian Music. Calcutta, 1963.

Ranade, G. H. Hindusthani Music. Poona, 1938.

Śārṅgadeva. Saṅgīta-Ratnākara. Madras: Adyar Library, 1943.

Singh (Sawai Pratapa Singha Deva). Saṅgīta-Sāra. Poona: Arya Bhusan Press, 1910-12.

Somanātha. Rāga-Vibodha. Poona, 1885. Also, Madras, 1933.

Someśvara. Abhilāsārtha-Cintamanī (Mānasollāsa). Baroda: Gaekwad's Oriental Series, 1925, I, p. 28.

Tagore, Sourindra Mohun. Hindu Music. Calcutta, 1875.

_____. Saṅgīta-Sāra-Saṁgraha. Calcutta, 1875.

_____, ed. Hindu Music from Various Authors, Calcutta, 1882.

Vaze, R. N. Sangit Kala Prakash, Poona, 1938.

Vyās, Krishnānanda. Saṅgīta-Rāga-Kalpadruma. Calcutta, 1916.

NOTES

PART I

1. See below, p. 40.

2. In South India the (Tamil) term is rāgam.

3. A. H. Fox-Strangways, The Music of Hindostan (Oxford, 1914), p. 122.

4. A work of the thirteenth century; see below, pp. 42 ff.

5. Saṅgīta-Ratnākara, i 3, 48 (see below, p. 42); the same text appears also in the later Saṅgīta-Darpana, i 125, 153 (see below, p. 51).

6. See below, pp. 123 ff.

7. Sanskrit Text Books on Music, Saṅgītasangraha, ed. S. M. Tagore, Calcutta, 1932.

8. For detailed information on North Indian drumming, drum words, drum phrases, etc., see Walter Kaufmann, Musical Notations of the Orient (Bloomington, Ind., 1967).

9. The North Indian term for the gliding from one note to another is mīnd ("deflect") and originates in the lateral deflecting of a vibrating string in order to change its pitch. According to Fox-Strangways (p. 183) there are other terms for mīnd in use: ghasīt (in the North), āsh and mīrh (in Bengal), and dhara or varek (in the South).

10. About the term rāginī see below, p. 41.

11. Arnold Bake, Indo-Iranian Journal, V, 2 (1961), p. 156.

12. Bulletin of the School of Oriental and African Studies, University of London, XXVI, 1 (1963), pp. 119-132.

13. For a detailed account see Walter Kaufmann, "Rasa, Raga-Mala and Performance Time in North Indian Ragas," Ethnomusicology, IX, 3 (1965), pp. 272-291.

14. See Ibid.

15. Walter Kaufmann, "The Forms of the Dhrupad and Khyal in Indian Art Music," The Canadian Music Journal, III, 2 (1959), pp. 25 ff.

16. Government Oriental Library, Madras, Nos. 1304, 13015.

17. The chapter dealing with these verses (dhyānas) bears the title Rāga-dhyāna-vidhānam ("raga-meditation-regulations").

18. Translated by O. C. Gangoly, Rāgas and Rāginīs (Bombay, 1935), pp. 107 ff.

19. The earliest copy (1440) is preserved by the Asiatic Society of Bengal, Calcutta, MS No. 5040.

20. Preserved in the Bhandarkar Oriental Institute, Poona MS No. 1026
(1884-1887).

21. "The Mirror of Music," reprinted in Calcutta, 1881; ed. S. M. Tagore.

22. Reprinted by the Arya Bhusan Press, Poona, 1921.

23. See Gangoly, pp. 115 ff.

24. Curt Sachs, World History of the Dance (New York, 1937), p. 219.

25. See p. 41.

26. See p. 40.

27. Thāta (or thāt) is a Prakrit word which means "model," "prototype,"
"array," or "mold." North Indian Sanskrit theorists use the word for "head-
scale," the material of which dominates to a greater or lesser degree a whole
group of rāgas. The thāta itself is no rāga, but only a scale, an "array" of
notes. In the past the concept of thāta could be found in the music of Islamic
India, where the term denoted a particular setting of frets on certain stringed instruments. As one setting of frets could be used in the performance of
several rāgas, the term thāta assumed the significance of a classifying and
ordering principle. The South Indian term for thāta is melakarta, or briefly, mela.

28. Samdhi (sandhi), Sanskrit: "transition from one to the other."
Pra-kāśa, Sanskrit: "visible," "shining." Thus Sandhiprakash implies the
transition from night to day or from day to night.

29. For a detailed account see Gangoly, pp. 72 ff.

30. See below, p. 41.

31. See p. 46.

32. See note # 16, this chapter.

33. See below, p. 42.

34. For further information on marga tālas see Bake, "Indische Musik,"
MGG, VI, p. 1180.

35. See below, pp. 51 f.

36. See Kaufmann, Musical Notations of the Orient, pp. 190 f.

37. Kaufmann, "The Forms of the Dhrupad...."

38. See Kaufmann, Musical Notations of the Orient, pp. 225 ff.

39. Ibid.

40. The kīrtana of Bengal, occasionally also found in other parts of
India, come close to a simple religious song (bhajan, etc.), which cannot
be considered as part of art music.

41. | 1 2 | 3 4 | 5 6 | 7 8 | 9 10 |
     | X | 0 | 2 | 0 | 3 |

42. | 1 2 3 | 4 5 | 6 7 8 |
     | X | 0 | 2 |

43. MGG, VI, p. 1175.

44. See below, pp. 183 ff.
45. See below, pp. 205 ff.

PART II

1. Pandit V. N. Bhatkhande in his treatise, "A Comparative Study of Some Leading Music Systems of the 15th, 16th, 17th, and 18th Centuries," (Saṅgīta I, 1-4 [Lucknow, 1930-31], 3-6) offers several lists of Sanskrit works, many of which are still unpublished. These works are preserved in the Palace Library of Bikaner, the Government Oriental Library of Mysore, the Palace Library of Trivandrum, the Central Library of Baroda, the Library of the former Maharajah of Kashi, the Tanjore Palace Library, the Government Oriental Library of Madras, and the Library of the Royal Asiatic Society, Calcutta.

PART III

1. Bombay, 1921 (ed. Bhalchandra S. Sukthankar).
2. Bombay, 1921.
3. Six vols. Ed. Sukthankar (in Hindi and Marathi, Bombay, 1937).
4. Written in Sanskrit verses in 1660. Ed. Joshi and Sukthankar, Poona: Arya Bhusan Press, 1918. The work also appeared in the Music Academy Series, Madras, in the early 1940's in Sanskrit and in Tamil.
5. A comparison between the thatas, Bharata's jatis, and the Greek harmoniai, as far as this can be done, produces the following:

thatas	jatis (Bharata)	harmoniai
Kalyan	Gāndhārī	Hypolydian
Bilaval	Nisādavatī	Lydian
Khamaj	Madhyamā	Hypophrygian
Kafi	Ṣādjī	Phrygian
Asavari	Pañcamī	Hypodorian
Bhairavi	Ārṣabhī	Dorian

6. See p. 11.
7. In Hindi; see p. 56.
8. Cf. the syllable pa in pater, father, père, etc.
9. See p. 11.
10. See p. 56.
11. See p. 44.
12. In Sourindro Mohun Tagore, ed., Hindu Music (Calcutta, 1882), p. 89.
13. See p. 541 f.

14. From Melakarta, "group-maker"

15. Tagore, p. 86

16. Poona, 1938, p. 23.

17. Yaman-kalyan, see pp. 63 ff; Shyam-kalyan, see pp. 109 ff; Shuddh-kalyan, see pp. 68 ff; Hemkalyan, see pp. 146 f; Hamirkalyan is a totally obscure mixture of the ragas Hamir and Kalyan.

18. Op. cit., p. 25.

19. See pp. 104 ff.

20. Also called Gorki-(Gaur-) Kalyan.

21. Calcutta, 1921, pp. 69 ff.

22. Tagore, p. 85.

23. See pp. 123 ff.

24. Or Nath, pp. 168 ff.

25. See pp. 117 ff.

26. Or Sorath; see pp. 213 f.

27. See pp. 394 ff.

28. Tagore, p. 85.

29. Also Rāga-Tatva-Vibodha, see p. 54.

30. See pp. 359 ff.

31. Sarang, Sanskrit, lit.: "colorful," "marvellous."

32. In Sarasvati, Nov. 1933. The author of the Rāg-Kutūhala (not to be confused with the Mān-Kutūhala), Gauda Brahmin of Jayanagar, called Rādhā Krishna or Kavi Krishna. He lived in the late eighteenth century and was in the service of Prince Bhīm Singh of Uniyār-gad (Jaipur).

33. O. C. Gangoly, Rāgas and Rāginīs (Bombay, 1935), p. 133.

34. See pp. 315 ff.

35. The work is a short treatise consisting of 27 verses. It was written in 1798 and was later published as a second part of the Rāga-Ratnākar (a collection of Hindi hymns by Khemraj Krishna Das) by the Vyankatesvara Press (Bombay, 1893). See also Gangoly, p. 135.

36. Translated by Gangoly, p. 135.

37. See also p. 61.

38. Gangoly, p. 136.

39. Gunakali subordinated to the Bhairav thata, often called Gunakari, is discussed on pp. 238 ff.

40. See pp. 79 f.

41. See pp. 257 ff.

42. H. Popley, The Music of India (Calcutta, 1921), p. 65.

43. See pp. 114 ff.

44. See pp. 130 ff.

45. See p. 143.

46. See pp. 138 ff.

47. See pp. 404 ff.

48. Tagore, p. 82.

49. See pp. 228 ff.

50. See pp. 224 ff.

51. Tagore, p. 85.

52. See pp. 99 ff.

53. For instance, in Sourindro Mohun Tagore, Six Principle Ragas with a Brief Review of Hindu Music (Calcutta, 1877).

54. See pp. 226 ff.

55. See pp. 389 ff.

56. See pp. 224 ff.

57. For the etymology of the word Sarparda see p. 19.

58. See pp. 205 ff.

59. See pp. 412 f.

60. See p. 413.

61. See pp. 277 ff.

62. Tagore, Hindu Music, p. 84.

63. See pp. 112 f.

64. Vol. V, 111-112.

65. See pp. 359 ff.

66. Gangoly, p. 108.

67. Tagore, loc. cit.

68. See pp. 228 ff.

69. See pp. 99 ff.

70. See pp. 168 ff.

71. See pp. 208 ff.

72. A thumri is a Hindu love song, frequently of light, popular, occasionally of religious, character. Its simple melody appears often in dance music and in theatrical shows.

73. The ghazal (often in dadra tala, 6/8) is the Mohammedan counterpart of the Hindu thumri. Its text is, of course, in Urdu or Persian.

74. The hori is a popular, religious Hindu song referring to the Holi festival. Of interest are the hori-dhamar songs (horis in dhamar tala), old folk melodies allegedly of the Mathura district.

75. See Kaufmann, Musical Notations of the Orient.

76. See pp. 465 ff.

77. See pp. 417 ff.

78. See pp. 183 f.

79. See pp. 382 ff.

80. Tagore, Hindu Music, p. 82.

81. See pp. 224 ff.

82. See pp. 389 ff.

83. F-mode; not the same as Bharata's MA-grāma.

84. See pp. 207 f.

85. A. Daniélou, <u>Northern Indian Music</u>, Vol. II (London, 1954), p. 187.

86. See pp. 359 ff.

87. Gangoly, pp. 72 f.

88. Ibid., p. 111.

89. <u>Sarasvati</u>, Nov. 1933, p. 426.

90. Gangoly, p. 133.

91. The descriptions of Shiva also apply to his incarnation. See also
     A. L. Basham, <u>The Wonder That was India</u>, New York, 1959, pp.
     307 ff.

92. See pp. 241 ff.

93. See pp. 277 ff.

94. See pp. 315 ff.

95. See pp. 359 ff.

96. See pp. 277 ff.

97. Gangoly, p. 116.

98. Tagore, <u>Hindu Music</u>, p. 81.

99. See pp. 279 ff.

100. Tagore, <u>Hindu Music</u>, p. 80.

101. See p. 138.

102. See pp. 323 ff.

103. See pp. 306 ff.

104. See pp. 465 ff.

105. See pp. 263 ff.

106. See pp. 323 ff.

107. See pp. 330 ff.

108. See pp. 465 ff.

109. See pp. 180 ff.

110. See pp. 359 ff.

111. See pp. 283 ff.

112. <u>Music of India</u>, p. 56. See also p. 53 of the present work.

113. See pp. 321 ff.

114. See pp. 189 ff.

115. Bombay, 1923-26.

116. Gangoly, p. 131.

117. See pp. 251 ff.

118. See pp. 279 ff.

119. See pp. 257 ff.

120. See pp. 233 ff.

121. See pp. 327 ff.

122. Gangoly, p. 108.

123. See p. 281.

124. See pp. 318 ff.

125. See pp. 321 ff.

126. A famous Hindi poet (1673-1745). His work Rāg-Ratnākar was re-printed among the collected works of Deo Kavi by the Nagari-Pracarini-Sabha (Benares, 1912).

127. Gangoly, p. 124.

128. Bhairav type, see pp. 248 ff; Purvi type, see pp. 300 f.

129. See pp. 123 ff.

130. Cf. Bibhas (Bhairav)

131. Gangoly, p. 115.

132. See pp. 114 ff.

133. See pp. 279 ff.

134. See pp. 318 ff.

135. See pp. 277 ff.

136. See pp. 318 ff.

137. See pp. 61 ff.

138. See pp. 70 ff.

139. Gangoly, pp. 145 ff.

140. See pp. 341 ff.

141. See pp. 351 ff.

142. See pp. 327 ff.

143. See pp. 295 ff.

144. See pp. 318 ff.

145. See pp. 277 ff.

146. The melody concerns the first ode of the Shih-ching, the "Book of Odes." For further details, see Kaufmann, Musical Notations of the Orient.

147. The name is taken from the music of South India.

148. Another type of Dhanashri is ascribed to the Bhairavi thata; see p. 543.

149. Tagore, Hindu Music, pp. 86 ff.

150. See pp. 380 ff.

151. Its author is Mohan Sen. See Gangoly, p. 145.

152. Gangoly, p. 147.

153. See pp. 362 ff.

154. See pp. 207 ff.

155. See pp. 365 ff.

156. See pp. 207 ff.

157. See pp. 439 f.

158. See pp. 499 ff.

159. See pp. 367 f.

160. See pp. 362 ff.

161. See pp. 364 f.

162. See pp. 499 ff.

163. The Music of India, p. 66.

164. Cf. raga Bindrabani-sarang, pp. 449 ff.

165. Tagore, Hindu Music, p. 88.

166. Another raga with the same name, similar to the fifth type of Gaud-mallar, is discussed below on p. 412; cf. p. 410.

167. See pp. 183 ff.

168. See pp. 186 ff.

169. See pp. 168 ff.

170. See pp. 99 ff.

171. See pp. 449 ff.

172. See pp. 503 ff.

173. See pp. 510 f.

174. See pp. 213 f.

175. See pp. 117 ff.

176. See pp. 211 f.

177. See pp. 503 ff.

178. See pp. 507 ff.

179. See pp. 228 ff.

180. See pp. 374 ff.

181. See pp. 211 f.

182. See pp. 449 ff.

183. See pp. 499 ff.

184. See pp. 517 ff.

185. See pp. 382 ff.

186. See pp. 439 ff.

187. See pp. 535 ff.

188. See pp. 533 ff.

189. See pp. 526 ff.

190. Patmanjri, pp. 195 ff.

191. See pp. 449 ff.

192. See pp. 368 ff.

193. See pp. 382 ff.

194. See pp. 112 f.

195. See pp. 453 ff.

196. See pp. 460 ff.

197. See pp. 453 ff.

198. Gangoly, p. 136.

199. See pp. 211 f.

200. See pp. 107 ff.

201. See pp. 472 f.

202. See pp. 365 ff.

203. Gangoly, p. 110.

204. In Suvarna-mala, Gujarati Quarterly, ed. Pursuttam Visram Mouji (Bombay, 1924), I, 4, pp. 32-33.

205. Gangoly, p. 131.

206. See pp. 211 f.

207. See pp. 233 ff.

208. See pp. 394 ff.

209. See pp. 233 ff.

210. Ibid.

211. See pp. 533 ff.

212. See pp. 449 ff.

213. See pp. 395 ff.

214. See pp. 499 ff.

215. See pp. 123 ff.

216. Tagore, Hindu Music, p. 83.

217. See pp. 535 ff.

218. See pp. 382 ff.

219. Written in 1798. Published in 1893 in Bombay in a work entitled Rāga-Ratnākar, a collection of Hindi hymns by Khemraj Kṛsna Das.

220. Translated by Gangoly, pp. 134 ff.

221. See pp. 551 ff.

222. See pp. 557 ff.

223. See pp.· 65 ff.

224. See pp. 535 ff.

225. See pp. 359 ff.

226. See pp. 394 ff.

227. See pp. 499 ff.

228. See pp. 449 ff.

229. Asavari with RE komal (D♭). See pp. 467 ff.

230. See pp. 233 ff.

231. For further descriptions see Gangoly, pp. 109 and 147 ff.

232. Calcutta, 1921.

233. It may be of interest to note that there are only three important ragas (in North Indian music) with MA tivra (F#) which are to be performed during the day; Todi, Gaud-sarang, and Multani.

234. See p. 552.

235. Gangoly, p. 109.

236. Tagore, Hindu Music, p. 89.

237. See pp. 485 ff.

238. See pp. 478 ff.

239. See pp. 216 ff.

240. See pp. 117 ff.

241. See pp. 147 ff.

242. See pp. 117 ff.

243. See pp. 507 ff.

244. See pp. 385 ff.

245. See pp. 359 ff.
246. See pp. 503 ff.
247. See pp. 385 ff.
248. See pp. 222 ff.
249. See pp. 382 ff.
250. See pp. 130 ff.
251. See pp. 343 ff.
252. See pp. 70 ff.
253. See pp. 68 ff.
254. See pp. 205 ff.
255. See pp. 138 ff.
256. Op. cit.
257. See pp. 222 ff.
258. See pp. 499 ff.
259. See pp. 224 ff.
260. See pp. 389 f.
261. See pp. 205 ff.
262. See pp. 535 ff.
263. See pp. 507 ff.
264. See pp. 168 ff.
265. See p. 138.
266. See pp. 449 ff.
267. See pp. 224 ff.
268. See pp. 205 ff.
269. See pp. 499 ff.
270. Gangoly, pp. 112 ff.
271. See pp. 183 ff.
272. Gangoly, p. 114.
273. See pp. 362 ff.
274. See pp. 533 ff.
275. See pp. 61 ff.
276. See pp. 185 f.
277. See pp. 372 ff.
278. See pp. 382 ff.
    279. A Vichitra-vina is a zither, the strings of which are stopped by
means of a glass ball.

INDEX

This book has presented some raga names and other relevant terms in two forms. The first two chapters show them approximated to the Sanskrit, Hindi, and Tamil spellings, while the third chapter presents them in simplified and commonly used anglicized forms without diacritical marks. Both forms are listed below.